The Lure of Tahiti

Fifteen choice extracts from the
rich literature of "the most romantic
island in the world"

The LURE of TAHITI

An Armchair Companion

Edited by
A. GROVE DAY

MUTUAL PUBLISHING COMPANY
TALES OF THE PACIFIC
HONOLULU • HAWAII

First edition

Printed in Australia by
The Book Printer, Victoria

Cover photography by Bernice P. Bishop Museum

Cover design by Jack Delaney

Library of Congress Catalog
Card Number 86-062756

Acknowledgments

"Sirens of the South Seas" by Annie Dillard. Reprinted from *Signature*, July, 1985, by permission of the author and her agent, Blanche C. Gregory, Inc.

"Sing: A Song of Sixpence" by James Norman Hall. From *Atlantic Monthly*, November 17, 1925. Reprinted by permission of Nancy Rutgers Hall.

"Povenaaa's Daughter," copyright 1951 by James A. Michener. Reprinted from *Return to Paradise* by permission of Random House, Inc.

"*Chez* Quinn," copyright 1946 by William S. Stone. Reprinted by permission of William Morrow & Company.

Tahiti, Island of Amour

Ever since I can remember, the name of this island has been one of the most romantic words in the language. Tahiti! The very word is like a bell, tolling the unwary to dreams of an exotic Eden in the far South Seas, where humdrum cares are forgotten and men and women live only for today and each other.

The island of Tahiti, in sober fact, has been a lure for dreamers for more than two hundred years. The rise of literary romanticism in the eighteenth century brought forth a nostalgia for the "primitive." Consequently, accounts of voyages and travels were high among the favorite books of the time for readers seeking earthly paradises.

Jean Jacques Rousseau can be credited—or blamed—for encouraging the idea that primitive societies were more happy and moral than civilized ones. Primitive men, he argued, were on the whole freer than others, because the equality intended by God was spoiled by social organization. Primitive life seemed also to offer the absence of conflict between the physical and moral aspects of sex, so that neither love nor jealousy troubled the innocent pagans.

The "noble savage" became all the rage in Europe. Since few uncorrupted savages could be discovered even in the Americas, the only place left on the globe where primitive people might be found was in the Pacific region that Balboa had named the South Seas.

The dupes of Rousseau were delighted when they learned about the greatest discovery of Captain Samuel Wallis, R.N., in command of an around-the-world exploring voyage in the copper-bottomed frigate *Dolphin*. His log records that on the morning of June 18, 1767, his crew sighted what appeared to be an enormous mountain with its summit covered by clouds. Next day, when a heavy fog lifted, the easternmost point of the high island was revealed with rearing green hills culminating in needlelike spires. Ashore, handsome brown people wandered among thatched houses scattered beneath breadfruit trees and tall coconut palms. Captain Wallis anchored here at

Matavai Bay, where in 1769 Captain Cook would observe the transit of Venus across the sun and Captain Bligh would spend months collecting breadfruit seedlings.

Wallis came on deck and found that his ship was surrounded by about a hundred outrigger canoes, manned by paddlers who had apparently never before seen a ship. These Polynesians showed their friendly intentions by waving shoots of the banana plant. At last a brisk young Tahitian climbed up by the mizzen chains and accepted a few trinkets. Several others then came aboard. As one was standing on the quarterdeck, a goat from the ship's animal pen ran up and butted him behind. He turned and, seeing the strange creature rearing on her hind legs for another attack, leaped overboard, followed by his friends.

This was the opening scene of more than a month of fraternization between the shipload of virile seamen and the enticing women of the island. Their menfolk seemed to encourage rather than condemn the exchange of courtesies — especially if the men might thereby obtain nails and other objects of iron, which they had never possessed. After a brief, unequal battle between the English crew and about four thousand warriors who were no match for the big guns of the *Dolphin*, Captain Wallis was welcomed ashore by a train of courtiers led by a buxom chiefess whom he called "Queen Oberea." Her influence enabled him to stock his ship with food, water, and wood for his continuing voyage.

At the end of five idyllic weeks, when on July 27 the captain finally decided to depart from among the noble, hospitable savages of Tahiti, the queen wept at the loss of her foreign friend. And when a pair of French frigates independently discovered the southern side of Tahiti on April 4, 1768, the description of the island's attractions by Captain Louis Antoine de Bougainville was so alluring and poetic that his government thereafter could never rest content until it had assumed a protectorate in 1843 over the entire archipelago of which Tahiti is the capital.

Nowadays the region of French Polynesia sprawls over an ocean area as large as Europe, but the land area is less than that of the state of Rhode Island. It is considered an overseas territory of metropolitan France, and all residents are French citizens who pay no income tax. The population of the one hundred and thirty islands is about 185,000, of whom about half live on Tahiti. From the capital of Papeete (pronounced Pah-pay-aye-tay) are administered two groups. The windward group of islands includes not ony Tahiti itself but its near neighbor Moorea (Moh-oh-ray-ah), Makatea, Tetiaroa, Maiao, and Mehetia. The leeward group comprises the twin islands of Raiatea and Tahaa, beautiful Bora Bora, Maupiti, and the atolls of Tupai, Mopelia, Scilly, and Bellinghausen. From Tahiti other groups are administered: the Australs, the Gambiers, the low Tuamoto or Dangerous Archipelago, and the Marquesas (from which Hawaii was presumably settled as early as the eighth century).

Tahiti is a volcanic island, not an atoll, and its tallest point is Mount Orohena (7,618 feet). Its area is roughly four hundred square miles. It is shaped like a figure eight. Its rudely circular main part has a smaller replica, the Taiarapu Peninsula, attached by a narrow neck, the Isthmus of Taravao. The road around the major part is about seventy-five miles long, running between emerald-clad peaks cut by many tumbling streams, and the ocean, fringed by coral reefs forming a sheltered, beach-dotted lagoon. Most of the settlements are along the shore; the interior is avoided by night because the Tahitians fear that it is infested by ghosts.

Tahiti's climate is warm and moist but not unhealthful, with temperatures ranging between sixty and ninety degrees. From cloud-topped Orohena and other mountains comes abundant rainfall all year, although a season falls between November and April, with most of it in January and February. Oddly, in July and August the nights are frequently cool. Daytime temperature variation amounts only to about ten degrees. Now and again a breeze springs up, often presaging a downpour. The air is aromatic with the fragrance of flowers that bloom year-round. Most of the people outside the town live in shuttered, thatched houses, surrounded by such trees as banana, breadfruit, mango, and guava, and especially the coconut palm, from which comes Tahiti's main agricultural export, copra. Paradoxically, after 1850, millions of oranges were shipped from Tahiti to California. Other products of the fields are yams, taro, vanilla, and pineapple. Visible from most parts of Tahiti is the sister island, Moorea, dappled with clouds and aflame at sunset.

Even more flamboyant than the scenery of Tahiti is the colorful variety of residents and visitors to be seen along the downtown waterfront. Most of the population is clearly Polynesian, mingled with the strains of foreign sojourners over more than two centuries. Of some three thousand European residents, most are French nationals born outside the region. Among them are workers on the internationally condemned nuclear-testing project conducted over two decades on the island of Mururoa in the Gambier group, some eight hundred miles from Tahiti. Only a few foreigners have special permission to reside in the islands; some of these are married to Polynesians. Notable is the Chinese and part-Chinese population. The first Chinese arrived to labor in the cotton fields during the American Civil War, when southern cotton was blockaded, and by 1866 there were more than a thousand on the island. However, the bottom soon fell out of the cotton market and many of the Chinese men returned home. Nowadays, through migration and natural increase, several thousand people of Chinese ancestry live in the islands. They still practice agriculture, but many have left the fields to engage in commerce, and it is a rare Society Island that does not have its main store operated by a shrewd Celestial.

The main product of these islands over the centuries has been Polynesian hospitality. The archipelago has continued to be a lure for thousands who come by sea and air. Currently, a white cruise ship of the American Hawaii Line, based at Papeete, is bringing pleasure to thousands of voyagers who spend a week visiting in seaborne comfort half a dozen other sunlit isles of French Oceania.

Further information about the fascinating island of Tahiti and its South Pacific neighbors can be found in many places. The most charming windows upon its attractions and inhabitants, present and past, can be viewed, it is believed, in the manifold pages of its rich literature—such as the selections that browsers may enjoy in the following sections: "The Sojourners," "The Travelers," "The Missionaries," and "The Explorers."

University of Hawaii   A. GROVE DAY

Contents

I. The Sojourners

Annie Dillard	Sirens of the South Seas	3
H. Allen Smith	The Smiths Keep Christmas	10
James A. Michener	Povenaaa's Daughter	21
H.E. Bates	The Grapes of Paradise	79
James Norman Hall	Sing: A Song of Sixpence	132
William S. Stone	Chez Quinn	153
W. Somerset Maugham	My South Sea Island	174
Rupert Brooke	Tiaré Tahiti	178

II. The Travelers

Jack London	Darling, the Nature Man	183
Paul Gauguin	Fishing Season	198
Pierre Loti	A Concert at the Palace	206
Herman Melville	At The Calabooza Beretanee	211
Charles Darwin	Darwin Climbs the Mountain	243

III. The Missionaries

Richard E. Lingenfelter	The First Printing Press in the Pacific	265

IV. The Explorers

George Robertson	The "Old Trade" at Matavai	281
Louis Antoine de Bougainville	The New Cytherea	288
James Cook	Captain Cook at Point Venus	301
William Bligh	Captain Bligh and the Breadfruit	319

I. The Sojourners

Annie Dillard

Sirens of the South Seas

The first contact between Europeans and Tahitians goes back to the year 1767, so that more than two centuries have passed of joyous intermingling of genes between the islanders and thousands of strangers of varied ethnic groups, including a strong strain from the Orient. It is amazing, however, that one can still define and view a "typical" Tahitian type — especially among the women of the island. This truth is noted by a recent visitor from the eastern United States.

Annie Doak, born in Pittsburgh in 1945, earned both a bachelor's and master's degree in English from Hollins College, and for seven years was married to her writing professor, R.H.W. Dillard. At the age of twenty-nine, she received the Pulitzer Prize for her contemplative volume, *Pilgrim at Tinker Creek* (1975). In the summer of 1975 she journeyed to the Galapagos Islands in the Pacific to write one of her contributions to *Harper's Magazine*. Mrs. Dillard is also a poet. Her latest non-fiction volume is *Holy the Firm* (1977), and her latest travel essay is "Sirens of the South Seas."

THE Tahitians are a beautiful, languorous people devoted to pleasure. That is how they were when the missionaries found them, and that is how they are again today.

The missionaries left the Tahitians demoralized and their culture dying — but that was a long time ago. Now Tahitian culture, never completely eradicated, is enjoying a strong revival. It is so pleasure-seeking that this visitor, at least, was struck with the comical thought that what these islands need at this moment is more missionaries.

There is in Tahiti a sweet ease, a voluptuous luxury, a sense of the compliance of nature and the abundance of

3

time. Nothing more fully embodies this sense of sweet ease than the *vahine*, the island women. Every visitor has re-marked these women — their faces, bodies, presences, motions, perfume — with good reason. They are admirable as objects, like flowers — and that is how they present themselves. Like flowers, they specialize in bright beauty, passivity, and sexuality.

Gauguin in no wise exaggerated the *vahine's* languor or simple purity of form. The girls and women you see in remote villages and on city streets and buses are just as lovely as hired bare-bellied dancers. They are wonderfully smooth of skin and round of limb, oval-faced, wide-shoul-dered, as flat-footed as any Gauguin woodcut girl, with long pliant fingers, cascades of scented hair stuck with blossoms, and dreamy, stony expressions that quicken when the music starts.

A girl of fifteen, wearing a red-flowered *pareu* and a white frangipani blossom over one ear, falls asleep on a leather airport bench. She languishes askew on the bench in the public lobby, unself-conscious, one smooth armpit bared, and her eyes roll back in her head completely. Her eyes roll back, and roll down, and roll back up again completely, as if she were a cat, before at last they roll up and stay up and at last her eyelids flutter and close.

The living is easy in French Polynesia, long ago and still today. Where else in the tropics are the people healthy, well-nourished, clean and prosperous? Breadfruit, coco-nuts, mangoes, papayas, and bananas grow on trees in the yard, among the orchids, and the clear ocean is full of snap-per, and giant edible clams. There is plenty of cash, too, as tourists circulate through the villages like bubbles in a fish tank and French businesses and military concessions thrive. The climate is so pleasant you scarcely need clothes or walls in your house. Consequently the ancient Tahitians — not a particularly artistic or intellectual people — had time on their hands, and they devoted it to playing, danc-ing, and, especially, making love.

For the ancient Tahitians, sex was "the focus of their lives." We have this from a sober, scholarly three-volume anthropological monograph (Douglas Oliver, 1974). When the ancient Tahitians weren't actually making love, they they were just getting ready to. Girls of all ranks, according to a disputed 1778 account, "passed through the embraces of hundreds" before they were married. Being married, then and sometimes now, narrowed the breadth of a young girl's interests only somewhat. ("We don't get divorced," one Tahitian told me. "We just have messy marriages.") For some few girls in ancient times, monogamy seems to have been the rule. For others, girls and boys, sex was a profession. But "for the majority," anthropologist Douglas Oliver is moved to comment somewhat giddily, "sexual intercourse was an avocation."

People of all ages and both sexes delighted in a steady stream of sexual conversation. People starting at about age seven made love on all terrains: in sacred chestnut groves, on black sand beaches and white sand beaches, in the rain forest and on dry stream beds. Public love-making afforded special amusement to spectators, the European explorers learned. In 1772 Bougainville described the hospitality natives extended to his shipmates. Tahitians invited strolling sailors into their houses, fed them, and offered them their daughters. Immediately the house would fill with curious onlookers who surrounded the couple and spread the ground with leaves and flowers. Musicians appeared and struck up melodies on their nose-flutes. The men were "confused," Bougainville noted, deadpan, but none, so far as he knew, "found it impossible to conquer his repugnance and conform to the customs of the country."

Such coquetry as there was in ancient Tahiti seemed to take the unambiguous form of outright proposition. "A desire for copulation," said one old manuscript, was "ceaselessly" signaled by unspecified gestures of women's hands, eyes, and — not quite imaginably — toes. In the forest, a girl signaled the boy she chose by hitting him with a softly

5

thrown piece of fruit while he was bathing. The boy would quit the water at once and head for the bushes.

In 1767 a British explorer was intrigued to discover a Tahitian woman making fingers at him. She held "her first finger up straight and smiled, then crooked all her . . . fingers and kept playing with them and laughed very hearty . . . ." At length he figured out she was offering herself at the price of one long iron nail. In 1803 a European man living in Tahiti was maddened by the sight of girls bathing in six inches of water. They choose pools by public paths, he said, and "take great care to show that they wash all parts of their bodies."

Today, European businessmen emigrating to Tahiti with their wives and children find those wives and families packed and headed homeward "within six months," said one resident. "Everyone takes a mistress — *a vahine.*"

Some upper-class Tahitian girls may remain virgins until their late teens. Some set their caps for European men. You see them at the best restaurants with these older escorts. Each wears a single, enormous black pearl at her throat. Each is beautifully groomed and smiling. If you address such a one directly in a language she speaks, as if she were a person, she is apt to be too meek to answer for herself. She is so vivid, motionless, and speechless, you feel yourself to be in the presence of a hologram.

What is it like to have a *vahine* as a lover?

"She was perfectly submissive," one French resident said. We were eating veal and mangoes under a wild hibiscus tree and a swaying casuarina tree, beside a white sand beach on the island of Tahiti. Beyond the calm lagoon a lacy fringe of breakers marked the reef. This white band of waves made of the lagoon and sky a bright bauble, a gift, like the day itself, whole and enormous, presented with a ribbon. In the ocean distance rose the volcanic and verdant slopes of Moorea, which, like nearby Bora Bora, many travelers consider the most beautiful spot on the face of the globe.

"Perfectly submissive." He grimaced. This French land-owner had kept his *vahine* for over a year, he said, to the delight of her large family, until his very loneliness caused them to break it off.

"She wouldn't even eat with me. 'This is for you,' she would say"— he made a graceful gesture with both hands — "'for you,' and retire, leaving me alone at the table. I never really got to know her." Now he savored his mango, his potatoes Anna, his pear tart. With us was the lively and well-educated Frenchwoman, a therapist, with whom he has lived for many years. On the beach beyond us, two bare-chested Tahitian men were launching an outrigger canoe. The outrigger's float was a piece of hand-carved, ba-nana-shaped wood; the outrigger's arms, tidily lashed to both canoe and float, were sections of an industrial rein-forcing bar.

"People say," the Frenchman went on, "that when you take a *vahine*, you should bring her friend also, so she'll have someone to talk to. For she'll never talk to you."

Tahitians are largely unmoved by the present indepen-dence conflict in New Caledonia. The Melanesians in New Caledonia are poor and chafe at their treatment by their French governors. They are black-skinned, short, and blunt-featured. The problem appears to be racial. ("Some of them are beasts," a French resident confided to *The New York Times.*) The Polynesians in French Polynesia are, by contrast, pale, rich, self-satisfied, and virtually self-govern-ing. The French keep their islands in luxury, like girls in a harem.

"Twenty years ago," the Frenchwoman said, "Tahitians were forbidden to speak Tahitian at school, even in kinder-garten. Now little children may be taught in Tahitian." I had seen 1950's photographs of Tahitians all dressed iden-tically— in skirts and stockings, dark suits and ties. Now I saw no stockings, no ties, but bright prints everywhere, and bare feet. I saw a man lounging in a palm tree on the shore of a lagoon, wearing only a blue *pareu* around his hips.

He sprawled like a sloth. "The people were more western-ized twenty years ago than they are today," the French-woman said. She passed a silver platter of sauteed veal, the platter gracefully strewn, as is so much in Tahiti, with red hibiscus blossoms.

"Now Tahitian dancing is part of the school curriculum."

I had just begun to understand that the sensuous cos-tumed dancing that *vahine* perform for tourists is not the cynical, moneymaking humiliation it had at first seemed, but instead a rather cleaned-up, neotraditional form of en-joyment for both the dancers and the musicians. The dancers are demure off-stage. I believe they enjoy dancing for its effort. Some troupes barely break even, for they must pay for their own costumes, instruments, and trans-portation. But who wouldn't like to sing and dance the night away? How their eyes flash and their hips roll as the grinning drummers change the pace and add a bump of syncopation! Some troupes are performing evermore traditional dances, both for tourists and for the big July festival and competition (at which everything is so tradi-tional in spirit that costumes must not be sewn with nylon thread).

Thirty years ago only lower-class young girls danced, according to historian P. O'Reilly. In 1956 a Papeete wom-an organized a dance troupe for proper girls, a troupe with well-made costumes and polished orchestration. Now everyone is getting into the act—not only the luscious young girls of all classes, but also their mothers and, with visible joy, their grandmothers.

What happens to old *vahine?*

Their faces grow lined, their hair turns gray, their torsos thicken, and, rapturously, they form a dance troupe in order to knock themselves out several days a week rat-tling their skillful hips before a crowd.

How I love to see these grandmothers dancing in rows! They wear missionary-style dresses from chin to bare ankles. They belt out rich-voiced harmonies to the deep

8

pounding of the big skin drum and the snazzy clatter of the wooden slit-gongs. Their worn brown fingers flirt in the air as their great hips roll and their expressions change from flirtatious irony to flirtatious enthusiasm and back again. They are, almost all of them, devout pillars of the Protestant church—such shaking hips on those pillars! Some of them are schoolteachers. It is they who tenderly teach their toddling great-granddaughters how to answer the big drums' hard bangs with their hips. They teach the tiniest girls to hold their heads and shoulders relaxed and still while their bare bellies romp and the melody's parts split and rejoin, and to smile with a faraway look as if they were seeing the white line of breakers at the reef over the audience's heads, and to keep their ankles together like nice girls, and perhaps—for aren't traditional things coming back in Tahiti?—to make a few wee come-hither gestures with their toes.

H. Allen Smith

The Smiths Keep Christmas

In the early 1960's, Harry Allen Smith (1907-1976) spent three months in the American colony at Tahiti. The result was one of his more than thirty volumes of humorous reportage, beginning with his highly successful volume *Low Man on a Totem Pole* (1941). Termed "the screwball's Boswell" by Fred Allen, Smith called his Tahiti book *Two-thirds of a Coconut Tree*, referring to a Papeete zoning law which restricted the height of a new building to "two-thirds of a coconut tree."

One of nine children, Smith was born in McLeansboro, Illinois, and attended St. Mary's parochial school in Huntington, but abandoned school in the eighth grade. His lack of formal education did not deter him from working on newspapers in Indiana, Kentucky, Florida, Oklahoma, Denver, and New York City. In 1927 he married Nelle Mae Simpson. The couple resided in such spots as Mexico, which produced *The Pig in the Barber Shop* (1958), and Hawaii, which resulted in *Waikiki Beachnik* (1960). In his Tahiti journal he referred to himself as "an anthropologist who operates not among the savage peoples of the primitive islands, but among the savage peoples of the civilized climes."

DECEMBER 24, 1962. Nelle said at breakfast this morning: "Let's see now, is today Christmas, or is it tomorrow?" Who would have ever dreamed, a year ago, that . . .

I went for a swim in the pool after breakfast, a thing I don't do often because of the litter that accumulates on the water. Now I was lolling and splashing around when I happened to notice the character of that litter. It is composed mostly of gardenia blossoms, and a few flowers blown off the nearby white ginger plant, and I thought, my God, people in Mexico drive two hundred miles over dangerous mountain roads to Fortin de las Flores and pay good money to swim in a pool with gardenias floating on the surface, and here I've got the same thing *au naturel,* if I may be so bold as to say so.

Later we drove down to the *Wanderlure* and I gave Carl Heintz some notes I have accumulated about little Norfolk Island, which lies off the east coast of Australia and which is to me what the Seychelles are to him. Many people have their own private dream island, a place they plan to visit before they die, and Norfolk is mine. I am unable to explain why it attracts me, but it does. I know an architect who yearns to visit the island of Dek, which is in Lake Tana in Africa. Dek is eight miles long and four miles wide and my architect friend has a great urge to see it and stand upon its soil. One evening at my house he got a bit drunk and grew so emotional about Dek that he wept. I can remember that I tried to soothe him by patting him on the back and saying, "God dammit, Harry, why don't you just drop everything and *go!*" I am hoping that later on, before leaving the South Pacific, I'll be able to make it to Norfolk. I have read everything I can get my hands on respecting its physical aspect and its famous pine trees and its somersetmaughamish administrators who say "Bugger you, Jack!" and its people who are descended from the *Bounty* mutineers. And I've talked about it so much lately that now Carl Heintz has developed an interest and says he'll try to put in at Norfolk after he leaves Samoa.

From the *Wanderlure* we drove out to Mataiea district to visit Baldwin Bambridge in his back-to-nature house. We found Baldwin with a seventeen-year-old Tahitian girl named Noeline, who is either his sixth wife or a candidate for that honor. Noeline's family lives near Baldwin's bamboo cottage and she is an attractive little girl with nice features and a splendid body; her skin, however, is a bit blotchy and she has a habit of picking her nose. Baldwin felt that there was a need for explanation of his relationship with Noeline, that we as Americans would not understand it and might even be a little shocked. He said that he and Noeline were simply carrying on in The Tahitian Way. We assured him that we thought The Tahitian Way was just fine and I even said that I would like to indulge in it a trifle. Nelle said shut up or I will give you some Tahitian Way right between the eyes.

Baldwin had me move the Dauphine, for I had parked it under a coconut tree, and he explained that coconuts are as heavy and as fast-moving as cannonballs and can do serious damage to the top of a car. I asked him if, with cannonball coconuts dropping all over the island, anybody ever gets hit in the head and killed. Never, he said. He could remember only one man who was ever hit by a falling coconut. "It only stunted him," said Baldwin.

We went over to the home of Noeline's parents, a sprawling establishment consisting mainly of a thatched house with a cook shack nearby and some chicken pens. The girl's father is a fisherman and a grower of taro root and at fifty-five is the father of twelve children, seven of whom live at home. We were invited into the house, where the mother was hastily putting on a shirt—she had been naked to the waist when we arrived. The main house consisted of one big room with five beds standing around the walls, each with clean white sheets and tents of mosquito netting suspended overhead. We adults sat down in a circle and the younger kids, naked or wearing only a shirt, stood around staring at us. I noticed that there were several prayer books and Bibles in the room, and some shell necklaces draped over the furniture, and an old family photograph on the wall. Everything had the look of decay except the floor, which was solid concrete and lent an air of stability to the place.

Baldwin told us that all these people live in The Tahitian Way and he pointed toward an older girl who was sitting on one of the beds and who was pregnant. "She has been away with Tahitian man," said Baldwin, "and now she has come home to have a baby because mama knows how to do. Nobody minds. Maybe she will not go back to the man. You must understand The Tahitian Way. The chiefs of each district, they are the real boss, they are the policeman, the court, the clerk, the mailman, everything. They keep records of those who are born and die and I have looked at these records. They say the name of the mother and it will be Nelle Smith and then the name of the father and it will be Rape by French Sailor. Ha! Some name for a father, huh? Mister Rape by French Sailor. A joke. You get it?"

I realized suddenly that it was Christmas Eve and I asked what plans they had for the holiday. They had none. The father said, and Baldwin translated: "We are happy because we have enough to eat." I wanted to know what all the little children would have for Christmas and he said the pastor of the district church had arranged to have Le Truck take the children all the way around the island the day after Christmas. Baldwin explained, with some bitterness, that most of the adults who normally use the bus would be drunk and immobilized on that day, and the buses would be available for giving the children an outing.

They showed us the cookhouse before we left, with its rock-lined pit, and the saw-toothed gadget that is used in the important work of shredding coconut meat, and under the thatch roof their proudest possession—a shiny new power mower. Baldwin said that these people would give us anything we asked for, including their chickens and their children, but that they would never part with that red-and-white power mower. Apparently it is a status symbol—there isn't any real need for it.

Baldwin now drove us to the Chinese restaurant, Atchoun's, out near the isthmus, and we had food of questionable quality. It was miserable. Bones and gristle surrounded by rice. The same as it is in the other Chinese restaurants of Tahiti. Baldwin and Noeline ate nothing but Chinese vegetables and drank nothing but cherry pop. Baldwin said that before he marries a girl in The Tahitian

Way, she had to promise that she will never eat meat or drink alcohol during the time she is his *vahine*.

An annex to Atchoun's restaurant contains pool tables and all of them were being used today, with much drinking of beer by the players, and a couple of guitars going on the sidelines. Baldwin spoke of the Tahitian love for music and said that the most popular instruments are the guitar, the accordion, and drums. He, a musician, believes that music can solve all human problems, that a person who sings and plays an instrument will always be happy and shorn of care and worry. Being a polite person I didn't say so, but that is a lot of bologna.

Baldwin also spent some time cussing out liquor. Then the name of a well-known Tahitian woman came into the conversation and I said that I had heard she was sick and in trouble, with a long history of heavy drinking. Said Baldwin grimly: "She ripped what she saw."

We drove back to Mataiea, where the people look upon Baldwin as a sort of king, and stopped at the *baraques* that have been erected for the holiday celebrations. Each district builds such *baraques*, prounounced barracks, whenever there is occasion for celebration. They are large pavilions made of bamboo or coconut wood framework and thatched with green pandanus and coconut leaves, with flowers added here and there. Inside are rude tables for eating and beer-drinking and a bandstand, and a floor for dancing. Every holiday, Christmas included, is observed in the same way, with eating and drinking and dancing, and usually there is a wheel-of-fortune by which suckling pigs and *pareus* are raffled off. Baldwin is a sort of benefactor to the entire district and he also is leader of the dance band. I had asked him earlier about Tahitian cattle ranches and cowhands, and now he was able to produce a real South Seas cowboy. I must explain that the natives of Tahiti are wild about cowboy movies and many of them consider Roy Rogers to be far and away the greatest man who ever trod earth. So now Baldwin introduced me to a young fellow who is a hero to the people of the district because he is, without question, a true cowboy. He was slim, quite handsome, with a shock of roached black hair that would qualify him for membership in the teen-age crowds back home. There was no suggestion of the Wild West in his attire—he had on a Tahitian shirt and an old pair of pants and a pair of go-aheads. I asked his name and had to have it spelled out for me: Theophile Toofa. I made a mental note of the possibility that he'd have to change his name if he ever made it to Hollywood and became a film cowboy. Or maybe not. Maybe a fast gun by the name of Theophile Toofa would go well in pictures. I offered to buy him a bottle of beer and he went to the bar and got it. A quart. Then I told him that I had read that Tahitian cowboys ride the range barefooted and with flowers in their hair. Theophile said it is not true, that he and his cowboy friends wear Western boots and sombreros when they are working. He was proud of the fact that he had been singled out for an interview and was grave and dignified in his responses when I asked if he was bothered by rustlers or if hired guns were a problem to him.

"We are too small," he said. "Our herd is only seventy. Some day we hope to have two hundred and seventy."

Theophile is ramrod of a spread of 270 hectares, owned by Baldwin's cousin Rudy Bambridge, who is a prominent lawyer and horseman. This Mataiea cowboy is twenty-six years old and when I asked if he is married he replied that he has five girls to sleep with. "He has five wives The Tahitian Way," Baldwin explained. Theophile doesn't carry a six-gun but often has a rifle with him on the range and uses it to shoot wild duck. He has three men working under him and they butcher as well as herd cattle. I asked him what kind of pasture is available to his herd. He said there are assorted grasses but the cows eat beaucoup bananas. This fruit is plentiful on the ranch, actually going to waste, and since the cows seem to love bananas, they are allowed to eat them as much as they want. They also

15

graze on mangoes and breadfruit, although the breadfruit has to be chopped up for them.

Out of this interview with Theophile Toofa came a constructive thought. If Mr. Rudy Bambridge can get his beef to the American market, the advertising agencies might have a great time playing around with such lines as: PRIME STEAKS FROM BANANA-FED COWS.

As the cowboy and I sat talking I noticed a pitch game in progress in a nearby banana-leaf shed. A pyramid of tin cans was set up on a plank and the contestants paid five francs for the privilege of trying to knock them down with a dozen rag balls. The balls were nothing more than hunks of blue-and-white pareu cloth—the same cloth that was designed in England by William Morris. Noeline asked Baldwin if she could play the game and we all walked over and took our turns firing at the cans. Noeline was good, and won a prize—a jelly glass. While we were admiring the prize a Tahitian girl about the same age as Noeline sauntered up to the shed, casually picked up a rag ball and let fly, and the tin cans went clattering over the ground. They were set up again and the girl wound up and cleared the board with a single shot. I'd hate to have that girl throwing rocks at me. She had speed and she had control and for all I know she may have had an effective change-up. We were all watching her and I was impressed by her beauty—she bore a strong resemblance to the Joan Bennett of twenty-five years ago and her tan skin was unblemished. Her loose-fitting cotton dress was faded and a bit frayed but that merely made her seem the more attractive. Inside the dress was something quite spectacular in the way of body. I came to a decision. This would be my Tahitian girl, my *vahine*. Adequate. Quite satisfactory. I moved up to the counter and picked up some balls and we were standing elbow to elbow. I turned to look at her, admiringly, and she was looking me straight in the eye. And she was giggling. I have been told that this is a sign of a fervent and deep-seated passion among Tahitian girls. A steady giggling that seems to have a few hiccups mixed in with it means that a Tahitian babe is ready for action. Her hair was down her back to her waist in two braids, and it was as black as a yard and a half down a shark's throat. I felt an explosive, volcanic heat rising within me, the same as those guys in that book *The Carpetbaggers*. I gazed steadily into her eyes, and she flashed a provocative smile. I suppose provocative is the word. I was provoked. Back of those lovely luscious lips were a few back teeth but none at all in front. In an instant she turned from a desirable, sensuous sex wagon into a crone. And in the same instant I abandoned all thought of becoming a dissolute beachcomber and resigned myself to continuing years of piddling around my vegetable garden and watching Buddy Nature Boy Rogers on T.V.

And so we returned to Baldwin's bamboo shack in the coconut grove and the maestro retired for a nap against the long night of music-making that lay ahead of him. Nelle and I got into swim clothes and went to the black sand beach. The shore had a deserted, primeval look for as far as the eye could see, as if nobody had set foot on it for centuries. There were remnants of old coconuts, and driftwood in grotesque shapes, the gnarled and misshapen stuff that is sometimes carved up and made into living-room pieces. There was a tropic mustiness, the smell of jungle decay. A misty rain was blowing off Little Tahiti's towering, soft-green slopes, and suddenly a rainbow flung itself across the landscape, sharp and clear, seeming to link the two islands more securely than the Isthmus of Taravao, and . . . git out th' way, Ole Donald Culross Peattie! I'm takin' over!

We returned to the bamboo house in time to see Noeline's mama coming through the palm trees bearing Christmas gifts for the *popaas*. There was a cardboard carton filled with fruit—two kinds of bananas, mangoes, papaya, and some others I didn't recognize. Then an ingenious package made of tightly-fitting banana leaves, formed into a leak-proof carrying container held together by sennit, and inside a quart or more of a purplish pudding, resembling Jello. I judged this to be a variety of the Tahitian *poe* which I've read about and which is said to be not only edible but tasty and flavored with bananas, as against the Hawaiian *poi* which is famous the world over for being ghastly. We carried the gifts home with us and the fruit was useful. I was puddin'-shy about the purple stuff and gave it to the hired girls.

As we drove home we took a turn along the waterfront. The only evidence that it was Christmas Eve was the six-foot lighted tree which had been raised to the top of the *Wanderlure's* mast. Below it there were lights and noise, for the Heintzes were having an eggnog party. We stopped in for a few moments, and on the deck ran into a young man from Alabama who is in the *Wanderlure's* crew. Nelle glanced at the lighted tree high overhead and said to this Secesh boy, "How on earth did you ever get it up there?" And he replied: "Drug 'er up with two hawgs and a mule."

And so we settled down at home to read a while, and to talk about the incredible beauty of the Tahitian land and sea, or those portions of it we had traveled through today. Christmas Eve in Paradise . . . and we were asleep soon after ten o'clock.

DECEMBER 25. Lay late in bed and it was six o'clock before I got to the kitchen and made us some breakfast of *pamplemousse* grown on the premises. An hour later, with the sun shining brilliantly, it began to rain — the fine, misty sort of rain called angel's tears, that brings out the perfume in all the flowers. Henryetta arrived bearing a load of Christmas food from Louise's kitchen — sliced turkey with truffles, great juicy succulent chunks of baby pig, and beautiful sliced tomatoes. I was sampling the pig when I heard a commotion on the terrace. The black cat was closing in on a young pigeon, already cripped and unable to fly. I chased the cat away and captured the pigeon and then had the

James A. Michener

Povenaaa's Daughter

Until he was forty, James A. Michener—born in Bucks County, Pennsylvania, around 1907, of unknown parentage and reared in poverty—had done almost everything except write a book. A Quaker volunteer for service in the Navy in World War II, he went, during a slack spell in combat, into a shed in an island plantation and began writing stories that appeared in 1947 under the title of *Tales of the South Pacific*. The book was awarded the Pulitzer Prize in 1948 as "a distinguished novel, preferably dealing with American life, by an American author." The world knows the sequel: a smash Broadway musical based upon the novel; thirty-five volumes that have sold twenty-one million copies around the world; and twelve Hollywood films inspired by his fiction. Some of his other books, such as *Return to Paradise* (1951), *Rascals in Paradise* (1957, with A. Grove Day), and *Hawaii* (1959), have contributed to the rich literature of the Pacific Islands.

One of Michener's finest stories is "Povenaaa's Daughter," set in Tahiti and its neighbor islands in the 1950's. The collision between outside cultures and the sturdy Polynesian tradition has never been better dramatized. The story is long because time must be allowed for Teuru to pass through her various involvements with men of four nationalities. Space is also required for the creation of the atmosphere of Papeete and Raiatea, regions that will never again be the same as they were during the decade after World War II.

NORTH OF TAHITI the *Hiro* began to roll, and before long all passengers were seasick. That is, they were all sick except a remarkable Polynesian woman of fifty who sat

21

on one of the forward hatches munching something she had pulled from a paper bag.

She was ridiculously fat. Her jowls seemed to run down onto her shoulders and her body, from neck to knee, was one unbroken ball of suet, covered by a blue-and-red Mother Hubbard which swayed solemnly about her ankles with each motion of the wallowing ship.

The bag from which she selected her dainties was quite greasy, and two men, long hovering at the vomit point, were thrust over when they saw what this large woman was eating. For Maggi — that was her only name — was eating fish heads. She would lift one from the bag, inspect it, then crack it with her teeth. There would follow a sucking sound, a smacking of lips and then more cracking, as if a dog were worrying a marrowbone. When she had quite drawn out all the goodness from the fish head, she would toss the skeleton in an arc over the rail and into the sea. Then she would loudly suck each of her eight fingers before probing once more among her inexhaustible supply of delicacies.

At the ship's rail hung a limp Chainman, so sick he thought he must die. Four times, just as he hoped he was becoming accustomed to the wicked roll of the *Hiro*, a fish head would go whirling past his face and he would collapse with retching. As the fifth head passed an inch from his nose, he stormed in outraged protest, "For the love of God, fat woman! Stop eating those fish heads!"

The woman in the Mother Hubbard put down her paper bag, wiped the grease off her huge cheeks, and looked at the miserable Chinaman. Placing her hands at spots where her hips had once been she taunted, "You've thrown over more than half of yourself. Jump after it!" Then, with ponderous grace, she rose and lurched over to the rail, where she swatted the sick man on the back. "Throw it up, Kim Sing!" she cried. She drew a greasy fish head from her sack and rubbed it under the Chinaman's nose, holding him by the waist as he heaved in agony. "That wasn't so bad, was it?" she asked like a mother.

Affectionately she dragged the near-dead Oriental to her hatch. After consuming two more heads she tossed the bag into the ocean and wiped her hands on the ample hem of her dress. Then, belching twice, she adjusted her huge bulk to the ridges on which she sat and asked, "Did you accomplish anything in Papeete?"

For a moment the sick man was unable to reply, but somehow the vast amplitude of the woman encouraged him and he said, "I made a contract for all my vanilla."

"Good!" she said with a crisp finality that meant she was saying nothing about her own mission to the capital.

But toward morning the Chinaman saw her smiling to herself in considerable satisfaction and he asked, "What did you find in Papeete that makes you smile, Maggi?"

She was not to be tricked. She laughed to herself for a moment, then rose and hurried to the rail. She peered into the stormy night and caught, along the horizon to the east, the first faint glow of dawn. It was a mere thread of pale light, yet as it played upon the tempestuous waters she could see, past the prow of the ship, waves breaking upon a reef. She studied the scene for some moments until she was satisfied that it was indeed her reef. Then she returned to the hatch and cried in a loud voice, "We'll soon be there!"

This caused a great commotion among the restless steerage passengers and they crowded the rail to catch the first sight of Raiatea, the ancient island from which all of Polynesia had been settled in the old days. In the dark mistiness of dawn they saw the island mysteriously appear out of the ocean, the spray high upon the reefs, the rain clouds low upon the historic hills.

Then suddenly, like the shifting mood of a wind that scurries across the surface of the sea, the passengers stopped mumbling to themselves, and Maggi, forgetting the Chinaman, elbowed her way forward to the prow of the ship, where she stood in the morning rain. She stood with her head cocked as if she were listening for a sound. But she was not, for on one of the offshore breezes came that most puissant of all island smells: the sweet, rich, perfumed, heavy, unforgettable odor of vanilla, ripening after harvest. The alluring sweetness filled the ocean. It was like the fragrance of many flowers, the richness of fine food, the sweetness of tropic sunshine. It was the smell of dawn. It rolled in blankets from the shores of Raiatea, the symbol of wealth, the reward of labor. Fat Maggi breathed heavily and thought, "I would give everything I smelled in Papeete for this. They speak of Paris! Pouf!"

As the *Hiro* warped its way to the creaking wharf, Maggi waited impatiently at the gangplank, and even before it was secured started to let herself down onto the dock. A group of cheering young men helped her, yanking her red-and-blue dress awry, but as soon as she felt the earth under her feet, she shook herself loose and plopped onto her head a pandanus hat, which she secured with one hand while running as fast as her bulk would permit through the copra sheds and down the main street of Raiatea.

As she hurried along many villagers called to her, seeking news of Tahiti. But on this day Maggi had no gossip to spare. She hurried on and at last half-galloped through the open doors of the island's only hotel.

"Povenaaa!" she bellowed. "Oh, Povenaaa!"

The hotel into which she had thus burst — Le Croix du Sud — was such a place as would have captured the imagination of Joseph Conrad had he voyaged to Raiatea. It was a two-story affair with an interior balcony off which opened several dismal rooms. The ground level was crammed with small, square tables, each attended by four chairs. An open kitchen, with many battered pots and pans, led to the rear and a dirty bar edged one side. A Japanese octagonal clock had run down some years before and now showed three-twenty, while a flyspecked portrait of Clemenceau surveyed the bar. And in one corner, barefooted and with a torn shirt, huddled a thin, unshaved

Polynesian man, sleeping off his drunk. This was her neighbor, Povenaaa.

Maggi's cries having had no effect upon the sleeper, she let fly with a solid kick and shouted, "Povenaaa! What a morning to sleep!"

The drowsy man twisted on his numbed hip, punched two dirty fists into his eyes, and looked up protestingly. When he recognized Maggi he scrambled to his feet, using her solid body as a post by which to haul himself to attention.

"Maggi!" he cried, embracing her warmly. "I didn't expect you!"

"Oh, Povenaaa! What news?"

He became all attention. He took off her hat and placed it carefully on a hook. He held a chair for her and banged furiously on the table for service. "Hey, there! Two breakfasts!"

A misanthropic servant stuck his head out from among the pots and asked dolefully, "Who's going to pay for two breakfasts?" Then he saw Maggi and smiled wanly. "For you, two breakfasts."

He produced coffee cups which weighed a pound each, great brutal things, cold brioches, and rancid Australian butter, served in a tin with a jagged edge. As Maggi sipped the chicory-laden brew, Povenaaa twisted his toes around the rung of the chair and asked impatiently, "What's the news, Maggi? Money?"

The big woman tried to play coy and savored her coffee down to the sticky sugar. Then she straightened her Mother Hubbard and said with tremendous import, "What we've waited for, Povenaaa. The Americans are back!"

The effect of this news on Povenaaa was electric. He rubbed his unwashed face, pressed down the front of his dirty shirt, and cried ecstatically, "Ah! *Les Americains!*"

"Yes. The yachts have begun to arrive."

"Lots of men?" Povenaaa drooled. "Lots of money?"

"Like the old days," Maggi replied, and the two neigh-

25

bors sighed nostalgically. Then abruptly, as if a deal had been concluded, Maggi slapped the table and cried, "Well! Why do we wait? Get Teuru!"

From a clapboard house down the road a young girl appeared. She had been interrupted at her toilet, for she carried a brush with which she tugged at her long black hair, which fell to her waist. She was barefooted and wore a cotton skirt with a skimpy bandanna halter. She was not a girl of extraordinary beauty, but she was handsomely proportioned and majestically straight in the Polynesian fashion. But her most memorable gift was a gamin smile and flashing black eyes that brimmed with an inner merriment.

She stood in the dust of the road, looking for her father, and when she saw him stumbling out from Le Croix du Sud she laughed affectionately and said, "Father! Stop the noise! You're drunk again."

"No, Teuru! Such news!"

His daughter remained in the road, brushing her hair until Povenaaa shook her by the shoulders. "Maggi's back!" he cried like a little boy relaying Christmas news.

"So soon?"

"And with such glorious news!"

With much nervous excitement Povenaaa led his daughter into the hotel and arranged a seat beside Maggi, who pinched her on the chin and cried, "I'm so happy for you!"

Before Teuru could ask why, some tourists from the *Hiro* entered the hotel and the men could not keep their eyes off the young girl, for it was deliciously apparent that she wore nothing beneath her cotton skirt, since Povenaaa had forced his daughter into her chair in such a way as to expose a splendid leg.

The men's eyes popping at the bar gave Maggi intense pleasure, but after the peep show had continued for some minutes, unknown to Teuru, the fat woman leaned over and with ostentatious prudery pulled down the offending dress. "Never show that much," she whispered, "except on purpose."

Povenaaa clasped his hands and giggled, "Teuru! You're going to Tahiti!"

At this Maggi clasped her young friend's hands and cried, "Oh, what I could do in Papeete these days if I was seventeen, like you."

"What's happened?" Teuru asked, caught up in the excitement.

Povenaaa giggled again. "The Americans! They've come back!"

"Yes, thank God!" Maggi drooled. "And you're going down to live on the best things dollars can buy."

"But I've never been to Tahiti," Teuru protested.

Maggi pulled her chair away from the bar and whispered, "You'll go, Teuru, and on the first day you'll meet a rich American on his yacht. All across the Pacific he'll have been dreaming of you."

"But I've never seen an American," Teuru pointed out.

Maggi ignored the interruption and said, "He'll let you live in his cabin. You'll eat your meals at the Yacht Club. Chinese girls will sew your dresses."

"You'll wear shoes, of course," Povenaaa interrupted. "White men like their girls to wear shoes."

"And if you find a handsome young lover," Maggi continued, "you'll have enough American money to pay his rent at the Hotel Montparnasse, where you can meet him at night."

"When the rich American is asleep," Povenaaa explained.

"And when the yacht sails there'll be another one coming in," Maggi said, recalling her boisterous youth in Papeete. "And who knows? Maybe later you will even get married."

Teuru listened to this recital with close attention. Povenaaa had always told her that some day the rich Americans would be coming back and it would be heaven for pretty girls. "And you'll be pretty!" he had assured her.

"But I wouldn't know what to do," she blushed.

27

"Do!" Maggi roared. "You don't do anything!" Then she dropped her voice and said, "With American men it's very simple. Look at that fellow at the bar. He's French, but all men are more or less the same. Povenaaa and I will leave. I'll manage to pull your dress up the way it was before. Watch what happens!"

As the big woman led Povenaaa from the hotel she hiked Teuru's dress accidentally, and all the men at the bar snapped to attention. A wife complained, "You haven't stared at me like that for ten years, Henri." To which he replied, "Ah, yes! But you haven't looked like that for fifteen."

Then one of them reacted as Maggi had prophesied. In three minutes he was trying to buy Teuru a drink. "I don't drink," she laughed. "My father does enough for both of us."

"Was that your father leaving here a moment ago?"

"Yes."

"Remarkably handsome fellow," the tourist said.

"You sound very silly," Teuru replied, whereupon the man coughed. At this point Maggi and Povenaaa returned. The Frenchman was completely confused and became more so when Povenaaa said, "Thanks, I'll have a cognac."

When the tourist had been eased away, after paying for the drinks, Maggi said, "See! It's simple! And with an American—much easier." Dramatically she fumbled in her bag and produced a slip of paper. *"Voila!* M'mzelle Teuru! Her ticket to Tahiti!"

The excitement of an actual ticket on the *Hiro* and the lure of Papeete were powerful, and Teuru's dark eyes bubbled with merry anticipation, but suddenly they sobered and she said, "I can't go."

"Why not?" Maggi snorted.

"I promised . . . Kim Sing . . . to work his vanilla vines again."

Povenaa exploded. "The Chinaman's vanilla! You compare that to a rich American!"

Maggi said quietly, "You were too young during the war, Teuru. We never smuggled you across to Bora Bora. But the lucky girls who did reach the American camp—they lived in paradise."

"A true paradise," Povenaaa cried. "Canned food. Jeep rides. Trips in the airplane. Whole cartons of cigarettes."

Maggi explained, "There's no reason to be afraid of Americans. I remember when they had a certain major who was what the men called an old bitch. Nobody could do anything with him. So I sent Hedy over and half an hour later she had his pants off."

Inspired, Povenaaa went to the door and roared, "Hedy! Come here!"

In a moment the heads at the bar almost snapped off, for into the doorway came a slim Polynesian girl of twenty-four. She held a very blonde child by the hand, and these two created a sensation of perfect beauty. Hedy—she had been so designated by the Americans—had the delicate quality of the actress from whom she had been named, but the frangipani flowers in her hair were her own device. When she spoke her voice was childish and musical. She did not want her daughter to enter the bar, so she said, "Major, you go back home." Then she saw Maggi and cried in her tinkling voice, "Good return, Maggi!"

"For you it's good," Maggi chuckled.

"You bring a message?" Hedy asked, keeping her eyes shyly upon the floor so that she would not have to look at the strange men along the bar.

"Such a message!" Povenaaa beamed.

"The Americans!" Maggi whispered, "They're back."

Unlike Teuru, Hedy knew how to appreciate this luxurious news. She smiled with delicate satisfaction, moved a little nearer Maggi, and sighed, "During the war they used to say, 'Come peace, Baby, you'll see me back here with a fist full of dough.'"

"She talks just like an American," Povenaaa said, proudly.

Hedy sighed again and sort of hugged herself. "I should

29

like to be in Papeete now!"

"And here's your ticket!" Maggi cried, producing another strip of paper.

"Oh, Maggi!" Hedy cried, embracing the fat woman. Then she pouted, "But what about Major?"

"I was thinking about Major," Maggi said softly.

There was a long moment while Hedy and Maggi stared at each other. Then, impulsively, the younger woman kissed the older and laughed, "You've always wanted Major, haven't you? Well, she's yours."

Povenaaa was sent to find Major and returned shortly with the fair-haired little girl, who ran promptly to her mother, but Hedy lifted the child deftly into Maggi's voluminous lap. "Maggi's your mother now," Hedy said gently.

The little girl looked first at her mother, then at her new mother. Both women winked at her and before the winks had rustled to rest, little Major — named after an American officer long since forgotten—accepted the new order. Hedy patted her approvingly and whispered, "You be good. Hedy's going to Tahiti."

Then Povenaaa spoke, officially, "You girls will love Papeete. I want you to behave yourselves. No drinking. Don't become bums like me. And remember that Americans do not shoot pistols all the time like the movies. I've known some very decent men." Then he stopped. He saw tears in his daughter's eyes. "What's the matter, Teuru?" he snapped.

"I want to see Papeete," she said haltingly. "I think I would like Americans but . . ."

"Poor little Teuru!" Povenaaa whispered. But her indecision frightened him and he realized he must tell the whole truth. "You must go," he pleaded. "For my sake if for nothing else. For if you could save only three hundred American dollars . . . Well, I could buy that surplus jeep on Bora Bora." He looked at Teuru in triumph, as if the coveted vehicle were already his. "And with a jeep! Why, I could be a very important man in Raiatea. With a jeep, that is."

The *Hiro* blew its whistle once. "I must pack!" Hedy cried. "Maggi! You must help me."

The two women bustled out of Le Croix du Sud and one of the men at the bar came to Poyenaaa's table. "Your pardon, sir. Who was that remarkable girl?"

"The big one or the little one?" Povenaaa asked.

"The . . . younger one."

"Name's Hedy. She's going to Tahiti." Then he grabbed Teuru's hand and started for the door, where he turned and added proudly, "And my daughter's going, too."

The *Hiro* blew its whistle twice, and then followed an amazing pageant of Polynesian life. Everybody on the dock began to weep. Maggi lowed and whimpered like a grief-stricken heifer. Povenaaa blubbered helplessly, repeating over and over again, "My daughter! My daughter!" Stragglers who had drifted down merely to watch the *Hiro* were caught in the lamenting and they too wept in an abandonment of sorrow. Tahiti lay less than a hundred miles away, and the ship sailed each week, but the sorrow in Raiatea could have been no greater had the passengers this day been destined for the Arctic wastes.

In a final debauchery of despair Maggi shrieked, "Hedy, look after Teuru!"

Hedy burst into passionate tears and screamed, "Povenaaa, I'll show Teuru what to do."

The *Hiro* blew its whistle the last time and stood out into the channel, and as it did so a transformation came over Hedy. She stopped weeping instantly, lifted her lovely head into the breeze, and looked southward. "Oh, Teuru," she whispered happily. "Tomorrow night we shall sleep in Papeete!" Then a frown puckered her forehead and she added, "But I wonder with who?"

Teuru blushed. A delicate color came to her cheeks, shining for a moment under the soft brown skin. "It's all very well to joke about such things, but . . ."

"Sssh!" Hedy warned. "Those gentlemen are looking at us. I'll bet they want to buy us some beer." But when

31

she turned she saw that Teuru was weeping. "Why are you crying now?" she asked sharply. "The boat's sailed."

And Teuru sniffled, "You've been away from home before. I haven't."

But by the following evening, when the *Hiro* like an exhausted porpoise rolled on toward Tahiti, Teuru's bubbling good humor returned and she shared in the general excitement as the glorious climax of their journey unfolded. To the west sprang the peaks of Moorea, crimson in sunlight. Ahead loomed the stumpy, cloud-wreathed hills of Tahiti. Seagulls dipped majestically about the ship, welcoming it as if it were a rich caravel, and even the seasick cattle revived as they caught the scent of land.

"Hedy!" Teuru cried, "look at those beautiful ships!"

"They must be the yachts," Hedy said, straightening her dress.

"And the white spires."

"Churches," Hedy guessed, keeping her attention focused on the yachts.

"But what's that?" Teuru cried.

To starboard, tied up to the quay that ran along the waterfront, stood a huge ship painted white. Along its deck moved sailors, also in white, each with a red pompom on his hat. "It's a French ship," Hedy sniffed scornfully. "You stay away from the French."

"It's lovely," Teuru said happily. "Even if it is French." Like most residents of the northern islands, she had inherited a revolutionary hatred of the French, who had subdued her islands last and with force.

"Ah!" Hedy cried. "Those yachts are American!"

But Teuru was fascinated by the warship, and as the tired old *Hiro* limped into port she stood at the railing and stared at the cruiser *Jean Delacroix* as long as it remained visible. Then, perforce, she had to look elsewhere, and for the first time she saw the rich panorama of Papeete.

Along the quay important Frenchmen bustled in coats that seemed too tight. Chinamen rode bicycles that teetered perilously, while handsome native men from the fishing boats hauled bonita onto the cobbled stones. Girls in Paris frocks walked slowly back and forth in twos and threes as officials in uniform bustled about giving orders, and a nest of tourists lolled in a rented sports car, blowing their horn at everyone. Three nuns waited on the dock for a sister reporting in from an outstation, and innumerable black and white and yellow boys ran screaming into alleys.

There was a color about Papeete that night that Teuru never would forget. The white clouds turning to purple. The silvery flash of bonita as they scintillated in the sun. The golden yellow towers of the Douane. The majestic motion of many people as their various colors blended, and everywhere the glorious flowers of Tahiti.

That was how Povenaaa's daughter arrived in Papeete. She stepped upon the dock barefooted, in a close fitting green-and-white pareu, her long black hair reaching her waist, a frangipani behind her left ear, a little wicker suitcase in her hand, and on the back of her head a straw hat. She took a deep breath of the new air and whispered, "We're here, Hedy."

The older girl presented a much different appearance. She wore shoes, very high in the heel, and a dress drawn tightly about her small waist. Her hair was done in plaited strands wound into a crown. For lips she had two scarlet dabs, but against the white flowers in her hair they seemed appropriate. She handed Teuru her suitcase, explaining, "American men don't like to see pretty girls lugging things."

As if she had lived in Papeete all her life, she led Teuru off the dock and westward to where the yachts were anchored. She knew she had little time, for the sun already had the peaks of Moorea aflame. Then abruptly she stopped. Suddenly she was no longer in a hurry. Motioning Teuru to stay behind, she sidled along the waterfront to where a yacht was tied stern to. A man of fifty was leaning over a board, cleaning fish. Hedy laughed musically and the yachtsman looked up.

"Watcha laughin' at?" he demanded.

"That's no way to clean a fish!" Hedy taunted.

"Whatsa matter with my way?"

"You'll cut yourself." She leaned slightly on the ropes, swaying with the motion of the ship. Then she laughed again.

"You think you could do it any better?" the yachtsman asked.

"Sure!" Hedy cried, using a French accent she had found irresistible during the war.

"If you're so smart, let's see." The man reached aft with a boathook and steadied Hedy as she swung herself aboard. "What's your name?" he asked.

"Fish-cleaner," she teased.

"No. Your real name."

"Hedy," she replied.

"Like Hedy Lamarr?"

"Yes. An American major said I looked like her." The petite girl leaned over to survey the mutilated fish, but she was careful to keep her lovely profile steady for several seconds.

"Say!" the yachtsman cried. "You do, at that!" He moved toward her, attracted by her extravagant charm, but as he did so she lifted the fish and laughed at him with tinkling music.

"You've ruined the fish," she said.

"Where'd'joo learn to speak English so good?"

"Oh!" she cried. "My bag!" She ran to the stern and started to shinny down the ropes.

"Don't go!" the American cried.

"I'll be back," she reassured him.

"What are you going to do?" Teuru whispered.

"Stop here for a while," Hedy said.

"What am I to do?" Teuru pleaded.

"Well," said the self-assured little beauty with a flip of

34

her head, "there's a lot more yachts."

"I couldn't do that."

Suddenly Hedy was all tender affection. "You're right! You've got to take these things very slowly. I remember when Maggi smuggled me ashore at Bora Bora. I was scared to death. I knew I'd never be able to talk with a major. An American, too."

"Were you?"

"Oh, yes," Hedy replied. She kissed Teuru good-bye and the girls began to cry.

"Whatsamatter down there?" the yachtsman shouted.

"My friend," Hedy blubbered.

"Whatsamatter with your friend?"

"She's never been away from home before!"

"Well, bring her along."

There was fresh sobbing, rising to a wail of remorse and lonely anguish. The American was totally bewildered as he watched his girl open her purse and hand the barefooted stranger a fistful of francs. He was even more surprised when Hedy wiped her eyes, flashed him a wonderful smile, pitched her bag aboard, and shinnied up the ropes with a wonderful cry, "All right! Where's that fish?"

Teuru was now alone in Papeete. Stuffing Hedy's benevolent francs into her suitcase, she pulled out a slim scrap of paper on which Maggi had scrawled two words: Hotel Montparnasse. She was about to seek a policeman when she beheld a sight that would have made the heart of any young girl dance with pleasure. Down the quay came three French sailors in dazzling white uniforms and red pompoms. Their shorts stopped crisply at the knee and they wore hard-ribbed white socks and highly polished shoes. They were laughing. They were laughing and making a great fuss, so that Teuru had to laugh, too.

They saw her hesitating at the edge of the road and quickly surrounded her. In French the tallest cried, "Ah,

the village maiden comes to the city!" Then they offered
her a cigarette.

"Ah! Virtuous maiden! She doesn't smoke!"

"I'm looking for a hotel," Teuru explained.

"*Voila!*" the sailors shouted.

"What happens here?" a policeman asked, patting himself on the belly.

"We're showing m'mzelle to her hotel!" the tall sailor
announced, making a little rhyme which his friends
mimicked in mincing style.

They grabbed her by the waist and swung her down
the street, so that she had to dance with them. Then they
lifted her high into the air and planted her bare feet on
the sidewalk. "The hotel of m'mzelle!" they cried, and
then the leader said very seriously, "Let it never be remarked that the men of *Jean Delacroix* were not gallant.
Your official welcome to Papeete." And he kissed her
firmly on the lips.

"So too the engine-room crew!" cried the next sailor,
holding her face to attention and wiping off his lips with
his shirt sleeve.

But the third sailor stood back. He blushed considerably and indicated that he would not force his attentions
on Teuru. His companions mocked him and the leader
cried, "M'mzelle! Our good friend Victor, he does not like
girls! Therefore, on behalf of Victor, I salute you again."
He lifted her into his arms, but this time Teuru did not
feel his lips, for over his shoulder she saw the confused,
scarlet face of Victor.

When the sailors left, their six handsome, white-
ribbed legs making rare patterns in the dusk, Teuru
watched them for a moment, then laughed and hoisted
her suitcase, turned on her bare feet, and marched into
the Hotel Montparnasse. This establishment, so inap-
propriately named, faced the peaks of Moorea, but
otherwise its facilities were unspeakable. It had served
wastrels and wanderers for almost a hundred years, and

in that time Rupert Brooke, Stevenson, Henry Adams, and Gauguin had lounged upon its dirty verandah, staring at the pantomime of Papeete. Now it was run by a German woman who wore stiff black lace collars, as if to bring to the hotel a respectability it had never owned.

"What do you want?" Frau Henslick snapped.

Teuru thrust the piece of paper onto the counter and Frau Henslick shouted, "What am I supposed to do? This says nothing."

"Maggi sent me."

"You mean the fat woman?"

"Yes!" Teuru beamed. "She said you might need help."

"I do," Frau Henslick cried. "I always do." She came from behind the counter and examined Teuru as if she were a horse. "Got your teeth?" Teuru opened her mouth and the woman nodded approvingly. "Can you work?"

"Yes," Teuru said. "I'm a good worker."

Suddenly the German woman screamed, "When you work here I want you to sleep in your own bed."

"What do you mean?" Teuru asked.

The German woman screamed even more loudly. "You island girls!"

That ended the conversation. Frau Henslick led Teuru to a dingy room, kicked open the door, and said, "You start work at six in the morning." Before the girl could reply, the angular woman had disappeared.

It was then seven, and Teuru was hungry, but before she could ask about food she heard the heavy shouting of a man: "Damn it! I want some hot water!"

There was some scuffling and Frau Henslick banged open Teuru's door. "You!" she shouted. "Take this upstairs to Mr. Roe."

Teuru lugged the pitcher to the upper hall and then wondered where she should deliver it. Reasoning that if she waited the man would shout again, she heard an irritated bellow issue from Room 16: "You old sow! Where's the water?"

Cautiously she pushed open the door and faced a young man standing in his shorts. He was redheaded and had a week's growth of beard. "Thanks," he said, turning his back on her.

At the door she asked, "Are you an American?"

"Yes," he said, swabbing his face.

"I've never seen an American before."

"We're pretty sturdy stuff," he said, lathering his beard.

She started downstairs, but he came to the door and called, "You eaten yet? Good. I'm just getting over a four-day drunk. How's about holding me up till I get to the restaurant?"

"I'll put my shoes on," she said.

"Don't bother. I never wear any."

He made her sit down while he shaved, cursing the blade. Finally he asked, "Do I look pretty awful?"

"You look pale," she replied.

He studied the mirror and shuddered: "Let's get out of here!"

He took her to the Yacht Club and insisted that she order the best of everything. He helped himself to poached eggs but couldn't manage them. Instead he sat back and admired the way she stuffed down the meat and vegetables. "I was hungry," she said.

"I feel nourished, just watching you," he laughed, but she made him eat some of her meat and he said it tasted pretty good, so he ordered some more, and while he pecked at it, she told him of Hedy.

"Which yacht was it?" he asked. When she described it he said, "She'll be a wizard if she gets a nickel out of that old bastard."

"Do you know him?"

"I came down here with him," Mr. Roe said.

"You will go back with him, too?"

"I'd sooner be dead." From the street came the sound of music and he said, "Would you like to dance?"

"I have no shoes."

"You forget, neither do I." He led her to Quinn's, a place Maggi had often mentioned, and there Teuru saw the gaiety of this island. As soon as Mr. Roe entered, everybody shouted to him and couples stopped by this table to ask what was new. He made no move to dance and she was not surprised when a very beautiful girl in shoes took him completely away. He did not return to Teuru at all but sat across the floor, drinking gin and growing more glazed each hour.

In her embarrassment Teuru was about to leave when there was commotion at the door and the three French sailors roared in. The leader saw Teuru at once and swung her onto the floor. He was good at native dances and flourished his hips as well as an island man. Soon Teuru felt her hair swinging about her shoulders, and then, as earlier that night, she saw across the room the penetrating stare of thin-faced Victor.

When she joined the sailors at their table, the young man rose properly, bowed and said, "My name is Victor de la Foret," and in those brief words he opened for Teuru a completely new vision of life, because when she said that she was from Raiatea, he replied, "I was born there."

"You were?" she asked. "I never heard of you."

"In spirit," he explained. "I had an uncle who served in these islands, and from the time I was a boy . . ." Nervously at first and then with a rush of golden words he told Teuru the history of her island: the hills that contained the marae, the straits from which the canoes set out to populate the Pacific, the forgotten groves where the lewd ritual dances were held. He was only twenty-one and he had never seen Raiatea, but he knew the island better than Teuru, who had left it only yesterday.

When Quinn's closed, the young couple walked along the quay until they found a bench, and then he told her of the map he had drawn of Raiatea, many years ago. "It was marked with a star," he said.

"What for?" she asked.

"Raiatea was the source. Women like you bore brave sons and they risked all the dangers of the sea."

For a moment these new ideas cast a spell over Teuru and she was back in the age when men of Raiatea ruled the oceans. Not until that night had she known that she carried such blood. Better than she could have liked any American, she liked this young sailor, and impulsively she reached out her brown hand and touched the red pompom. "It dances," she said, "on your white hat."

Victor drew back and even in the faltering light she could detect his blush. "You shouldn't have done that," he said nervously.

"Why not?" she asked perplexed.

"It's a rule," he said. "A silly rule."

"What is?"

"A girl . . . who touches a pompom . . . a sailor's red pompom, that is . . ."

"I'm very sorry," Teuru apologized.

"It's nothing," he assured her. "A stupid rule. But she must kiss him."

This was not play-kissing and Teuru rose in embarrassment and started to leave, but Victor caught her by the hand and said quietly, "Tonight . . . when the others were kissing you . . . I was afraid."

In stately grace the barefooted girl bent down and placed her lips on his. Her long hair fell about his shoulders and across his eyes. At first he did not move. Then, in an excess of joy, he flung his arms about her and pulled her down upon his knees. "You are like the queen of my island," he whispered.

These words were very sweet to Teuru, but she was somewhat perplexed—recalling all that Maggi had told her about how men behave—when Victor made no move to kiss her again but spent the night asking her detailed questions about Raiatea. Toward morning, when pale light was quivering upon the tips of Moorea, a bugle sounded on the *Jean Delacroix* and Victor said he must leave.

40

"I must see you each day," he whispered. Then, staring at his shoes, he confided his secret. "I joined the *Jean Delacroix* to see these islands. Because, you understand, I am going to write a great poem about Raiatea. In the ancient days, of course."

A policeman stopped by the bench and said, "You'd better get back to your ship, vice-admiral."

"Will you talk with me again tonight?" Victor begged, and Teuru said that she would. She reached the Montparnasse at five minutes to six and Frau Henslick screamed, "Come in, you baggage. Are you sober enough to work?"

"I'm all right," Teuru replied. Indeed, she thought the words had never really applied to her before that moment. She felt all right.

"Then go up and see what Mr. Roe's making such a noise about."

There was a wild clatter at the head of the stairs, followed by a bucket bouncing down, step by step. "I said I wanted some ice!" Mr. Roe stormed.

"Get him some," Frau Henslick ordered.

Teuru hauled some up to Room 16 and Mr. Roe shouted, "Bring it in!"

Gingerly Teuru pushed open the door, keeping her eyes down, for Mr. Roe was wearing almost nothing and in his bed slept the pretty girl, who now did not have her shoes on. By no gesture did Mr. Roe acknowledge that he had ever seen Teuru, and it was apparent that he knew nothing of the evening before.

All that morning Frau Henslick kept Teuru hopping, so that when siesta time came the girl did not even bother with food but fell into a deathlike sleep for two hours, awakening only when the German woman shook her. "Mr. Roe wants you again," Frau Henslick said.

"He makes a lot of trouble," Teuru said sleepily.

"He pays his bills," the landlady said simply, and thus Teuru was introduced to the rules of Hotel Montparnasse. People who paid were let alone. Teuru learned

41

never to enter any room unless invited. Each night after eleven, stray girls from all the outlying islands wandered through the hotel, checking up to see if all the men were sleeping well. It was not uncommon for two or sometimes three girls to spend the night in one visitor's room: one in bed and two on the floor. If no other place was available, they crowded into Mr. Roe's room, for he never bothered them, and if, as was often the case, he found them in his bed when he got back, he woud curl up in a chair on the verandah, unless he was very drunk, when he would roar, "Get the hell out of here. I've got to get some sleep." And there would be a scurry of bare feet down the corridors.

Teuru was not bothered by the Montparnasse because she herself lived in a kind of dream world. During almost every free moment she was with Victor de la Foret. On rented bicycles they rode and then clambered up to the pool of Pierre Loti, where, generations before, the romantic novelist had wooed his island girl. They danced, went to boxing shows, and sat in the movies. But most of all they talked. Teuru, who had been a quiet girl — Povenaaa's chin was always bobbing — now found herself able to speak for minutes at a time, relating her memories of Raiatea. True, she sometimes wondered when they were going to get around to those things that Maggi had said "were all that men wanted, anyway!"

When Victor finally did, Teuru was completely shocked. It happened one night while they were sitting on the bench. The young sailor caught Teuru by the waist and cried, "We are going to get married!"

"Married!" Teuru repeated. She was astounded at the idea. After all, she was only seventeen, not nearly of an age to marry. She had not yet lived with a man, she had borne no children, knew nothing of life. She suspected that it was both unfair and ungallant of Victor to propose such a thing, and in extreme perplexity she told him he had better go back to his ship.

"But will you marry me?" he begged.

"Not right away," she parried, and as soon as he had left she scurried across the quay to Hedy's yacht and scrambled aboard. In the darkness she upset a bucket and heard a gruff voice cry, "Get off'n this boat, you crooks!"

"Hedy!" she whispered. "It's Teuru!"

There were muffled protests but soon the Polynesian girl appeared. She embraced her friend and said, "The skipper complains a lot, but he bought me this robe."

They sat on the deck and Hedy listened carefully while Teuru explained about the wedding proposal. "I warned you!" Hedy cried indignantly. "I told you Frenchmen were no good. To expect you to marry him. So young! And no money!"

"What shall I do?" Teuru begged.

"You go back to Raiatea. Maggi and Povenaaa will tell you I'm right."

"Will you ever get married, Hedy?"

"Of course. In two or three years."

"Then why can't I?"

"At your age! You haven't even had a baby yet. You go home."

So next morning Teuru informed Frau Henslick that she'd be sailing on the Tuesday *Hiro*. The German woman bawled at her for being an ingrate, but Teuru was determined. Nevertheless, as the day ended she nervously watched the *Jean Delacroix*, waiting for the white suit and red pompom she had grown to love.

She was surprised, therefore, when Victor did not appear at the accustomed hour, and she was wandering idly along the quay when a young man in civilian clothes . . .

"Victor!" she cried. "I hardly knew you!"

"I was keeping it as a surprise. My enlistment's up and I cabled Paris for special permission to stay out here." He dropped his voice and added, "So that we could get married."

"But we can't!" Teuru objected. "I'm going home next *Hiro*."

"That's what I planned, too," he said eagerly.

"What did you plan?" Teuru asked, half in tears.

"To go with you . . . to Raiatea. Our first home! We'll get married on Monday."

"But Povenaaa would never let us!" Teuru protested.

"We'll talk with M'sieur Povenaaa," Victor insisted, and on Tuesday they were aboard the *Hiro.* There was a fine cry as Hedy and her American saw them off, with many flowers. Frau Henslick was there, too, with more flowers, and an old woman from Raiatea who just came down for the general lament. Victor said, "I am sure it must have been like this when the canoes set out for Hawaii. But Raiatea's only a few miles."

Teuru said, between tears, "It's always so sad to part."

That night they sat upon a crate of knitting yarn and watched the timeless race of the moon across the tropical heavens. As new constellations appeared, Victor named them, and all around was the music of a small ship plowing through starry night: the lowing of cattle, the whispers of women talking, the patient throb of the reluctant engines, the cry of a night bird, the echo of waves against wood.

Teuru sat close to Victor and in spite of Hedy's warnings, in spite of what she knew Povenaaa and Maggi would say, she wanted to marry this Frenchman. She was about to tell him so when a mysterious sound came from the port quarter and Victor rose. He peered into the darkness and asked, "What is that noise?"

Teuru stood beside him, her face pressed into the wind, and before she could speak the first probing dagger of light cut across the waves and poised above the hills of Raiatea.

"My island!" de la Foret cried, and there was something in his passionate recognition of a land he had never seen that bewildered Teuru, yet at the same time she felt that she had found the one man with whom she could live forever happily. They stood like enchanted voyagers from another age as the pitching *Hiro* approached the island. These were the hills that had bred the bravest navigators the world has ever known. These were the valleys of the most pagan rites, the sacred altars where human sacrifices had been dragged by the hair, the living monuments of a towering civilization—lost.

But their reverie was broken by shouts coming from the wharf. Some children had caught sight of the lovers and were screaming, "Povenaaa! Teuru has her American!"

The happy message sped through the crowd, for all the island knew of Teuru's mission, and all the villagers beamed approval of the handsome young American. Then, as the *Hiro* docked, there came a fresh commotion and the crowd fell back to make a pathway for Maggi, puffing and on fire. She took one look at the young people and shouted, "By God, girl! You've done it?" Then she turned and shouted, "Get Povenaaa!"

In a moment half the children on the quay were paging the town bum, and soon he appeared, barefooted, his pants falling away from his hips, his face a thicket of whiskers. Then, as his bleary eyes focused, he saw de la Foret and he cried in Polynesian, "I knew my daughter could catch herself a rich American!"

The gangway was lowered and Povenaaa received his first shock of the day, for when Teuru led Victor ashore, the first thing the young poet did was to stoop down and kiss the earth of Raiatea. "My God!" Povenaaa cried. "Is he sick?"

Maggi shook her fist at the *Hiro* and swore, "You'd give Jonah the seasickness."

Povenaaa led the procession to Le Croix du Sud and when the rancid butter appeared with the sour brioches he asked expansively, "And what part of America do you come from?"

Victor smiled and said, "I am a Frenchman."

There was a horrible silence while Maggi stared dumbly

at Povenaaa's gaping jaw. Teuru tried to help things out by saying that Victor was really a French sailor, but that he'd been discharged on Saturday.

"Oh, my God!" Maggi groaned.

Now Victor tried to soothe things. "I've come here to marry your daughter."

"No!" Povenaaa exploded. "No French pig shall . . ."

"Father," Teuru pleaded. "Let's go home."

"I think we better," Maggi said limply. With anguish she paid Povenaaa's bill—what a hollow celebration this had been—and then started for the weatherbeaten house. Once inside Povenaaa miraculously produced four rickety chairs and demanded, "Now what's all this about?"

"I want to marry your daughter," de la Foret said forcefully.

"No! She's too young!"

"And besides," Maggi added. "Frenchmen are not welcome here."

"She's right!" Povenaaa stormed. "No Frenchman will marry my daughter."

Now Teuru spoke. "But I love him. He's very gentle. He's a poet."

This caught Povenaaa off guard. He stopped blustering and leaned forward. "Poets are very famous. Do they make a lot of money?"

"No," Teuru interrupted. "Not yet. But some day he will. He's writing a long poem. About Raiatea."

"Son of a pig, it's strange!" Povenaaa mused. "The world full of rich Americans and my daughter picks a poor French poet."

Ignoring de la Foret completely, Maggi took Teuru's hand and said, "I understand Hedy got herself a beautiful yacht. How did she get a yacht and you a poet?"

Teuru blushed and explained, "She didn't fall in love. I did."

This was enough for Povenaaa. He rose to his full

height and announced dramatically, "There will be no marriage! Not between a poet and a girl only seventeen."

"What shall I do?" de la Foret cried, anguished that he must lose Teuru.

"You stay here, of course," Teuru replied.

"Here?" he repeated.

She lifted his bag and carried it into her small room. Next she fetched hers and placed it beside his. Then she stood in the doorway and motioned to him.

"You mean . . . I'm to stop here? With you?"

"But there's to be no marriage!" Povenaaa warned, defending his daughter from the unwelcome intruder. When de la Foret remained rooted in bewilderment, Povenaaa reached out and pushed him into Teuru's room. "You can stay here for the time being," he said grudgingly. "But no marriage!"

Disappointed and disgusted, Povenaaa slammed the door on the young lovers and slumped down beside Maggi. "A dog's luck," he mused bitterly.

"It's too bad," Maggi consoled. "But it'll work out . . . in time. The important thing is, be firm! Don't let them get married. He'll leave one of these days."

Povenaaa scratched his bewhiskered face and asked, "A poet? Do you suppose that's much better than a sailor?"

The disillusionment of young Victor de la Foret was catastrophic. It was not the disillusionment of love, for never had he been so happy. In the morning Teuru rose from their bed and polished the thin bamboo wafer she used on the vanilla flowers. Then she threw around herself a blue-and-white *pareu* and combed her radiant hair. Sometimes she would bring in a pawpaw, some limes, a mango, or a pot of black coffee. They would eat together while the morning birds made a symphony among the trees. Then she would kiss him good-bye and walk like some ancient goddess toward the vanilla plantations.

Nor was it the disillusionment of life with Povenaaa,

who worked each night to bring America into the conversation. The disappointed father made it emphatic that a Frenchman was a pretty poor substitute for a Yank. He also delighted in dandling Major on his knee, adding that he guessed no babies in the world were as pretty as American babies. He said— staring boldly at Teuru— that he guessed any girl in the world would be mighty happy to have a child as intelligent as Major. He taught the child to sing an amazing version of "Yankee Doodle." Worst of all, in an old copy of *Life* he found a full-page color shot of a jeep. This he posted right where Victor and Teuru had to face it as they ate. But for the most part Povenaaa proved a decent sort, even though he used to ask Maggi almost every night, in a voice so loud that Victor had to hear, "I wonder when he's leaving."

No, the tragic disillusionment that overtook Victor de la Foret was that of Raiatea itself. Where had the once great civilization fled? How could the godlike subduers of the vast Pacific have degenerated into Povenaaa? Why, only last week sailors of Raiatea had fled back to port when a trivial storm overtook them at sea. He studied the relics of the island, hoping of find an answer, but in no stone could he detect a trace of the grandeur that had once inhabited this land.

Strangely, he found his only solace in Maggi, who often sat with Major on her lap, droning about the old days. She could recite the names of all the canoes that had penetrated the oceans even to Peru.

"But what happened, Maggi?"

"Now we stay home."

"But where did the grandeur vanish?"

"It's still here. You ever see Major's mother? Very grandeur, Hedy!"

"I mean the spirit of life."

"It's here. Some time Teuru will take you to a real island dance."

Word arrived that there was to be one on nearby Bora Bora, and Victor arranged for a longboat to make the trip. He rode aft with Teuru and for a breathless moment he could believe that he was sailing with the immortal canoes. Ahead rose the fantastic cliffs of Bora Bora, radiant in the sunlight. About him the birds wheeled as they had generations ago during the hegira. In counterpoint to the throbbing of the engine he could hear the men of Raiatea chanting songs whose very meaning had been lost in the dust of years. This was the historic grandeur of Polynesia: brown bodies thrusting forward into the unknown sea, frail boats riding to the sunrise. Ahead the sure knowledge that somewhere there must be an island. Behind the security of a beautiful homeland.

He had a further sensation of historic reality when he decamped onto the shore of Bora Bora, where the cliffs dropped into the fairytale lagoon. As dusk came on, lovers from all over the island gathered and a tomtom beat out traditional rhythms. Men leaped into the ring and began furious gyrations. Soon they were joined by handsome girls. They danced, as if demented, a sexual ritual that probed far back into the past, until with furious cries the men caught the girls by the waist and threw them toward the jungle's edge. There was a timeless moment when the men leaped beside the girls as lovers ages ago had done before dragging the women into the bush. But now came a nervous giggle and the girls rejoined their friends.

The spell broken, de la Foret had to recognize not some dim memory of the past but the harsher actualities of now. This once godlike people! Look at them! Their teeth falling out from white man's food. Their health ruined with white man's diseases. Even the flaming moon that had once risen above the volcano to shine down on rare, savage bodies now limped up from a dead volcano and shed a pallid light upon a doomed and dying race.

49

"Teuru," he whispered, "let's go back." She understood his disillusionment and tried to round up the Raiatea sailors, but they were afraid to set forth in the darkness.

That was the beginning of de la Foret's illness. He had no fever, no disease. He was sick of that almost incurable malady: today. When he watched Povenaaa trying to sell his daughter to some rich American, he was sick. When he dissected the trivial life of modern Raiatea, he was sick. There had once been a glory, but today it was vanished. Therefore he was ill with today's illness.

His poem never got beyond the first canto. True, that fragment was superb and was published with distinction. It dealt with Polynesia as a physical world: the sky, the stars, the lonely islands. It was when people were introduced that the poem turned to rot. Victor was aware of this and stopped writing. "I am sick," he repeated.

"You must come with me while I work the vines," Teuru laughed, and it was there that de la Foret rebuilt himself. Day after day he watched Teuru move among the vines, grasping in her firm left fingers the flowers that looked like orchids. In her right hand she carried the bamboo wafer, which she deftly stroked along the stamen, collecting pollen. Then, with a twist of her left thumb, she snapped open the flap the protected the pistil and deposited upon it the pollen from her bamboo. Then she allowed the flap to snap back in place, whereupon she squeezed the pistil to be sure the pollen penetrated it.

"It's so tedious," Victor complained.

"Vanilla's too important to trust to luck," she explained. She said that every flower impregnated by her gentle method would produce a vanilla bean. Those she missed would die that night. "I do the work of bees and flies," she said.

Since the flowers opened at eight and closed at four, Teuru and Victor spent most of each day in the sunny fields, reworking the same vines daily to pollinate each new flower. "Povenaaa must be a rich man with so much vanilla," de la Foret observed as he watched the long beans ripening in the sun.

"They're not Povenaaa's!" Teuru laughed. "They belong to Kim Sing."

Then the sickness returned. The sunny islands of Polynesia were now owned by Chinese and Frenchmen and Germans. Everyone prospered. Only the Polynesians withered. "You spend so much care on a Chinaman's vines," Victor protested. "Who cares for you?"

Teuru blushed. "Yes. Povenaaa was asking that last night."

"What do you mean?"

She would not reply but that evening Povenaaa was most blunt. He had Major on his lap and asked, "When will you have a white baby, Teuru?" His daughter blushed and made no reply. "Well!" Povenaa continued. "You have a man for eight months now. What's the matter?"

Victor was outraged. "You shouldn't talk like that," he protested.

Maggi looked at him and sniffed. "Poets, hmmmm. I'll bet Hedy isn't fooling around with poets." She sucked at a bone and then called for Major. Swinging the child onto her lap she counseled, "Don't you ever bother with poets, Major."

Humiliated, young de la Foret left the table. Teuru found him along the shore. "What kind of father is Povenaaa?" the poet cried.

"He knows I ought to have a baby pretty soon," Teuru replied.

"Stop it! Are you trying to drive me mad?" He pushed her away and stormed along the beach. When Teuru tried to keep up with him he shouted at her in a high, tormented voice and told her to go home. She sought out Maggi and reported the strange behavior.

"Was he crying?" Maggi asked.

51

"Yes," the perplexed girl replied.

"Good!" Maggi said, straightening her Mother Hubbard. "When a white man cries it means that pretty soon he's going home."

"Why?"

"I can't explain it," Maggi said. "Every time you think you understand a white man, something like this happens. But I noticed that whenever one of my men cried I could start packing his things."

"Why are white men so hard to understand?" Teuru asked.

"Because they're all fools," Maggi explained.

"But you yourself said there were some wonderful white men on Bora Bora."

"Yes, but they were Americans."

"But Hedy told me that when the major found she was going to have a baby, he cried."

"What about?" Maggi asked suspiciously.

"About his wife in America."

Maggi shrugged her shoulders. "It's as I said. White men are very strange."

Victor returned late that night. Lighting a small lamp by Teuru's bed, he scanned the poetry he had tried to write. It was apparently very bad, for one by one the sheets were burned. Teuru feigned sleep and watched him. Then finally she asked, "Have you nothing you want to keep?"

Startled, he dropped a flaming page and had to extinguish it with his foot. When he had done so he sat on Teuru's bed and held her dark head close to his. "Yes," he muttered. "I have one thing to keep."

"What?" she inquired prosically.

"My memory of you." Then, as if he wished to explain exactly the meaning of this day, he launched into a long apostrophe to the fact that in the midst of a dying and degenerate world he had found one clean, pure symbol of the ancient grandeur: Teuru's placid beauty.

"What's 'placid' mean?" she asked.

He realized that she had not understood anything of what he was trying to say, and she, realizing that he did not intend making love, sighed and pulled away. "I've got to sleep," she said. "I must be up early."

When she rose, he had gone. He did not return and she heard that he had slept on the hotel floor like an ordinary tramp. When the *Hiro* arrived Major came running in with her childish news: "Victor go away!"

At first Teuru felt nothing. Victor was going back to France. Good. She went about her work, but as she did so she saw a vision of the young sailor in crisp whites, with a forbidden red pompom on his hat, and she burst from the house and dashed along the dusty road to the dock.

The *Hiro* was standing out into the channel, but she could see Victor against the railing. She was disposed to call out to him, but instead she stayed among the shadows and watched the boat recede into the distance. It was strange. As a girl she had often come to see the *Hiro* sail and aboard there might be some girl she had never really liked, but at the moment of departure she would break with weeping over the loss of this unimportant girl. Now Victor was leaving and she felt nothing. But then he put his hand over his eyes, as if he were shielding them from the morning sun in order to locate someone on the quay. She started to wave her hand and cry "Victor!" but she realized that the *Hiro* was already too far from shore.

At last she turned to resume her work in the vanilla fields, only to find Maggi and Povenaaa weeping bitterly, consoling each other. "He was a fine young man," Maggi said.

"For a Frenchman," Povenaaa said, "he was all right."

Then Maggi with fortitude wiped her eyes and announced, "But we must forget him. Look!" And she produced a ticket for Teuru on the next *Hiro*.

"Only this time," Povenaaa begged. "An American. Please."

There was a somber quality in Teuru's return to Papeete. The day was overcast and the brooding hills were enveloped in fog. Along the beautiful quay there was a gaping wound: the *Jean Delacroix* was missing. There were no sailors with red pompoms, and the waterfront looked as if it had been betrayed. Even Hedy's yacht was gone.

But Hedy herself was waiting at the gangplank. The slim girl had a scar across her right cheek. After she had fallen into Teuru's strong arms she said, "He hit me with a dish. Night before he sailed."

"Was he a good man?" Teuru asked.

"Pretty good," Hedy said reflectively. "I managed a lot of presents and some money."

"What are you doing now?" Teuru asked as she trudged back to her old job at the Montparnasse.

"I have another American," Hedy reported.

"You're lucky," Teuru said.

At the hotel Frau Henslick screamed, "So you've come back! Put your things in your old room. There's a Hikeroa girl in there now. Kick her out. She's no good."

Teuru was unpacking when the German landlady returned and announced, "Under no circumstances are you to give any food to that bastard Johnny Roe." This, Teuru figured, meant that Mr. Roe had stopped paying his bills. She was alarmed, therefore, when the American shouted for some ice. She filled the bucket and started upstairs.

"Remember!" Frau Henslick warned. "No food!"

Teuru was quite unprepared for what she saw. In bed lay the young American, very drunk. That was normal, but the once neat room was a shambles. Clothes were scattered everywhere, men's and women's, and as she picked her way among them she saw that Hedy was perched in the armchair, peeling an orange.

"Surprise!" Hedy cried. "I live here now!"

"Let's have the ice," Mr. Roe moaned.

"Don't worry about him!" Hedy laughed. "This is no

yacht, but Johnny's a lot more fun."

"You ought to keep the room cleaned up."

"Johnny don't care. And besides, I can see where things are."

Mr. Roe was in as bad a condition as his room. His face was a pallid white and his hair needed cutting. "I think he ought to have a doctor," Teuru said.

"He's drunk."

"How does he live?"

"Traveler's checks. They're wonderful. I sign his name here, and a Chinaman cashes them."

"Then why don't you pay his bills? So I can bring him food?"

"We go out to eat now and then," Hedy assured her, but it was obvious that most of the money went for her clothes and his gin.

So from time to time Teuru spent her own money to provide Mr. Roe a decent meal. She delivered it secretly so that neither Hedy nor Frau Henslick could berate her. One day she was sure that Mr. Roe was dying, but that very evening he and Hedy appeared at Quinn's. He was handsome in pressed whites. Hedy was breathless in a halter bra, a sweeping dirndl, and gold slippers. Mr. Roe recognized Teuru and asked her to dance.

"I must owe you a lot of money," he apologized.

"You ought to stay sober and eat more," she advised.

She hoped that he would invite her to dance again, but he soon became staggeringly drunk and danced no more. There were moments, these days, when Teuru was almost unhappy. She would step out of the hotel and see that gaping empty space where the *Jean Delacroix* had anchored, and she would recall Victor and his flashing white uniform. At such moments she would wish that somehow they could have married.

But it was difficult for Teuru to remain melancholy for long. Her happy, bubbling nature would assert itself and she would be swept once more into the rich pattern of Papeete life. In the evenings she would walk through the colorful streets, her head high, and she would find a dozen things to laugh at: tourists avoiding Chinamen as if they were killers, little girls acting like big girls and whistling at sailors, a Paumotu fisherman wrestling with a turtle. One night she stood for some time chuckling at a tiny Chinese seamstress trying to fit a very sour white woman with a white dress. Teuru's eyes bubbled with merriment as she watched the white woman trying to look important. Then she heard a rasping voice cry, "Don't move. Keep the light on your face."

She turned and saw a wretched little man of more than forty, pencil in hand, sitting in a doorway. His head was large and dirty. His clothes were borrowed and also dirty. He did not have good teeth and he was sketching Teuru's head.

"I must go now," she laughed.

"No!" he pleaded, and there was something in his voice that commanded her to stay. So she continued to laugh at the Chinese seamstress and the white woman, while the little man made hurried scratches on his pad.

"What are you doing?" she asked.

He showed her the sketch. "That's you," he said.

On that first night she talked a long time with Earl Weebles, even bought him some beer, which they shared in a grubby cantina while he explained what sculpture was. "I can take a piece of marble," he began. Then he laughed nervously and said, "Damned little marble I see these days. But I can take mud or cement or even butter. And a human being grows right out of it."

"I don't believe you," Teuru laughed.

So he took her to his small room and for five successive evenings she returned and posed for him while he hacked away at a chunk of tree he had somehow lugged into the room. "You understand," he said in his rasping voice, "that I can't pay you."

But she was so convinced that this little man loved

what he was doing that she sat willingly, amused by his earnest comment. "England's a rotten place to live," he said. "Too cold. I almost died there. Tuberculosis. But I always dreamed of Tahiti."

"How did you get here?" she asked.

"Damned near didn't. Got caught passing bad checks."

"Where did you learn to carve?"

"Never learned. Just started one day. Used to spend my last thruppence on museums. Went to Paris, too. Fine museums there. You ever been to Paris?"

"I've only been here twice," she laughed.

"You are very beautiful," he said. "Now! Would you like to see yourself?"

He stepped aside and allowed Teuru to see her portrait. She was astonished that wood could be hacked away until it looked like a human head: "My face isn't as lumpy as that!"

He explained, "I didn't try to make your face exactly as it is. I wanted to show it springing from the deep heart of Polynesia."

"What do you mean?" she asked.

"Your people," he said earnestly. "They are the most beautiful human beings I've seen. You are intended to represent them all." Then he tied a rope around the head and started lugging it into the street. "We'll see if we can sell it."

He hawked it through Quinn's, but nobody wanted it. He tried the Col Bleu with no more luck. There was a steamer in from Sydney and he offered it for two hundred francs, five dollars, thirty bob, any sum at all. He asked Teuru to stand beside it so the passengers could see the likeness.

"Don't look much like 'er," an Australian fireman growled, but he bought it for ten shillings. With the money Weebles took Teuru to Quinn's and ordered drinks. He danced, too, coming not quite as high as her forehead. Later, in his studio, he uncovered a three-foot piece of marble and said, "I've been saving it for something worthy. Would you pose for me?"

"Sure," she laughed, resuming the chair.

"I mean . . . undressed?"

She slipped off her clothes and stood in the wavering light, unconsciously assuming a pose that illustrated her strong peasant blood. "It is perfect!" Weebles said, but on that festive night when Teuru first stood in his room, he did not start to work upon the statue.

Teuru now entered upon a complicated life. During the day she listened to Frau Henslick's ranting. Occasionally she slipped out to get Mr. Roe some food, and in the evenings she posed for Earl Weebles as he carved out the series of heads and torsos that he peddled hopelessly through the streets of Papeete. But once after midnight, as she was preparing her bed in the studio, where she now slept, Weebles started to cough and blood came.

Often Teuru had seen this blood-cough in the islands and she knew its meaning. She tried to stifle her cry of pain, but it escaped, and Weebles, with his death sentence smeared redly upon his fingers, said, "That's why I stole money to get out here."

"But you musn't stay in this tiny room."

"I can work here. That's what matters."

"No!" she protested. "You are killing yourself."

"What else can I do?" the pathetic little man asked, chopping away at his work.

"You can come home with me," she said simply.

She would accept no argument. Earl Weebles was dying, that was plain, and if he remained in this narrow, choked Papeete hovel he would die very soon. But in Povenaaa's big house in Raiatea he might live for many years. Accordingly, she took her savings to the shipping office near the cathedral and said, "I want two tickets to Raiatea. There'll be a lot of baggage." She spent three days trying to sell Earl's accumulated statuary but in the end she had to give it away. His tools she packed and sent aboard the *Hiro*.

As the little ship rolled northward to the rich vanilla lands, it would have been natural for the eighteen-year-old girl to contemplate on why she, a girl of bubbling vitality, should be dragging along with her a consumptive and dying Englishman, old and ugly; but she did not engage in such speculation because what she was doing had been done in Polynesia since the first day Captain Wallis discovered the islands. The natives, rich and happy in their relaxed life, had instinctively reached out to protect the embittered or confused or deteriorated white man. It was a rare Polynesian family that did not have a record of some outcast cured of despair. The easygoing, sun-drenched natives kept white men as families near London or New York might keep beloved puppies. They were welcome to sleep with the unmarried daughters. And if the time ever came when they were able to return to what they called civilization, there was a pang of regret in the bosom of the Polynesian family that had — perhaps only for a brief period — protected them as treasured pets. So on the northward journey Teuru stood barefooted, her fine head and chest forward to shield little Earl Weebles from the rain.

The arrival in Raiatea was not gala. Maggi took one look at the little shrimp and washed her hands of the whole affair. "Another passage wasted," she snorted, adding in a loud voice so that all on the dock could hear, "They tell me, however, that Hedy caught herself another rich American."

To Povenaaa an Englishman was no better than a Frenchman. He made it a point to stumble over chunks of statuary and then moan as if his shin had been fractured. At night he would sit on his porch and shout across to Maggi, "I wanted a jeep and look what I got. A stonemason that don't even know how to build a house."

But Povenaaa's troubles were only beginning. Teuru made him haul clay to Weebles' room and big rocks and stumps of trees. She bought him not a jeep but a broken-down old mare, and it became a common sight to see sweating Povenaaa, his pants slipping down, straining along the roads, cursing bitterly while he dragged behind some huge object that raised a storm of dust and flies.

For the closer Earl Weebles came to death, the grander became his designs. His largest group showed Povenaaa, Maggi, and Teuru standing by the prow of a ship at the critical moment when it hesitates at the edge of the ocean. Povenaaa was transmuted into a fearless navigator. Maggi was the symbolic matriarch bearing food and determination into the canoe. Teuru was pregnant, carrying the seed of Polynesia to a new part of the world. In this majestic group there were no fragments of a dying race, no wormy, whining Povenaaa. Here was depicted the dayspring of Polynesia.

It was this way with every statue that Weebles carved. He did not record the death about him in Raiatea, for in the midst of his own death he saw life. He witnessed the eternal on-springing of humanity, and in his Raiatea pieces he created a testament of life. Consider only his figure of the fisherman. He wanted to use Povenaaa for this, but Teuru's father said he'd be damned if he'd take off his clothes again for that shriveled-up Englishman. So Weebles found an old man, useless for anything, and handed him a spear. What evolved was the figure of a man, rich in years, poised for one last try at the reef bonita. There was grandeur in the sagging belly line, compassion in the old head.

Earl Weebles saw these things. He said, "Raiatea is the most beautiful spot on earth." It was also apparent that he considered Teuru the most beautiful woman he had ever seen. Endlessly he copied her placid beauty. She would come home from working the vanilla vines, laughing, her hair about her waist, barefooted and strong, and he would insist that she stop just as she was, and he would prepare the sketch upon which he would work that night.

It was curious that she never thought of him as an artist. He was merely an unfortunate man who needed a last home. She worked for him, posed for him, slept with him, and comforted him when coughing spells attacked. She even enlisted the aid of her cautious employer, Kim Sing.

This happened when she found that Weebles needed new tools, a sketch book, and some medicine. Her own money had been used up and Povenaaa had none. So she went to Kim Sing. "Why do you need so much money?" he asked.

"To buy rocks with."

"Rocks!"

"Please, M'sieur Kim. My friend needs many things."

"Can he pay back the loan?"

"He could give you a piece of sculpture, perhaps?"

The canny businessman laughed. "None of that stuff!"

"Then I'll pay it back," Teuru said.

"How?"

"You yourself said I was your best workman."

"It would take a long time."

"I'll be here a long time," Teuru insisted.

"But why should you do such a thing?"

"Because Weebles needs the money. Now."

"Are you in love with this man?"

"Of course not."

"Then why do you seek the money?"

"Because he's very sick," she said.

By such persistence Teuru mustered the help of many people in behalf of Earl Weebles. In time she even wore down fat Maggi's contempt, whereupon she arranged for the sculptor to take his lunch at Maggi's, so that he could have hot food.

"I don't object to feeding you," Maggi puffed. "Most island families have some no-good bum eating their food sonner or later."

"Why do you tolerate it?" Weebles asked humbly.

61

"When I was young I liked to have a white man around. It was fashionable."

Weebles wiped his chin and said, "I could never express in words . . ."

"I know," Maggi broke in. "I must say that for you. You're grateful. You take the French poet that lived with Teuru last year. What a simpleton! Used to ask me, 'Maggi? Where has the grandeur gone?' I told him if he ever got a good hold on Hedy he'd have more grandeur than he could handle."

"The grandeur gone?" Weebles repeated incredulously. "I've never seen such grandeur before. The hills quiver with meaning."

"And you haven't seen Hedy yet!" Maggi added. In time she grew to like the wizened Englishman. "Weebles!" she cried one day. "Why don't you move over here with me?"

The little man looked up in amazement at the woman who weighed more than twice as much as he. "Not that," she roared, banging the table until the plate of fried fish clattered. "I was thinking that if you left Povenaaa's . . . If I took care of you . . . Then Teuru could go back to Papeete."

"Does she want to go?" Weebles asked quietly.

"Of course she does. She's got to catch herself a rich American."

There was a long silence, one of those hazy, fly-buzzing pauses during which the bedraggled Englishman stared at the fat woman. Finally he muttered, "I won't be there much longer."

"The sickness?" Maggi asked, banging her chest. "It's bad, eh?" Weebles nodded and Maggi changed the subject abruptly, "But you've got to do something with all that junk."

"What junk?"

"Those heads. Those things you carve."

"What do you mean?"

"I mean," she said, banging the table, "that pretty soon it's going to cave in Povenaaa's floor." That was when she started hauling one piece after another down to the *Hiro,* peddling them among the passengers. She sold by weight, asking a dollar a pound, but she was usually so sweaty and puffing when she lugged the stuff aboard that she would accept any reasonable offer.

Weebles was delighted. He had, in his lifetime, sold very few pieces and he glowed with satisfaction when Maggi reported good luck. "Remember that head of Teuru that looked like a cow? This morning I stuck a Swiss woman with it."

Weebles loved beer and in the evening, when a sale had been made, he would stand treat at Le Croix du Sud. Once, as Teuru raised the amber glass to her amber lips, the sculptor stopped, enraptured. He put down his glass, deeply affected, and begged to be excused. They heard him coughing outside, and he waited in the road until Teuru left the bar. They walked through the deserted streets, down to the wharf where the sweet vanilla beans were waiting shipment.

"I've never been able to talk well," he said.

They had never said much, Teuru and Weebles, but this night great agitation gnawed him and he said, "You're very young . . ." but the precise words would not come, and he stood there by the straits from which the great navigators had set forth. His hands reached for hers and he felt the subtle structure of her bone and flesh. Finally he blurted out, all at once, "You have wasted these months on me."

There was a world more he wanted to say, but he was silent, an inchoate chunk of confusion which no chisel like his own had ever quite polished to completion. When they got home he begged her to pose for him once again, and Teuru stood there naked in her father's room. The statue was never completed, of course, for that night he died.

He was buried, as he would have wished, near the straits of Raiatea. When the funeral was over Povenaaa said, "Now we can get some of this junk out of here." He ordered the whole collection to be hauled away, but this was a silly command because he had to do the hauling. The smaller pieces he gave to people about the island who had posed for Weebles at one time or another. But he was stuck with the big ones. He tried to make Maggi take some, but she would have none of them.

"If I look like a blown-up whale," she snorted, "I at least don't want a picture of me around the house."

It was she who finally talked some sense into Teuru's head. She said, "It's all very well to be nice to men. A girl ought to be. Lord knows, I was in my day. But it's also necessary to look out for yourself. How do you suppose I bought this house? A rich American, that's how. Now you get on back to Tahiti and find yourself a real man."

She bought Teuru her third ticket to Papeete and whispered consolingly as the *Hiro* blew its whistle, "You've had a no-good Frenchman and a half-dead Englishman. Get yourself a strong American and start having babies."

This time Hedy did not meet Teuru at the Papeete quay. Alone, the nineteen-year-old trudged back to the Hotel Montparnasse, where to her surprise Frau Henslick greeted her with an embrace. "You're the only girl I've ever been able to trust," she shouted. "That Hikeroa girl has your room again. Throw the tramp out."

Cautiously Teuru motioned up the stairs with her thumb. "Hedy still here?"

Frau Henslick put down her pencil and beamed. "She's the smart one. She's married."

"To the American?"

"That good-for-nothing drunk?" And although Teuru could hear no disturbance, Frau Henslick suddenly screamed, "Shut up, you lazy bastard."

"What's the matter with him?" Teuru asked.

"Nothing. Hedy stayed around till the traveler's checks were used up. Then she married this rich Austrian refugee. He runs the new curio shop."

Frau Henslick directed Teuru along the quay to a bright new store. Inside, a nervous Austrian tended shop, hovering like a frightened hummingbird above trays of exquisite jewelry. "Is Hedy here?" Teuru asked.

The Austrian fluttered to the back of the shop and with obvious uxoriousness called for his wife. In a moment she appeared, gloriously pregnant. She posed for a moment beside her birdlike mate and then said, "M'sieur Kraushoffer—you must never call him Herr Kraushoffer. He wants no more of that. He's a real sculptor, not like that dirty Englishman." She pointed out the delicate filigree work that M'sieur did. "It sells very well."

In proof she led barefooted Teuru onto the sidewalk and pointed to a spanking new Renault. "Ours," she said simply. She made Teuru climb in, and they took turns blowing the horn. Then she kissed her friend and whispered, "M'sieur Kraushoffer has a rich friend. Tonight put on your best dress and eat with us."

The dinner was excellent, and Hedy was quite the grandest lady Teuru had ever seen. She commanded the servants what they must do, served the wine with a dazzling smile, and continually referred to how clever her husband was. The other guest was a moody Bavarian, Herr Brandt. He was, he announced, considering a business in Tahiti. He used many words that Teuru did not understand and wound up by trying to rip off all her clothes. She was not averse to lovemaking, for Maggi had long ago instructed that this was natural for a girl after she was fifteen and that men seemed to enjoy it greatly. But Teuru compared rough, cold Herr Brandt with kind, gentle Earl Weebles and as a logical conclusion she smashed the German across the nose and ran back to the hotel.

In the morning Hedy appeared. She was furious, said

that Teuru had insulted her husband's friend and that she must never come back to the shop again. Never. Tears followed, with Hedy admitting that Herr Brandt had tried to do the same with her once and that she had struck him too. She gave Teuru a wrist-watch and said, "Take it up to Johnny. We broke up in a terrible row, and I stole most of his things. But I'm not mad at him any more." She fluffed out her pretty dress, said good-bye, and walked down the quay, calling *"Bon jour"* to all the other respectable married women of the town.

It was some time before Teuru found occasion to deliver the stolen watch, but when she did she was dismayed at what she found. In a dark room, surrounded by filthy confusion, red-headed Johnny Roe lay sprawled on a bed he had not left for four days. He had not shaved. He had not washed. He had not eaten. He was a horrible cartoon of a man, so that even the stray island girls now left him alone at night.

"Mr. Roe!" Teuru called gently. In a month-old stupor he rolled his head slightly and stared at her.

"Who's there?" he mumbled.

"I've brought your watch back. You must get up." She threw him a pair of shorts and insisted that he crawl into them, but when she tried to lead him along the hallway to the bathroom he collapsed. Teuru called for Frau Henslick, who hurried to the top of the stairs. When she saw it was Roe again she became raucous.

"I'll never touch that drunken swine again. I've hauled him back to his room for the last time." She stood over the crumpled body — the most recent in a distinguished line of men who had tried to drink themselves to death in the Montparnasse — and reviled the American while Teuru ran along the quay searching for someone to help her lift the inert form. Finally she got Johnny spread-eagled on the sheets. Then she washed and shaved him, holding his face tightly when the dull razor grabbed. He was bleeding when she finished, but he was beginning to look like a human being.

It was three days before he could walk to a meal. In that time Teuru had actually to chew small portions of meat and place them between his lips. She had also to buy him the gin he whimpered for, giving him a little less each day until she had weaned him back to strength.

Frau Henslick was outraged. She said that Johnny Roe should be tossed into the bay. "Shark's meat! That's what he is!" She said that as soon as he could move she was going to have him tossed in jail. And as for that room! Out he must go!

Teuru solved this by moving him down to her room, and it was there, in a grubby back hallway of the Montparnasse, that she finally learned how truly sweet it was to be in love. It was as Maggi had said, "Quiet bits of heaven." For Johnny Roe had come so close to wrecking himself that he could appreciate what Teuru had done for him.

"See what the Chinaman will give us for the watch," he suggested. She became adept in haggling over prices with the pawnbrokers and she hoarded both her salary and the loans on his jewelry. Like a French housewife she husbanded their wealth and spent it on things that would be good for Johnny. It was very good to watch him come alive.

"What happened to you?" she asked.

"I'd always heard about these islands. After the war I wanted to see them."

"Were you in the war?"

"Like everyone else."

"Why is it so many white men want to come to Tahiti?"

"You've got to have somewhere you want to go," he replied.

"What did you want to find?"

"You, I guess."

"We're out of money," she replied, changing the subject.

"I'll have to get a job—somewhere."

"What can you do?" she asked.

"Best thing I ever did was fly a plane."

"Maybe I can figure out something," she said.

And that was how Teuru, Povenaaa's daughter, finally arrived one day in Raiatea with an honest-to-God American. As the *Hiro* docked Maggi and Povenaaa waited ecstatically. They studied the clean-shaven, good-looking young man, and Maggi cried in Polynesian, "I knew you could do it!"

It was a much different story, however, when the four of them faced the rancid butter of Le Croix du Sud. Povenaaa got right to the point. "I better hurry over to Bora Bora, because there's only one jeep left."

"You buying a jeep?" Johnny inquired.

Povenaaa winked broadly and patted Johnny on the arm. "It's good to see you here, son. How long you intend to stay?"

"As long as Kim Sing . . . that's his name, isn't it?"

"You know our leading merchant?" Povenaaa asked expansively.

"Not exactly. I hope to work for him, though."

"Work?" Maggi gulped.

"Did you say work?" Povenaaa gaped.

"Yes. Teuru told me . . ."

Now Povenaaa became all diplomacy. "Do you mean," he probed, "that you have to work?"

"Yes."

"You mean . . . you're broke?"

"That's right. If it hadn't been for Teuru . . ."

This was more than the man could bear. Povenaaa became choleric and then spluttered, "Pigs! Dogs! Chickens!" What this meant he did not stop to explain. In majestic outrage he stamped from the hotel and did not show his face in the bar for three days. As for Maggi, she sank back in her chair and studied Teuru. Three times she started to ask questions but each time she shuddered and ended by ordering herself more beer.

By this time Kim Sing had opened his vanilla sheds and the rich smell permeated the bar, so Teuru said, "You'll get used to that smell. We'll go now."

She led Johnny across the road and presented him to the merchant. "An American?" Kim replied. "I couldn't pay an American decent wages."

"Any wages would be decent," Johnny confessed.

So each sunny morning Johnny Roe hauled out into the hot sunlight huge tarpaulins bearing the harvested beans, now five to seven inches long, laden with essence which the heat would tease into condition, so that in time the patiently tended beans became pliable and wonderfully odorous. At night he hauled the tarps in out of the dew, and when the beans were cured, he arranged them upright in big tables.

Then Teuru went to work. Sitting with her eyes at the level of the bean tops, she bundled the licorice-colored beans into the quarter-kilo packages which were shipped to Paris. Forming her left hand in a circle, she would cull from the large assortment a few choice beans to make the outside of the bundle attractive. For the middle she saved the scrubs, being attentive to select each bean so that when the longer outside ones were pulled into position all beans would appear to be of the same length. Kim Sing said that Teuru's deft bundling earned him an extra twenty per cent.

These were happy days for Teuru. She watched Johnny thriving under the new regime and saw that he was growing brown and strong. It was fun, too, to have him working with her, and she enjoyed watching him spend the money she allowed him at the bar. He drank only beer himself, but he was a great favorite with the young men at Raiatea, standing them whiskey and gin, beating them at darts. Sometimes Teuru told herself that she had been luckier than most girls, and the more she grew to love Johnny the more clearly she remembered fright-

69

ened Victor and triumphant Earl Weebles. One night she told Maggi, "I've been lucky."

Maggi leaned back to count up the score. "By and large you have been," she agreed.

Only Povenaaa held out. Each time he saw Johnny he was humiliated anew. Pushing his forlorn mare along the roads, the cruelly betrayed man would dream of that last jeep in Bora Bora. Then he would hammer the mare and imagine it was Johnny Roe.

But when Povenaaa did finally accept Johnny it was completely, said he was the finest American he had ever known. The two men got roaring tight and stopped every stranger to tell them the news. Teuru was going to have a baby!

Yes, Teuru was pregnant. Maggi, of course, had been the first to detect the happy secret, and she commissioned Major to dash through the streets informing everyone. When Povenaaa heard, he left the mule right in the vanilla fields and came storming into the shed and informed Kim Sing, "We're going to the bar and get drunk." Then he had a better idea. He whispered to Johnny, "We'll stick the Chinaman for the drinks." Unctuously he said to Kim, "It wouldn't be a celebration without you." So the merchant paid for the bottles and Povenaaa giggled at having made the Chinaman a fool. But Kim Sing had plans of his own, and when they were discovered, they almost drove Johnny Roe crazy.

It happened one morning when Johnny came to work and found Maggi, Kim Sing, Povenaaa, and three other men rolling dice. Teuru stood nearby, watching the game with interest, advising Maggi, "You'd better try harder! You need three more sixes!"

"What's the game?" Johnny asked.

"Dice," Teuru said.

"I can see that. What's it about?"

Teuru blushed and looked away, so Johnny asked Povenaaa. "Don't bother me now," the excited man cried. Suddenly there were shouts of triumph and Maggi swore the Chinaman had cheated, but Kim Sing grinned happily and picked up the dice.

"The damned Chinaman gets the baby," Povenaaa spat.

"Gets what?" Johnny asked.

"The baby."

"Whose baby?"

"Teuru's."

"I didn't know Teuru had a baby."

"She doesn't . . . yet."

"You mean . . . my baby?" Johnny fell back with his mouth gaping. Then he yelled, "Hey! What's this about my baby?"

"He won it," Maggi said disconsolately.

Grabbing Teuru the American cried, "What are they talking about?"

"When it's born," Teuru said. "All the people in Raiatea would like to have it. So we rolled dice."

"But it's your own baby!" he stormed.

"Sure," she said. "But I can't keep it. I'm not married."

"Your own flesh and blood!"

"What's he mean?" Teuru asked Maggi.

Johnny Roe looked beseechingly at the fat woman and asked, "Would you give away your own baby? Would you give away Major?"

The crowd in the vanilla shed burst into laughter and Johnny demanded to know the joke. "It's Major!" Povenaaa roared, punching Johnny in the ribs. "Major's not her baby. She's Hedy's."

"You mean that Hedy . . . ."

"Of course," Maggi explained. "Hedy had to go to Tahiti for good time before settling down. So she gave me Major."

Johnny Roe had heard enough. He stormed off and bought two bottles of gin, and when Teuru found him he had returned to his Montparnasse days except that now

71

he blubbered, "Our baby! You raffled off our baby with a pair of dice!"

He kept this up for a whole day and Teuru became afraid that it was the start of another epic binge, so she broke the gin bottles and said, "All girls give away their first babies. How else could they get married?"

Johnny sat upright, suddenly sobered. "What do you mean, married?"

"What man in Raiatea would want a girl who couldn't have babies?"

"You mean . . . the men don't care?"

"Very much! Since people find I'm to have a baby several men who never noticed me before have asked when you were going away."

"What happens then?" Johnny asked suspiciously.

"Then I get married."

Johnny fell back on his pillow and moaned, "It's indecent. By God, it's indecent."

So Teuru consulted Maggi, who said, "I'll talk to him." She puffed into the bedroom and asked, "What are you moaning about?"

"This whole affair. It's indecent."

"What's wrong about it? Tell me, why did you come out here?"

"I was a drunken Papeete wreck, so Teuru brought me here."

"I mean why did you come to Tahiti?"

"Well, in California I was even a worse wreck."

"Why?"

"The war, I guess."

"We had a war, too."

"Mine was different."

"Oh, no. Eighty men from Raiatea volunteered and went into the desert with the Foreign Legion. We lost many men from Raiatea."

"They have a statue in Canada which says something about the ones who didn't come back being the lucky ones."

72

"Don't ever believe it! Is that what you thought, Johnnny?"

"Something like that. I got all mixed up."

Maggi started to laugh. "I'll never understand white men."

"How do you mean?" Johnny asked.

"Like you," she said, puffing heavily. "You get sick at heart about something, so you come out here to cure this disease, and when you're cured you despise us for how we manage it. That seems ridiculous to me."

"It's even more ridiculous, how a girl's own father— how Povenaaa can send Teuru to Papeete."

Maggi exploded with laughter. "Povenaaa? Did you say Povenaaa?" She held her fat sides and shook her head hilariously. "Didn't anybody tell you? Povenaaa could have no children. That poor skinny man. We felt sorry for him in Raiatea so somebody gave him a baby to bring up."

"Who did?"

"I did."

Johnny Roe was stopped dead cold. They were pitching curves at him now and he was stopped cold. He started to laugh and finally kissed fat Maggi on the cheek. Seeing her chance, she grabbed him by the hair and kissed him back.

"You're a smart woman," he cried. "You're about the smartest woman I've ever known."

"I been around," she joked, talking like an American movie.

Johnny finally sat on the bed and asked, "How come you gave up Teuru?"

"I heard the rich Americans were coming to Papeete . . . about the time of Zane Grey. I wanted to see things before I married."

"Did you marry?"

"Oh, yes."

"Where's your husband?"

"He was killed in the war. In the desert."

That was that. Johnny had no more to say, but as she left, Maggi added, "When you get back home . . . Well, if you should ever make any money, send Povenaaa a jeep."

But Povenaaa did not have to wait upon such a miracle, for a more astonishing one took place right on Raiatea. One morning, about seven, a yacht put into the straits and an expensive launch, manned by men in white, hurried ashore. An elderly gentleman with white moustaches asked many questions at Le Croix du Sud and ended by going to Kim Sing's vanilla shed. He stood in the doorway for a moment until his eyes became accustomed to the shadows. Then he saw what he was seeking.

"Hello, Johnny," he said.

The young American turned, clean, bronzed, solid-looking: "Hello, Mr. Winchester."

"I told your father I'd look you up."

"How is Dad?"

"Fine, fine. I think he'd like to have you back."

That night on the polished yacht Povenaaa and Maggi ate off silver plates, but Teuru was not there. "I'm too fat," she told Johnny, insisting that he go. After brandy Mr. Winchester said he thought it was about time for Johnny Roehampton to be heading home. Johnny blushed nervously and agreed it was about time.

"He's been here long enough," Maggi said expansively.

"Too long," Povenaaa observed.

Johnny had much to do before shoving off. He thanked Kim Sing for the job. He gave presents to each of the gang at the bar. He bought Maggi a shawl and even promised to send Povenaaa a jeep.

But Povenaaa had been disappointed many times in his life and he was not to be taken in by any more tricks, so while Johnny was packing he rowed out to the yacht and consulted Mrs. Winchester. "I don't ask much," he said. "I'm reasonable, but I've had dreadful bad luck with Teuru."

"Who's Teuru?"

"My daughter."

"Is she sick?"

"No, she's pregnant."

Mrs. Winchester gulped. "You mean . . . she isn't . . . married?"

"Certainly not!" Povenaaa snapped. "It's my bad luck with her men I'm speaking of."

"What do you mean, her men?"

"I don't think she has good sense," Povenaaa explained. "First she brings home a Frenchman. He lives with us eight months and I don't get a sou. Then she brings home an Englishman. Not a sou. Now it's Johnny Roe. Still no money."

Mrs. Winchester grew pale. "You mean . . . you would take money . . . for your daughter?"

"Well, seeing that Johnny is leaving behind a baby that I'll have to feed . . ."

Weakly Mrs. Winchester cried, "Griswold! Grisworld!" When her husband appeared she whispered, "Get this creature out of here."

"What's going on?" Mr. Winchester blustered.

"It's unspeakable! This wretched man's daughter has had three lovers. Now she's going to have a baby and her father"—she shuddered—"wants to be paid off."

Mr. Winchester took out his wallet and said, "My dear, I warned you that Tahiti . . ."

"Don't give it to him! Give it to the girl, if she's not some cheap . . ."

"I've seen the girl," Mr. Winchester said. "She's very decent."

He took his wife ashore and led her to the vanilla shed, where she gasped when she saw how lovely Teuru was.

"You're very pretty," Mrs. Winchester said.

"Johnny told me you were an old friend."

"Yes, we've known his family for years."

"What will Johnny do . . . when he gets home, I mean?"

Mrs. Winchester perceived that she had stumbled upon the classic island tragedy: the deserted native girl and the handsome white man. So she said gently, "He'll probably go back to college."

"And get married?" Teuru asked, smiling warmly as she whipped cords about her bundle of beans.

Mrs. Winchester knew that the brave smile masked the heartbreak of betrayal, so she said consolingly, "And you? What will you do?"

Teuru started a new bundle in her left hand and said thoughtfully, "I guess I'll get married, too. After I get rid of the baby."

Mrs. Winchester swallowed. "What do you mean? Get rid of the baby?"

"Kim Sing won it. After a few weeks I'll give it to Kim Sing."

"He . . . won . . . it?" the American woman asked weakly.

"Yes. He threw eleven sixes."

Mrs. Winchester retreated in a flood of nausea. At the door she bumped into Povenaaa and said to her husband between clenched teeth, "Give this despicable creature some money." Then she stared at Povenaaa and said bitterly, "You had to take care of the baby!"

Yet it was Mr. Winchester's money that finally settled many problems for Teuru. After the yacht left, with red-headed Johnny Roehampton staring at the dock until the headland had been breasted, Povenaaa slipped over to Bora Bora and came home with the last jeep. It was badly battered and carried a garish sign across the front: Shore Patrol. But it ran and it had a horn. Povenaaa's first use of it was to drive up to Kim Sing's establishment and blow the horn like mad. When the Chinaman appeared, Povenaaa stood up and announced to his former employer, "You, M'sieur Kim Sing, can go to hell." Then he drove off down the middle of the road.

Teuru immediately came to apologize. She told Kim

he had always been kind to her family and that she appreciated this. "And now what will you do?" Kim asked.

Teuru looked at the bundles she had tied and said, "After the child is born, Maggi wants me to go back to Papeete."

"Papeete is very fine," Kim said.

"But the rooms are so small and dark. I don't want to leave Raiatea any more."

Kim Sing thought a long time and said, "You should tell your father."

So Teuru sought out Povenaaa at the new pier where he was hauling rock. "I'm not going back to Tahiti," she announced.

To her surprise Povenaaa said, "Good! We're people of importance now. We still have lots of money left from the yacht." Then seeing Kim Sing approaching, he shouted, "And no daughter of mine is going to work for a damned Chinaman, either!"

Kim Sing came to the pile of rocks and said haltingly, "I did not come to ask Teuru to work for me again."

"Then get out of the way. Can't you see I'm a busy man?"

"I came to ask . . . since Teuru does not wish to leave . . . since I'm to have the baby anyway . . ."

When the meaning dawned on Povenaaa he slammed the jeep into low gear and tried to murder the Chinaman with it. "My daughter!" he bellowed. "Living with a Chinaman!"

From behind the rocks the merchant said quietly, "I am not asking her to live with me. I am asking her to marry me."

Then Teuru stepped boldly beside Kim Sing and said, "Yes, Povenaaa, we are going to get married." Povenaaa let his hands fall from the steering wheel and started to gulp, but Teuru said softly, "I went to Papeete three times for you. Now I shall stop in Raiatea."

Povenaaa washed his hands of the whole affair. He

announced, at Le Croix du Sud, that if a daughter of his insisted upon such a thing he wished to hear no more about it. Maggi arranged the wedding and exacted from Kim a written pledge that he would not beat Teuru, as some of his countrymen did their wives, and that he would allow her spending money so long as she continued to wrap bundles of vanilla. But on one point he was adamant. Povenaaa came sniveling around and said that since his only daughter was leaving home he might as well sell the house, but Earl Weebles' big sculptures still cluttered up the place. "Why not move them into the vanilla shed?"

But Kim Sing—even though he had sworn not to beat his wife—was not a complete fool. So years later when hungry collectors from London and Paris reached Raiatea they uncovered the precious masterpieces in the most unlikely places. The classic bust of Maggi, for example—the one now in the Louvre—it was found propping open the door to the barn where Povenaaa kept his jeep.

H.E. Bates

The Grapes of Paradise

That a serpent may lurk in a Pacific Garden of Eden is dramatically shown in a masterly novella by one of Britain's finest authors, H.E. Bates. The local Tahiti scene—especially on the hideaway neighbor island of Moorea—is depicted in increasingly suspenseful style by this cunning artist in fiction, and the action culminates in a shocking tragedy that clashes with the tourist-folder image of the islands.

Herbert Ernest Bates (1905-1974), born in Northamptonshire and educated at Kettering Grammar School, taught himself to be a prolific and popular storyteller, and even wrote a text, *The Modern English Short Story* (1941). He was working on a local newspaper when at the age of twenty he published the first of a score of novels. A number of them deal with the people of the English countryside. One of them, *Love for Lydia*, became a mini-series on Masterpiece Theatre.

During World War II, Bates was a squadron leader in the R.A.F., and stories of service life were published in three collections under the pseudonym of "Flying Officer X." Towards the end of the war he was sent to Burma, and from this experience resulted two novels: *The Purple Plain* (1947) and *The Jacaranda Tree* (1949). His best-known novel is *Fair Stood the Wind for France* (1944), about a bomber crew forced down over the war zone.

Few visitors to the Pacific have returned with more treasure than the following long tale, "The Grapes of Paradise."

I first caught sight of him about three o'clock in the afternoon, at the start of a humid and torrential squall of rain on the waterfront of Papeete. He was tall, lean, and

English to the bone, with eyes of transparent whitish blue and receding fair hair that made him look much older than he really was. The hair badly needed trimming at the neck. His shirt of pale lavender, sun-faded and worn outside his crumpled brown trousers and with a small design of darting indigo fish across it, was remarkably subdued for those parts and had not been washed for some time. It was too early to tell whether he was ill, drunk, or troubled, or perhaps all three, but he was completely oblivious of the rain.

He was in fact not drunk. He had not been drunk for some considerable time. All he was doing was to watch the passage of a little motor schooner beating shorewards through the gap of coral reef a mile or two out to sea. The flow of ocean in and out of the gap was very fast there and he kept beating his hands together like a man watching a horse race in which he is afraid his favorite cannot win.

I watched all this through the open door of a barber's saloon. He stood quite alone on the waterfront in the rain, staring at the schooner, the breadth of the street away. Inside the reef the squall of rain became sometimes so dark that beyond it there appeared to be continuous plumes of dirty smoke where normally the vast breaking crests of spray on the collar of rocks would have shown like the rearing waves of pure white horses.

Somewhere between plumes of smoke and rain the schooner, rolling like a squat white drum, occasionally disappeared. All the time, far beyond her and the smoking reef, the Pacific flared in sunlight, a harsh clear glitter outside the storm, and beyond it all the fantastic mountains of another island glowed like half-melted pale green candles in the sky.

When the rain suddenly stopped he stood watching for nearly another ten minutes until the schooner drifted in at last and tied up below him, fifty yards away. As soon as she tied up he started to walk towards her. Then he suddenly stopped, seemed to change his mind completely, and turned on his heel.

That was the first time I ever saw his face. My impression had been that he was about to meet someone off the schooner, that they hadn't arrived and that he was disappointed. Instead I saw that his eyes were extraordinarily savage: not savage with anger or the intensity of disappointment but inwardly savage, with pure blind melancholoy, perhaps against himself.

That was the second impression I got: that, when he came and sat in the barber's chair next to me, hair and face and the balding reaches about his temples still streaming with rain, he was living in a state of emotional sightlessness. He picked up a towel from a washbasin and started to rub his face and hair. His shirt was open down the front, showing a chest of pale amber hair, and he dried that too. When he had finished he lay back in the chair, shut his eyes and stretched out his arms to the wet knees of his trousers. The hands went limp, turning downwards, loosely, as if he were very tired, and as they did so I saw a scar, ten or twelve inches long, a raw brown-pink slash running from above one wrist to the muscle of the upper arm.

The barber began to comb and cut his hair without a word. Soon after he had started a girl came along the pavement outside, wheeling a bicycle. She stopped, leaned one foot against the bicycle, and stared at the four men in the saloon.

"Hullo, Harry," she said.

She spoke in good English, but he made no effort to open his eyes or answer. She was not wearing the customary *pareu* of Tahitian girls but a sleeveless dress of pale green, with no design at all. Her hair was not plaited but was brushed in two dry black bunches, like combed rope, over her bare shoulders. She was pretty in the pert and delicate way, light and birdlike, that comes when Chinese blood is mixed with Polynesian, and her waist and legs were wonderfully fine and slender.

For another ten minutes or so, leaning on the bicycle at the open door of the saloon, she went on talking to him, saying that she hadn't seen him lately, asking if he'd seen this person or that, and why did he never come dancing at the New Pacific now? All the time he neither opened his eyes nor answered.

"They tell me you're off on the next flying boat," she said, but even that had no effect on him.

By this time the sun was shining again and the air, delicious after the rain, was steaming hotly. The handles of the girl's bicycle glittered as she twisted them. Her hair had steel blue lights in it as she flicked it back over her shoulders and she said, for the last time:

"Well, tell me if you do, Harry. I'll come and see you off. I'll come and say good-bye."

Impassively he ordered a massage. He seemed to know instinctively, without turning his head, that she had left. A few moments later he actually opened his eyes. All the keener edge of their savagery had now become blurred and their queer white blueness was merely glassy as he turned to me.

"English paper you're reading?"

"Yes," I said. "Have it if you like. You're welcome."

"No thanks."

"Absolutely the latest," I said. "Only two weeks old."

Jokes that fail with strangers in strange places are colder than icebergs. He did not answer.

Outside the saloon the street had already steamed to concrete dryness. At the extreme end of the reef the rearing lines of sea foam pranced with splendor in the sun. Beyond it the distant island slopes glowed with deeper, clearer green, the candle fissures almost purple in the far brilliant air.

"They tell me the other island is very beautiful," I said.

"Not been there yet?"

"Not yet."

"Schooner twice a week," he said.

His voice was unexpectedly soft. The short cryptic words that ought to have made it sharp had in fact the opposite effect. He gave an impression of talking quietly to himself, meditating.

"Anywhere to stay when you get there?" I said.

"Rest-house."

"Any good?"

"Don't know," he said."Haven't seen it for a month or two. Daresay it's good. Daresay they'd fit you up."

This, the longest piece of conversation he had offered so far, was also remarkable because during the final part of it he actually turned and gave me a glance that had in it the beginnings of a smile.

"What are you here for?" he said. "Usual thing? Looking for the lost Loti Lotus Land or the Gauguin ghosts?"

These sentences were neither cryptic nor bitter. Nor were they exactly sarcastic or sad. The odd thing about them was their emptiness. They might have been a few spiritless puffs of air let out of a paper bag.

"I'm not sure what I've come for," I said. "It's like eating mangoes for the first time. You know they won't taste like oranges but what else do you expect? You don't know."

He may have thought that this showed, perhaps, a slightly higher degree of intelligence than anything I had said before because he then said:

"That'll save you a load of disappointment. Oh! the girls are beautiful—some of them. Oh! They'll give you what you ask for."

The barber, who had finished my hair, now gave me the towel. For a few minutes I sat reflectively rubbing my neck and face and ears. It was so hot already after the rain that my eyes were damp with sweat and my throat was parched.

"Like to join me in a drink?" I said. "When you've finished? It's pretty hot in here."

"I don't," he said. "Don't drink, I mean."

"We could get a taxi and drive back to the hotel," I said. "It's cooler there."

"I'll be ten minutes yet," he said.

I couldn't make up my mind whether this meant he was coming or not until he said, "I'm afraid I'm only an orange-juicer. Or passion fruit." He actually gave a laugh in that dry puffed way of his and again nothing, I thought, could have been more passionless.

Twenty minutes later we were driving along the water-front, past the *Postes et Telegraphe* building, the last shops and the thick bright hedges of hibiscus and bignonia that flank the gardens along the black sand shore. Heat beat up in slaty glittering waves from the tarmac, sprang from waste stretches of dust under thin high palms, and turned the yellow bells of creepers on fences to fleshy shimmering gold.

At the hotel, he ordered, as he had promised, an orange juice. The handsomest of Tahitian girls brought it, with a glass bowl of ice and a soda siphon, on a bamboo tray.

"Nice to see you up here again, Mr. Rockley," she said. "Soda? Have you enough ice in there?"

He made no answer. Instead he sat looking beyond the low tidal stretches of water inside the reef and then far beyond the rearing crests of the reef to where, more fantastic than ever in the more westerly angle of sun, the mountains rose like pale green candles melting but never lessening in the harsh fine air.

"Cheers," I said.

"Good luck," he said.

He lay back in his chair, white-blue eyes empty again and almost completely transparent, his arms flat out, the palms turned down, the fingers twitching. The scar was like a jagged brown bootlace. And suddenly I realised that his habit of sitting with his palms downwards, twitching his fingers, must have grown unconsciously out of pain.

Then he saw me looking at it. He looked surprisingly neat and respectable now, with his fresh-trimmed, fresh-massaged hair, but the barber had not been able to trim his voice or change its tone at all. It was still remarkably soft, passionless, and unabrupt as he ran one finger down the scar, and stared at it in silence for a moment and then said:

"Take good care nobody does that to you."

He was single, unassuming, friendly, and about thirty-five. He had come down to Tahiti from Vancouver, crossing the Pacific by way of Fiji, Samoa, and the Cook Islands, three months before, full of conventional thoughts about romantic places.

He had in fact been overworking and had been given three months' leave by the firm of industrial bankers for which he worked in Vancouver, and when I talked to him that first afternoon, over his modest orange juice, with his eyes almost always fixed on the mountains, he had already taken a month more than his time.

At first there was nothing at all unconventional in what he had to say. There is a common expression about Tahiti which is, I suppose, often made about other places but is made with more truth about this island that everyone so much expects to be a paradise. Two weeks there are too long, it says, and a year not long enough.

He had not been on the island more than a day or two before he felt convinced of the truth of the first part of the expression. When he arrived by flying boat, in the cool of a tropical evening, an hour before dusk, the waterfront was gay with a great crowd of girls in brilliant crimson *pareus*, women in pretty summer dresses, men in bright-patterned shirts, almost all of them carrying leis or *couronnes* of orchid, gardenia, hibiscus, jasmine, and tiare flower. Most of them were shouting, laughing, throwing kisses and waving their hands; a few were weeping with joy. There were so many flowers that he

85

felt that every garden had been stripped. The air was sweet and sickly with the scent of them.

Out of all this, as he stepped ashore, a plump Tahitian girl came forward, put her gold-brown arms on his shoulders, laughed softly and kissed him splendidly on the lips. After that she put a lei of frangipani round his neck and then suddenly went away to do the same service for another visitor. Then another girl put another lei round his neck, this time of small cherry-colored hibiscus and jasmine, and then another girl a third. He felt slightly embarrassed by this excess of flowers, which were by now piled like Elizabethan ruffles up to his ears, but he laughed too when he saw that all of his fellow passengers were also hidden under flowers, some of them under six or seven leis of purple, white, orange and vermilion, some of the women wearing enchanting *couronnes*, gay little hats of purple orchid bloom.

That night at the hotel, on the edge of the lagoon, under electrically lighted coconut palms that sometimes fluttered in a wave of cool wind coming off the sea, where until long past midnight fishing boats with flares were floating about the black water, he drank champagne and did a little dancing to the three-piece orchestra of two men and a girl, who played mostly Tahitian tunes. The girl also sang songs and as time went on he thought all the songs had in them the same indescribable sadness. Two other girls, one of them not more than twelve, both bare to the navel except for a strip of covering across their breasts, did several native dances, swinging and rolling their hips, making gestures of voluptuous and graceful supplication with their light-brown hands, swishing their light skirts of hibiscus bark — not grass, as he had always imagined — dryly in the night air.

He had several dances with one or two of the women passengers from the plane and one each, out of courtesy, with the two air hostesses, pleasant girls from Adelaide. He bought a drink or two at the bar. The atmosphere had in it a great sense of careless easiness. Frenchmen danced with Tahitian girls; Frenchwomen with Tahitian men.

"It was all very nice and free and easy and fresh to me," he said, "except that I might just as well have been in Nice or San Francisco or Paris or Sydney, though I didn't know it at the time."

In the morning he took a taxi, drove into the town, cashed a check at the Bank of Indo-China, and looked at the shops. The cashing of the check took him the better part of an hour and a half, and in less than half that time he had looked at all the shops. The town had something of the air of a dusty and flyblown French provincial town crossed with a midwestern shack-town populated mostly by Chinese. A few ancient white-painted schooners were being loaded with crates and barrels and bicycles and all manner of goods on the waterfront, where loafers sat about drinking milk out of green coconuts or bottles of fruit juice out of straws, spitting at the dust.

"It all looked so bloody flyblown and so tatty," he said. "I could have vomited."

That very morning, in fact, he went into the offices of the Pacific Navigation Company, cancelled his passage of three months hence, and took a ticket on the next plane outward.

"It was as bad as that," he said, "and what made it worse was that nobody seemed to care a damn whether I went or stayed."

Then he went back to the hotel, stripped out, put on his swimming trunks, and went down to the sea. The beach of black sand, such as there was of it, looked like a foundry yard. The lagoon of black water illuminated by the flares of mysterious midnight fishing boats had become a stretch of tidal junk yard, one foot deep, filled with countless black clusters of sea birds and lengths of what looked like yellow intestine.

At the end of fifty yards of jetty sprouted a lump of

coral rock. On the rock a French girl with a figure as flat as a boy's and legs like white peeled sticks sat staring down into forty feet of dark blue water from which rose shadowy mountains of rust-brown coral, murderous as steel.

"I'm glad you came," she said. "If there's someone watching, the sharks don't follow me."

He decided not to swim. Instead he went back to the bar, sat on a high bamboo stool just as he was in his swimming trunks, and dejectedly ordered himself a whisky. He sat drinking till three o'clock.

He was still drinking, but still more dejectly, three weeks later. By that time he had toured the island twice, had eaten suckling pig several times, and had not taken a single swim in the repulsive, sea-edged lagoon. The dazzling beaches of white coral of which he had heard so much and of which he had actually seen pictures on posters simply did not exist. In the shops he bought as presents a few shells of polished mother-of-pearl, a boar's tusk, and a piece of native wood carving in the form of a pineapple cut in half. He sat in bars and watched dust blow out of pot holes in the road outside and then blow back again. He drank with all sorts of people in all sorts of places and tried to laugh, above the sound of loudspeakers that might have been blaring out of any street between Sydney and Southend, at the jokes they made.

"Better take a *vahine*," someone said, "and settle down and get it out of your system.

He agreed that the girls were beautiful. Their willingness in the realms of cohabitation was not simply legendary. He was fascinated with the splendid handsome readiness of their laughter. He liked above all a certain air of surface shyness in them, the grace of their walk on flat feet, and the black strength of their waist-long hair.

"Anyway that's neither here nor there," he said. "I

88

never saw one I really wanted. The point is that I suddenly realized that what they say is true. Two weeks are too long and a year isn't long enough. Just before the plane was due out I cancelled my ticket and booked myself on the next one. Then I did the same with that one. And at the end of the month I was—"

He stopped speaking. Since he had hardly given up, for a single second, looking at the fantastic molten candles of the island across the lagoon, it cannot be correct to say that he suddenly looked across at the mountains. It is truer to say, perhaps, that he woke up. The remarkable air of sightlessness in the very pale blue eyes was dispersed for a moment or two, enabling him to focus properly on something that it was now obvious he had not been seeing before.

He also pointed—with, I noticed, his scarless arm.

"At the end of the month I was over there." He turned to me now, as he had done in the barber's shop, with the beginnings of a smile. "I don't suppose you saw the schooner come in this afternoon? The one in the squall?"

"I did," I said.

"That's the one," he said. "Takes four hours. That's the way you get there."

The schooner, throbbing and rolling like a butter churn, loaded with everything from cows and bicycles to barrels of *vin ordinaire*, took him over to the island almost exactly a month after he had first arrived in Tahiti. By that time he had drifted into a habit of getting mildly drunk every night and sometimes also at the lunch hour: not because he particularly wanted to get drunk but because of all the pleasant pointless things there were to do this required least energy and passed most time.

As the schooner drew nearer to the island he gradually realized that the mountains he had previously seen only from a distance were really less like candles than gigantic chimneys, massed to the very ridges with vegetation. Their outline made a strange green graph, rising and falling violently, against the sky. Along the coast and a mile or two out from shore the reef was locked like a stupendous jagged collar on which the sea rode with unremitting roar, magnificently springing with high snow-white arches of spray.

After two or three stops at little village landing places where boys sold him slices of frost-fleshed watermelon on the quayside, the schooner finally ran, about mid-afternoon, into a long still lagoon. He had already noted with some pleasure that the sand about the villages was white. Now the schooner began to run so near to the coast that he could have leaned out and thrown a stone on to the strips of pure white coral beach that ran everywhere out from the thickets of breadfruit, wild plantains, palms, and the tall yellow-flowered hibiscus from whose bark the so-called grass for skirts was made.

The water in this land-locked lagoon was so still and undistorted that it made him feel extraordinarily peaceful. In occasional shallow bays it was pure yellow, turning to greenish blue, then pure bold indigo as the water deepened. The only disturbance on it was the wash of the schooner and occasionally, far off on the flat sun-white surface, a flight of little fish, pure frantic silver, scared from the water by some predatory chaser like a flight of birds.

His destination was the last stopping place but one along the lagoon, a wooden landing stage behind which was a solitary palm-thatched house and at the side of which stood, on stilts, in shallow yellow-blue water, what he took to be the rest-house. Like a fairly large square bamboo bandstand, it rose from the strip of pure white shore.

A boy of twelve came down from the house to greet him, to smile enormously, and to take his bag. He stood for a moment in the glare of sunshine, waving his hand to the departing schooner. As it throbbed down the lagoon, farther into the intensely green shadow of the mountains, the sound of its engines dying away, he was aware of his sense of tranquillity deepening. This was it, he started thinking, this is what I came to see.

Then, as he turned to go up to the house, an extraordinary thing occurred. Perhaps it was merely extraordinary, he explained to me, because he hadn't expected it. He had told no one he was coming there but now, as he turned, someone was waiting there to greet him.

It was a girl, holding an enormous crimson lei in her hands. He supposed, he said, it was the largest lei he had ever seen, a great flowery boa of petals minutely crinkled, so that they looked like feathers packed together.

But it was not this in itself that was remarkable. What immediately struck him as so extraordinary was that the girl, though quite young, eighteen or nineteen, was the ugliest he had ever seen. It was difficult to convey the peculiar quality of her ugliness but it was, he explained to me after several attempts, exactly that of a primitive idol hacked out of a golden-colored wood, and not very well hacked at that.

She was so ugly, in fact, that she was, in a peculiar way, quite handsome. Her frame was tall and massive. Her bare feet were immensely broad and flat, with gripping toes. Her hands, which would have made a lesser lei look no longer than one of the necklaces of pink coral he had often seen in the shops, were like great golden-brown crabs with extended claws. Her legs, he said, were like those of a billiard table built in smooth shining mahogany, and her arms, no less powerful, were as broad as hams where they joined the wide naked shoulders.

These were his own descriptions and he apologized for mixing them up a little but he went on to say that all the skin of her body was very fine, with a look of being oiled and polished. It was her face that had the rough-hewn look. The big dark brown eyes seemed not

91

quite squarely fixed and the mouth seemed to have been plucked severely sideways and upward out of shape, curling the inner edge of the upper lip so that it looked like a half-healed scar. Later he saw in fact that it was a scar, as if at some time she had been violently struck across the face by a blow that had also flattened and broadened the square snoutlike nose.

Crowning all this was a mass of overpowering jet-black hair that she wore unplaited. It was like a gigantic wiry horsetail that reached to her massive buttocks. Later she was actually to put on lipstick and an occasional bangle, and sometimes a pair of earrings, but that day the only decoration she was wearing was a large pure yellow hibiscus over her right ear. That too was an out-size flower, with a big stiff central pistil that stuck out at him like a darting tongue.

Her only garment was the *pareu* in the usual pattern of crimson and white, in this case of leaves and flowers, and it had been wound so tightly across her enormous breasts that she actually seemed to have outgrown it. It left all the upper part of her chest, her arms, and her shoulders naked.

When she smiled at him the scarred lip seemed to give a raw flare and he saw that she had one tooth missing just underneath the twist of it, exactly as if it had been knocked out by the blow that had caused the scar.

She placed the lei round his neck and greeted him, at first, in French.

"You don't speak English?" he said.

"A little."

"And the boy?"

"My brother? Just little words of French."

She led him up to the house. To one side of it, the shady side, a sort of bamboo and palm thatch lean-to hut had been built, and there she showed him into a simple room where later he used to lie in bed and stare at the whole tranquil seaward stretch of lagoon.

He continued to speak in English, asking her one or two questions, such as her name and where he would be able to eat and so on, and every time she attempted to answer in English she gave a great cackling laugh, throwing back her head and opening her mouth to its widest, revealing her thick animal tongue stiff and quivering.

He could not quite grasp her Tahitian name. He thought it sounded, at first, like Tavae. He was not sure and tried to repeat it and she laughed again.

"They call me Therese too sometimes," she said. "Therese I like better."

From that moment onwards he called her Therese. "My name is Rockley," he said. At first she pronounced it in the French way, as if it had an accent at the end, but later, as time went on, she simply called him Rock.

"Will you have something to drink now?" she said. "Tea or coffee? Wine or coconut juice or orange?"

He thanked her, said he would have orange but that what he wanted to do most of all was swim.

"Good. You swim," she said. "I'll make orange and bring it down to you."

"Good swimming?" he said. "No sharks?"

"No. No sharks," she said and she laughed, raucous, showing her tongue again. "If sharks come I frighten them."

He started to unpack his bag. She stood watching for a second or two, then said "Please excuse," and started to go to the door. For so large a girl she moved with remarkable silence, and it was several minutes later that he looked up, thinking she had gone altogether, and saw her still standing at the open door.

Then, for the first but not the last time, he got a totally different impression of her. The hut had only one small window, so that it was fairly dark inside, and in the strong outside light she stood partly framed in shadow. He could not see the details of her face. She stood with

93

one arm brushing back her hair, looking back at him, one leg crooked in an attitude of being arrested in a turn.

For a moment you could forget then, he said, how ugly she was. You could see how superbly and splendidly she was built. She made on him for a moment the same impression as an inanimate object, something magnificently executed: a well-made boat, an idol, a piece of sculpture, even a mountain.

"If you want something," she said, "you must ask me. Or Timi, my brother. Or my mother. How long will you stay here now?" He hesitated, more than anything because he was fascinated by the way she stood there, to all appearances ugly no longer, and she said: "Oh! well, you tell me later. Doesn't matter. You stay one week — one year — two years!" and then she turned on her heel and went away with a curious massive gracefulness, laughing with throaty splendor.

There was just one more incident that stuck in his mind that afternoon before darkness fell. After he had been swimming for a good hour or more he came out and sat on the landing stage, deliciously wet and refreshed after the first swim he had taken.

Evidently she had been watching for this moment from the house, because a second later she was coming down to the landing stage with a pitcher of orange juice and a glass on a tray.

"You swim long time," she said. "You must be thirsty now."

She sat beside him on the landing stage and poured his drink. She sat with legs curled under her, watching him, pushing back her hair.

"You swim good," she said. "I swim every day too. Could you swim to the other side?"

He was still panting from exertion and was able, for a few seconds longer, only to shake his head.

"Sometimes I swim there and back," she said.

"Oh! not me, not me," he said. "Too far. Out of practice."

"Not so far."

She laughed, enlarging her scar, and he sat drinking his orange juice, staring across the lagoon. Across the skin-smooth shadows, far off, a shoal of tiny fish burst from the water, as in the earlier afternoon, like fragments of silver. The crests of the mountains, far up, smouldered in sun. The deep far shadows under the thicket of the opposite shore grew greener and greener every moment, solid and glassy and finally untranslucent in the changing air.

He looked along the shore, tired but not too tired, blissfully and completely entranced by the tranquillity, the rapid embalmment of air and water and sky under approaching twilight and by everything he saw from the flaring tips of the mountains to the flick of a canoe paddle far down, seaward, towards the end of the lagoon.

Then he became aware, as he watched, of an unusual thing. In the afternoon, coming along by schooner, he had noticed the flowers of the tall grey-green hibiscus trees, those from the bark of which the so-called grass was made. Like soft pollen-dusty yellow cups they covered the boughs, the sand below the boughs and floated where they fell in water.

Now, to his surprise, the same flowers were red. Both where they grew and where they fell they glowed in a shade of cinnamon, warm and deepening.

His surprise, when he spoke of it, made her laugh again.

"Every day they change," she said. "In the morning they begin one color and as they die they become another color. In the morning yellow. In the evening red. And then in the morning the new ones yellow again."

And that, as he said to me, was how he felt about himself. Between morning and evening he had become a different person. It was unquestionable, he thought, that he had found there what he had come to see. And as he looked along the shore, where little fiery jungle cocks, quite tame, strutted scarlet and green about strips of well-watered grass, under palms and among crimson clumps of ginger lily, he felt that everything was in perfect, ordered pattern, absolutely ordained and right from the changing colors of the hibiscus to the crow of jungle cocks still giving to their hens among the tree ferns fierce territorial warnings that hawks still hovered somewhere about the steely leaves of palm.

He was ready, he felt, to stay a million years. The pure absolute tranquillity had already started to hold him like a drug. He felt glad already of every breath of it. He was even glad of the big, overpowering ugly girl who sat with him for nearly an hour longer, telling how she swam the lagoon, how she speared shrimps in fresh-water streams at nighttime by shining a lamp into their eyes, and about the changing colors of hibiscus flowers: the soles of her big feet dark and horny like the feet of a bear.

He lived, for the next month, the happiest days of his life. The girl, the boy, and her mother, a blousy, prematurely paunched woman who spent most of her time in the open kitchen shed at the back of the house, looked after all his wants with tireless attention and yet left him free.

At the hotel he had eaten mainly European food, more French than anything in character, the sort of food he would have eaten anywhere, and he had liked it very well. Now he learned to eat, and also to like very much, mostly native food: dried raw fish, hot crabs, breadfruit, fried plantains, sweets of guava and coconut cream, and curries of various kinds, including the delicate fresh-water shrimps found in the mountain streams. In a sort of dugout at the back of the house stood a great barrel of *vin ordinaire* from which they drew him wine by the jug. He found it made him sweat a great deal but he drank it constantly.

Every day he swam, before and after breakfast, and

then again in the afternoon and evening, half a dozen times between dawn and sunset. When he was tired of swimming he slept; when he was tired of sleeping he walked along the lagoon, either towards its landlocked end where a cluster of fifty or so dwellings lined the road, or seawards, where he could swim again or watch the Pacific hurling itself with its towering, white-horse waves against the reef, on one part of which, by the gap, the iron skeleton of a wreck struck up as a mass of twisted junk, rust-orange through the glittering mist of ocean spray.

Occasionally he walked inland, climbing to the lower part of the foothills. In part old plantations of guava trees had been felled to give more grazing for cattle; the grass was green and fertile. Great jungles of banana flapped overpoweringly above groves of orange and *pamplemousse*, the big pinkish grapefruit of which he never tired at breakfast. Narrow rapid streams watered pleasant little valleys of breadfruit, wild lime, and avocado pear, and jungle cocks kept up their ceaseless crows of warning, invisible about the thickets, proud against hovering hawks.

Sometimes, this being the rainier season, it rained torentially as he walked. He started by running for shelter. In a few days he was walking on through hot quick squalls, his shorts and shirt soaked, taking a bath as he walked. Sometimes, after these storms, he stripped out, hung his clothes on a rock in the sunshine, and swam naked while they dried.

Occasionally the girl came with him. Once as they walked together a sudden squall obliterated half the lagoon, flooding the sandy path under the palms to a depth of six inches. The faces, bodies, and clothes of himself and the girl were sluiced as if under warm fire hoses, so that when it was over she looked like some enormous water animal that had just dragged itself, blubbering and dripping, from the sea. Then, her hair matted and drenched, the lines of her body more gross than ever under the soaked *pareu*, she looked even uglier than before.

There were two things, all this time, that he liked about her. He was fascinated, first, by her great strength; it impressed him enormously. And the other was, as he put it, that she didn't care a damn.

By that I thought he meant, at first, that she was very free, generous, or in some way promiscuous. On the contrary, he said, the very opposite was true. She had a strange, proud, almost virginal sort of dignity.

What he meant, I gathered, was that she was a sort of tomboy. Perhaps, with her great strength, she would naturally have done nothing but heave boats about, swim the breadth of the lagoon, spear fish, roll barrels of *vin ordinaire* up from the schooner, and slog through the thickets with cordwood on her shoulders. His impression was also, since any girl looking into a mirror could hardly have failed to have grasped the ugliness of that kind of face, that she might have given up, as fairly hopeless, the idea that any man, drunk or sober, would find her attractive. Free of feminine obligations, as he saw it, she could behave before him with the physical ease, lack of embarrassment, and sheer strength of another male.

She too swam a great deal. In the water, as in every other way, she was massive and powerful in all her movements. At the same time water gave her gracefulness. Wearing an ordinary two-piece swimming costume of black material, she swam with superb and easy power, her long black hair trailing out like water weeds.

One morning she challenged him to swim the breadth of the lagoon with her. He knew that his powers as a swimmer were really not up to this but she said:

"Swim slowly. You can do it. We can rest for an hour on the other side."

To his surprise he made the opposite shore without much difficulty. He found that he was, in fact, in better physical condition than he had ever been. He felt taut, springy, and in splendid shape all over. The wide Pacific air had given him an incredible feeling of buoyancy.

Then, as they swam back, they caught sight of a large indefinable water object rolling straight before him in the lagoon. Like a gray sloppy shadow, it made a huge rippling wave as it swam. He took one swift look at it, yelled, "Sharks! My God, sharks!" and started to lash out in panic in the opposite direction.

He had no sooner turned than he heard her laughing. He turned back to see her waving a knife above her head.

"Ray! That's all!" she was shouting. "A big ray. That's no harm. That won't hurt you."

The giant ray, looking as he described it like some sort of india rubber submarine, rolled ponderously off as he turned and swam back to her. The look of fright on his face must still have been remarkably vivid by the time he reached her because she burst out laughing a second time and said:

"Now you really look like a white man. Very white— *so* funny."

He did not, he confessed, feel funny at all. He felt more than a little sick. His buoyancy had gone and his legs felt queer and shaky.

"You're not afraid, are you?" she shouted. She held up the knife above her head, cutting at the air with a slash. "Shall I kill him? I can go after and kill him if you like. Shall I go?"

"Good God, no," he said. "Leave the damn thing and let's get out of here."

"Funny! So funny," she said.

Then as they swam back, he taking continually involuntary glances over his back to make sure the ray had gone, he said:

"I didn't know you carried a knife. I didn't notice that before."

She turned in the water, swimming on her back.

"I keep it inside here," she said. She tapped the folds of her costume about her enormous hips. "I make a pocket inside."

He knew that meant there must be sharks and he felt a little sick again.

"You never know," she said. "Shall I make a pocket for you? It's easy to sew one in."

"So is sitting on dry land," he said and at that she started laughing again.

It was his first and only swim across the breadth of the lagoon and he had to confess he hadn't liked it very much.

"At the same time, when I looked back on it," he said, "I got an odd comforting feeling about it. There was nothing to account for it then, but I somehow got the feeling that if there had been trouble she'd have gone through hell to get me out of it."

After that he kept his swimming to within short distances of the shore. When he wanted to cross the lagoon or change the monotony of swimming he took the outrigger canoe and paddled about instead.

Besides the little outrigger the family had a large craft that carried a single sail. Most of their fishing was done with long five-pronged spears, sometimes at night, by the light of torches of palm frond, or communal fashion, whenever a shoal moved up the lagoon. Sometimes these shoals took several days, perhaps nearly a week, to move the full length from the reef-gap to the last upper finger of shore. Then the great communal net was thrown out, to be drawn gradually about the shoal, in the upper narrowing reach of water, until the fish could finally be pursed and drawn ashore.

On the last day and during the last hours of this netting every villager, except perhaps a few Chinese sharecropping vanilla up the valleys, came down to help with the great task of pulling in the net. Men, women, and children sat on the sand beneath the palms, chattering excitedly until the final hour when every hand was needed for the pulling. After that the catch was distributed communal fashion, according to the degrees of labor, and men who had handled the net for days would find themselves with so much fish to spare that they could make it up for market in long strings, sending it over by the next schooner to Papeete.

About a month after Rockley's arrival on the island a shoal of great size, moving very slowly, came up to the lagoon. It took several days to travel the three and a half miles of water. It was often difficult, Therese said, to gauge the rate at which a shoal could travel, especially a large shoal. There would often be days of tedium, false alarm, rising excitement, and much tension before the net could finally be closed.

Rockley had greatly look forward to helping at one of these catches, but the shoal was so slow that on the fifth day he found himself, at midday, rather bored with waiting.

"It's always the same," the girl said. "It may be this afternoon. May be tonight. We have to have patience. We can never tell."

Then he asked her if she would be going to the net that afternoon.

"I must go to the net," she said. "It may happen suddenly. If I don't help with the net I get no fish."

Some time later, after she had served his lunch, he watched her going away to join the boy and her mother at the net. As she walked down the path she turned, waved to him and said:

"You sleep. When it's time I'll send Timi with a message. Then you can come down and you will have fish too."

"How many do you suppose they'll give me?"

"Oh! plenty. Plenty for strong men. You must pull hard. I'll show you how to pull."

He slept for a couple of hours, woke suddenly, and went down to the landing stage. Across the lagoon the boy was paddling shorewards in the outrigger. Rockley was sure the time had come for closing the net and that the boy had come to fetch him.

"Not yet," the boy said. "Long time yet. Perhaps tonight. Hours."

Rockley sat down on the landing stage and watched the boy beach the outrigger. Then the boy climbed up on the landing stage too and they sat for a few minutes talking.

The afternoon, Rockley said, was very beautiful, with great clusters of sea-packed cloud on the mountains and a light of sheer purity, miraculously soft and limpid, across the glassy water. It was very hot and the fronds of the palms were so still in the heat that they looked as if scissored out of stiff green metal. The only sounds were the crowing of the jungle fowl and, from so far off that they seemed strangely small and toylike, the voices of villagers waiting at the net.

Suddenly he realized that for the first time, in the middle of this exquisite stillness, he was really bored. He had had his fill of swimming; he was tired of waiting for the shoal.

"I felt," he said, "as if I'd like a damn good talk to somebody. You know, a good yarn. In fact, to be honest, I was a bit lonely. I suddenly felt a hell of a long way from anywhere."

Then he made, he said, the first of three serious mistakes. It was a very simple thing and at the time it seemed quite impossible that it could have, as casual things sometimes do, significant consequences.

Without thinking, he asked the boy if he would take him down the lagoon for an hour, in the outrigger, as far as the gap. The boy hesitated. He even looked, Rockley realized afterwards, a little uneasy, almost scared. Then he made various excuses, including the main one that the shoal might be landed at any moment, and Rockley said:

"Oh! Just half an hour then. After that I'll come back with you to the net."

Distances by water are always deceptive and he had never really had to calculate how long it would take to paddle to the seaward end of the lagoon. It took, in fact, an hour; and then not quite an hour, because of a strong incoming drift, to paddle back again.

It was all so pleasant, unspectacular, and dreamy between the walls of palm and the higher jungle thickets that he did not realize that the flowers of the big hibiscus were already turning from yellow to red by the time he and the boy were again opposite the landing stage.

Then he saw the boy suddenly lift his head, brown eyes sharp and startled. From the upper end of the lagoon there was a deep murmur of voices. The boy started paddling furiously, quite agitated now, and Rockley knew that the final netting had begun.

By the time they reached the net, ten minutes later, the water at the end of the lagoon was like a white living cauldron of struggling fish. The boy was so quick to beach the outrigger and run along the shore that he actually tripped, fell, and then rushed on, wiping his sandy hands on his bare thighs, quickly spitting on them afterwards.

Perhaps seventy or eighty people, Rockley said, were pulling at the net, and presently he found the boy, the mother, and the girl among them. With her colossal mahogany legs locked in the coral sand the girl was not only pulling with all her enormous strength but with a remarkable expression on her face. Her dark eyes were large and blazing, with a peculiar fanatical light in them.

As he took up his place beside her, taking hold of the net, he had no idea that this in fact was anger.

"You said you would show me how to pull!" he said.

She did not speak. She neither turned nor looked at him. She simply stared at the net, the water, and the leaping fish and lugged with all her astonishing strength at the net, her expression never altering.

He supposed, he said, that he must have spoken to her

a dozen times or more that afternoon as they pulled together at the net, but each time she gave him no hint of a
word or look in answer. It was pretty hot and strenuous
work and he was glad when it was over. By that time
darkness was falling and there were still some hours of
work to do with the sorting, sharing, and stringing of the
fish. He knew that the stringing would in fact go on all
night, so that the strings of fish would be ready for the
incoming schooner on the following day.

Soon after half past six he started to walk back to the
rest-house alone. As he was leaving the net he passed the
girl, stopped for a moment and said:

"I am going back to the house. Will you be coming
back?"

Again she made no answer.

"No need to come back for me," he said. "I can find a little fruit and eat that. Fruit and a little wine—that's
enough for me."

She had not even paused to listen and now by the time
he had finished speaking she was already some yards
away, striding strongly out of reach of him.

He went back to the rest-house, sat on the little verandah, too tired even to wash, and then drew himself a
pitcher of wine. Then he sat on the verandah again,
watched the stars in the lagoon and above the fantastic
graph-like ridges of the opposite mountains and also the
flares burning in a great cluster at the end of the lagoon.

Normally the wine, the evening, the stars, and the
mysterious waving half-drowned lights of the flares
would have soothed him deeply. That evening, instead,
he felt bothered—not worried, as he was careful to explain, but bothered—bothered, mystified, and slightly
irritated. He couldn't think what on earth he had done.
The incident of the boy and himself going down the
lagoon never occurred to him as the remotest possible
cause of anger in anyone. He couldn't explain it at all.

Then, much later that night, he thought he caught a

glimpse of what the causes might be. He woke about midnight to the sound of quarrelling. In the house the girl was reviling someone, with great fury, in words he didn't understand. He heard the boy's voice in answer. He got out of bed, went to the door of his room and listened. He thought he heard the sound of beating. After that he went back to bed, listened for a time, and thought he heard an even odder sound—that of somebody weeping. But whether it was the boy or his sister crying somewhere outside in the darkness he never knew.

"Before I came down here I read somewhere," he said, "that these people were lighthearted, frivolous, courteous, generous, but deceitful and cruel."

He paused and before going on he gave one of those odd smiles of his.

"But that night," he said, "I started to find out they could be something else besides."

Next morning, he said, it was impossible to recognize, or even believe in the existence of, the girl of the evening before. If the flowers of the hibiscus trees had been purple that morning instead of yellow, the change could not, he said, have surprised him more.

She was smiling broadly as she brought him his breakfast of *pamplemousse,* coffee, fresh-baked Chinese bread and butter, boiled eggs, and a basket of oranges, papayas, limes, and avocado pears. She actually prepared the *pamplemousse* in front of him. Then she poured his coffee. Then while he was eating the *pamplemousse* she cut a large papaya in half and began to prepare it too, knowing he liked to finish his meal with that. In the bright orange cradles of flesh the black-grey papaya seeds glistened like fat beads of caviare.

All day she remained smiling, attentive, rather talkative, and extremely sweet to him. There was no mention either of the incident at the net or of the boy. In the late morning she rolled up the skirt of her *pareu* above her knees, stood in a shallow part of the lagoon, and washed her hair. Fresh-fallen hibiscus flowers floated on the water and under and about the landing stage small fish of brilliant blue, with stripes of bright ocher, swam tamely in and out of the sunshine.

One of the pleasantest things about life there, he said, was to watch the Polynesian girls wash their hair. Its great length, its strong blue blackness, and the way it glistened as it dried quickly in the sun were all beautiful things to see.

"I watched her half the morning," he said. "And she chattered as if she hadn't seen me for years."

Soon it occurred to him that she was spending more time than usual on her hair, combing it and recombing it, shaking it out and spreading it over her shoulders to dry. At last he spoke about this, teasing her very slightly, and she said:

"Tomorrow night there will be dancing. Had you forgotten?"

Occasionally on Saturday nights young men and girls came up from the village, sometimes bringing a drum, a banjo, and a guitar. There would be a good deal of wine drinking, singing of songs, dancing, noisy frivolity, and provocative laughter. A lot of flirting went on and the girls swung taut rubbery hips, their tight skin golden in the lamplight, and curled their fingers in subtle invitation, making the men excited. Most of them wore lipstick, generally of much the same carmine shade as the big hibiscus flowers in their hair.

The following night she too wore lipstick. It was, he said, the first time he had ever seen her wear it, and it made a difference to her face that was sharp, uneasy, and startling. He was not sure, at first, that it did not make her uglier than ever. The big mouth became more than ever like a scar. But the chief difference, he said, was that it gave her a sort of defiance, a certain touch of savagery that made her look out of place among the smaller, prettier girls.

That evening he danced with her several times and once or twice the banjo played European or American tunes. He drank a fair amount of wine, thought the stars of the southern hemisphere had never looked so huge, soft, and flower-like above the lagoon, and in general enjoyed himself greatly. She too seemed very happy. The most remarkable thing about her, he said, the thing that never failed to surprise him each time he held her in his arms for the dances, was the lightness of her enormous body. It was quite unbelievably perfect, he said, in its sheer balance and poise.

About midnight he walked outside to light a cigarette, relax a bit, and get a breath of air. An exquisite little wind, heavy with warmth and tree perfume, blew for a moment or two across the lagoon, died suddenly, and then sprang up again, stirring the fronds of the palms. He stood for a time under a palm tree and watched the stars.

He had drunk, he thought, quite enough wine, though not too much to prevent his remembering, after a few minutes, that he had been told not to stand, sit, or lie under palms. Coconuts falling from a great height are projectiles of considerable nuisance, and he laughed to himself as he remembered it and moved away.

Then the wind sprang up again across the lagoon, giving quite a gusty shudder in the fronds of palm, almost as if a storm were blowing up. He heard it stir the water, creating a sudden rush of waves that lapped against the outrigger and rattled the boat chain.

A moment later he saw her come out of the house and down to the landing stage. The fact that she went straight to the boats made him think that possibly she too had heard the stir of wind and had come down, as she sometimes did at night, to see that the canoes were safely moored.

She stood for some minutes on the landing stage. In the rest-house the banjo and the drum were thumping

107

with low regular rhythm, softly, and a long bar of light came from the open walls and across to the landing stage.

She stood just beyond the edge of this light, hands on her hips, looking at the water, and for some time he stood some distance away, uncertain whether to speak or not, watching her.

"Then I made another mistake," he said. "Another damn *faux pas.*"

It was four or five days after our first meeting that he got as far as telling me this and up to that time I hadn't attributed to him any great sense of humor at all, but now across his face there went, I thought, the flicker of a grin. A moment later I realized it wasn't a grin. It was a deadly stab of pain.

He walked over to where she was standing on the landing stage. As she heard him coming she turned, moved a step or two, and lifted her head. The light from the rest-house was shining behind her now and suddenly he saw her like a big muscular idol, all black except for pure edges of light glimmering along the massive curves of her shoulders, her thick upper arms, and the fringes of her hair.

She looked exceptionally dark, powerful, and magnificent. The individual features of her face were lost in shadow. All he could see was a great carved head, sharply poised, well up, with its flowing mass of hair. Then she moved again, her eyes glinted quickly in the house lights, and he saw her shake back, with a splendid roll of her neck, one side of her hair, showing suddenly the bright yellow saucers of flower above her ear. He saw the sumptuous heave of her breasts and then suddenly, more than a little drunk, he forgot for the first time how ugly she was.

A moment later he was kissing her. Or rather, after the first impact of his lips, she was kissing him. As with everything else she did, it was powerful and massive. It was an affair of overwhelming physical splendor. She gripped him with great strength, locking him against her passionately, and in a queer melancholy fashion repeating his name.

He realized, next morning, what a stupid mistake he had made. He only hoped she would forget it as soon as he wanted to do.

"The confounded trouble was," he said, "that I couldn't forget it. I'd really got quite fond of her—not in love or anything like that, but just fond, in exactly the same way as you get fond of a great big ugly dog. Except for her face there was nothing you couldn't admire and like about her. She was very, very likeable."

And not only, as he explained, the girl. All of them were very likeable. The mother was eternally pleasant, smiling and soft-eyed. The boy was quick, good-looking, light in frame, and surprisingly energetic. He was always fishing, making or mending the long elliptical baskets of bamboo for keeping fish alive and fresh under water, doing jobs on the boat or the outrigger. Occasionally Rockley helped him with these things.

After the incident of kissing the girl he began to welcome more and more the chance of slipping away to swim or fish with the boy. He welcomed a chance of mere companionship. That was one of the ways in which he hoped the girl would see that the affair of the kiss and what followed it was merely an episode he didn't want repeated. He was desperately anxious not to become involved in anything deeper.

"It had just the opposite effect," he said.

Whatever he did with the boy aroused her to terrible silences: moods that lasted, sometimes, the greater part of a day. Two or three times the boy and himself took the outrigger as far as the seaward end of the lagoon, but on the third of these trips she was so inexplicably sullen, black, and mute against him that he was determined never to make one again.

Another day he and the boy walked up the mountainside, a distance of four or five miles, to where, on the edge of the thicket, eight or ten men were felling a tree for a dugout canoe. He had very much wanted to see how these canoes were made, and he spent a very pleasant day. After the tree had been felled and trimmed, the men began the preliminary work of hollowing out the tree with axes. After they had roughly shaped it, lightening it a good deal in the process, they would steer it, on rollers, down the mountainside. The whole business would take a week, perhaps ten days, according to the size of the tree.

It was very pleasant there in the brisker upper air of the mountainside, sitting under the shade of a big breadfruit tree, watching the men, quenching his thirst by sucking sweet oranges gathered from the neighboring trees, and listening to the sound of a stream running down somewhere under a jungle of glinting elephantine banana leaves. Then as he watched the flesh-golden bodies of the men sweating while they worked on the tree he remembered how he had once read, probably as a boy, how the North American had shaped his canoe by filling the hollow with water, throwing red hot rocks in it, and thus giving it curvature.

It was all so interesting that he was glad he had taken his camera with him. It was the kind with the viewfinder at the top. He took about a dozen pictures, first of the men working on the hibiscus trunk, then of various groups of them standing on or about the tree, then one or two of the boy, either alone or with the men.

Finally he decided he would like a couple of pictures of himself with the men. He had never let the boy use the camera before, but the viewfinder was so simple that it took less than a minute to show him how it was used. The boy was not merely delighted about this; he was innocently, worshipfully overjoyed. He fairly danced with the camera, Rockley said, so much so that finally

Rockley had to leave the group and demonstrate how the boy must press the camera against his chest in order to prevent it shaking. He found then that the boy's hands were actually quivering, almost shuddering, with excitement.

There was a great deal of jollying, golden-bellied laughter about this, and the boy responded by behaving, in a charming way, as if he were a person of singular privilege, almost a hero.

"It did your heart good to see him," Rockley said.

Later in the afternoon, as he and the boy came down the mountainside, a single cloud on the upper crest of mountain enlarged itself, descended suddenly, and broke in a storm. They ran for shelter in a shack owned by a toothless Chinaman who sharecropped vanilla farther up the hill. The rain, warm, steamy, and torrential, beat into the great leaves of surrounding forest like a sluice while thunder walked up and down the dark precipitate valleys between strange fires of sun and lightning.

In the middle of all this the Chinaman hobbled out, bandylegged, into lakes of rain, coming back some minutes later with half a dozen oranges and a spray of vanilla orchid and two vanilla beans. Rockley sat under the wide eaves of the shack and sucked oranges and watched the Chinaman explain, with neither French nor English but only little gestures of a pair of yellow dirty hands and a matchstick, how the cream lips of the little delicate, self-sterile ghost-orchid had to be fertilized.

Presently the rain stopped as suddenly as it had begun and there was more laughter, very high-pitched and tinny, from the little Chinaman, as Rockley allowed the boy to take another picture of himself and the Chinaman standing by the door of the shack. All about them the forest sparkled and dripped with water. On Rockley's hands was a strange combined fragrance of oranges and vanilla, at once fresh and exotic, and he felt it had been an enchanted, exhilarating day.

111

"But that was only half what the boy felt," he said. "He was still so excited when we left the Chinaman that I hadn't the heart to take the camera away from him. I let him keep it slung around his neck and he went down the rest of the mountainside like a king."

Then, as the two of them reached the rest-house, the boy started to run forward. He was twenty yards or so from the house when Therese came out of it. As soon as she saw him she stopped. He was still very excited, waving his hands about, making demonstrations with the camera and calling her name.

Then, four or five yards away from her, the boy stopped too. He flicked open the viewfinder of the camera and started to look into it, laughing, as if about to take her picture.

"The next thing I knew," Rockley said, "was that she had snatched the camera from his neck and was swinging it wildly round her head, like a prehistoric sling or something, as if she was going to bash his brains out."

The boy ducked in terror, put his hands up to his head to protect himself, and then ran to the house. She took a dozen or fifteen furious barefooted strides after him, screeching madly and still swinging the camera about her head.

It wasn't until the boy disappeared into the house that she seemed to come to her senses. Then her arms suddenly dropped. She stared in a stupefied sort of way at the camera, as if not sure now whether it was a camera or a sling bag or something else, and then came slowly back to Rockley.

"She just stood there, gave me the camera and stared," Rockley said. "No recognition in the stare. No contrition. No apology. Nothing like that. Just a long, empty, sightless stare."

This episode perturbed him so much that he could not sleep that night. After some hours he got up, put on a pair of straw slipppers, and walked down to the landing stage. He started to smoke a cigarette and think things over. In the pure dark sky the stars seemed more brilliant, more beautiful, and more voluminous than ever. He stared at them and their reflection across the lagoon for a long time and then, in spite of them and the pleasure everything about the place had given him, he came to a decision.

"I decided," he said, "to get out. The schooner would be arriving in a couple of days. I could catch it and go back to Papeete."

There wasn't, he said, much reasoning about the decision. He still had several weeks of his leave to go. He disliked Papeete. The trouble was that he had begun to be much more than disturbed. He did not know why, but he had a queer, fatalistic feeling of impending disaster.

He had already started to walk back to the house when he saw her coming down the stone steps to the landing stage. She suddenly halted halfway up them. This time there was no light from the house behind her. She was simply a shape of vague patterns, her *pareu* hastily wrapped around her, under the brilliant stars.

He was determined that, this time, there should be no nonsense: no more kissing. He was perfectly sober this time, with no fancy illusions about anything, and he walked straight past her, not stopping or turning until he reached the top of the steps.

Then he spoke to her. "Therese," he said.

She neither turned nor spoke to him.

"Therese," he said, "I'm going away. By the next schooner."

There was no sort of movement from her. She was simply an enormous shape carved out of the darkness.

"Good-night," he said. He had already turned on his heel and was walking away. "I'll be going the day after tomorrow."

"The schooner doesn't come until the day after that," she said.

113

"All right. Good enough," he said. "The day after that."

He walked on. She didn't speak again. He went on and into the house with a feeling of relief, mingled with sudden wretched twinges of regret. There was absolutely no reasoning in his going; he did not want to go. But he was convinced, absolutely certain now, that it was the thing he must do.

But before the schooner arrived, three days later, something else happened. He made, he said, the third of his stupid mistakes about her.

He was determined to leave in the friendliest possible fashion. He ever started to plan little gifts for everybody, and for the first of the three days he behaved with polite neutrality. He began by avoiding the boy. He deliberately swam, fished, walked, and idled about the place alone. Whenever the boy approached him, he made an excuse about a book, a towel, a letter, or something and went away.

The immediate result was, as he said, that she couldn't have been sweeter. She was her old friendly, laughing, almost frivolous self again. She prepared his fruit at table, made jokes as she watched him eat, and threw back her head in gusts of superb, sumptuous laughter.

It was only when the boy came into sight that her attitude and her expression changed. Then she seemed to go blank before him. A sort of blight came over her. Every vestige of light and friendliness was suddenly extinguished. He began to understand then what was the matter with her. For the first time, fully, he realized how jealous she was.

"That was the Polynesian virtue the guide-books had left out," he said. "So jealous she couldn't bear to share me with the kid, her own brother. So possessive that she was frantic about a boy, another male."

The second day, having put his finger on the cause of

114

everything, he decided to keep himself more to himself than ever. As a result, after breakfast, he walked the entire distance to the point at the end of the lagoon. A white sandy track wound pleasantly under high palms past occasional abandoned gardens of half-wild gardenias, croton, and tiare trees. A few wooden shacks, some empty, some with a few cockerels crowing about them, were dotted about the thickets. From far off came the inexhaustible thunder of the reef and then, at the very tip of the land, in from the open ocean, the great blown cloud of spume, white and glittering and sometimes rainbow-shot, in the brilliant air.

He was half way back from the point when a voice hailed him unexpectedly from one of the houses in the thickets on the shoreward side of the track. He turned, stopped, and saw a girl waving her hand.

"Hullo there," she said in English. "Good morning." She was walking across the garden towards the thin cane fence that flanked the track. "I thought it was you."

He said good morning, staring blankly, and did not know what to do.

"You're staying at the rest-house, aren't you?" she said. "Don't you remember me?"

He said he was sorry: he didn't remember.

"I saw you quite a few times at the New Pacific Hotel," she said. "Dancing. Over at Papeete."

"Oh! yes," he said.

"I really come from here," she said. "I go over for a few weeks sometimes."

She smiled: uncommonly small, pale, and compact, with a delicate upward cast in her eyes that he afterwards knew came from the mingling of Polynesian blood and Chinese. She moved with grace. Her voice was soft and rather high. To look at her after looking at Therese was, he said, like looking at a little yellow paraqueet after a buzzard, or at one of the little angel-finned, blue-and-white ocher fish after that giant sloppy ray that had scared him in the lagoon.

"Like it here?" she said. "I saw you go past once before, but you were with Timi that time and I didn't like to call."

"I like it very much."

"How long do you think you'll stay?"

"As a matter of fact," he said, "I'm off tomorrow. Catching the schooner."

"If you like it so much, why are you off tomorrow?"

It was altogether too complicated to explain and he said he didn't know.

"Catching the next plane?"

"No," he said. "The one after."

"You look hot," she said. "Wouldn't you like to sit down on the verandah a minute and I'll get you something to drink? Some lime or orange—whichever you prefer."

A few minutes later he was sitting down on the verandah of the little house. Going in and out of the house, getting his drink of orange, she moved with pert grace, not wearing the ordinary *pareu* but a simple waistless dress of yellow with several circles of emerald at the edge of the skirt, her dark hair plaited.

"Pretty as hell," he said. "But then, no point in describing her. You've seen her already. That was her outside the barber's shop, that time you first met me."

He stayed for another hour. She lived with a mother, three elder sisters, and an aunt, but that morning they were up at the plantations of vanilla, some way in the hills, fertilizing flowers. It was a job, she explained, for which the big Polynesian girls were far too clumsy but which the delicate fingers of Chinese or part-Chinese did rapidly, skilfully, and with perfection.

He could not help being fascinated by her own thin, delicate hands as she sat there telling him those things.

"Don't you work in the plantations too?" he asked her.

"Not often," she said. "I look after the house mostly and do the cooking. I have a little trouble with my heart sometimes. Nothing much, but the hills are too far for me."

She put her left hand on her chest, just above her heart, and held it there. She was wearing in her hair not the big customary hibiscus flower but a little cluster of *tiare*, not more than six or seven blooms of small wax-white stars. Her breasts were sharp and upstanding, her arms were almost pure ivory, the nails shapely on the fragile little fingers, and he could smell the fragrance of *tiare* in the air.

The following day the schooner sailed without him.

Therese was delighted by his sudden change of plans. During the next few days, as she sat about the place at the various tasks of grating coconut, crushing herbs, preparing breadfruit, topping and tailing shrimps, washing and drying her hair, he knew that she was very happy. He heard her singing a good deal. He would not have been surprised if her voice had emerged as a baritone but it was in fact a rather thin soprano, high and pure. The songs she sang were repetitive, a little melancholy and most fairly slow and dreamy, like lullabies. A few weeks before he would have asked about these songs and perhaps have got her to tell him the meaning of the words; but now he was wary of doing anything, even in the most casual way, that she might interpret as affection.

For this reason he made a series of excuses for getting out of various things she wanted him to do. He had, for instance, asked several times about fresh-water shrimps and how she caught them at night, in the little streams, by the light of flares. For some time he had wanted to go one one of these shrimping expeditions, but now he made excuses of some sort whenever she mentioned it.

Soon she began to grow more and more persistent about this. In fact, as he said, she started pestering.

"Why don't you come with me? You say you want to come. All the time you say you want to come with me and now you don't come. Why don't you come?"

He would make some excuse about being too tired at night or the wine making him sleepy; or he would change the subject completely.

"I'd rather go fishing for tuna," he would say. "Out in the open ocean. They fight so much better than shrimps do."

This, though it made her laugh, did nothing to stop her persistence.

"We can do both," she said. "Tonight we can catch the shrimps. Tomorrow we can take the boat and catch tuna."

He wanted, in fact, to do neither. What he chiefly wanted to do now, and he found it more attractive every day, was to walk along the lagoon to the house among the thickets and play, as he put it, with the little paraqueet there. The little paraqueet was, it seemed, amusing in many ways. Her heart not quite strong enough to stand work in the vanilla plantations or the gradients up into the forests, exercised itself freely in other directions. On hot still afternoons he lay for hours on the beach with her or on a cool truckle bed inside. Paraqueets, as he explained, are extremely affectionate creatures. They are also very teachable and quick to learn. And sometimes darkness was already falling when he walked back to the rest-house along the lagoon.

Then, when he got back, Therese would say:

"You walk a long time, don't you? How far do you walk every day?"

"I like to look at the wreck," he would say, "and wonder how it got there. I like to watch for tuna. I thought I saw tuna leaping yesterday."

All this time he was afraid she would be suspicious. To his relief and surprise she was not suspicious: not, at any rate, at first. She seemed absolutely content, perfectly happy, simply to have him there. It was enough, it seemed, that he hadn't gone away.

Then, after about a week, she said:

"Don't you get tired of watching the wreck? Soon I shall begin to think you go there to look at something else besides."

"Such as what?" he said. "It's beautiful. I like looking at the ocean. I saw a little plane yesterday."

"Such as the little Chinese girls in the house along there," she said. "They're very beautiful too, the little Chinese girls."

For the moment it was on the tip of his tongue to say that the house was always empty when he passed it, but he saved himself in time.

Even then there was no sign of her suspicion. There was not the faintest hint of jealousy. At the same time he felt disturbed. Women, as he remarked, are not compared with cats for nothing. They have infinite capacities for awaiting their time to strike. Gossip, moreover, is the fastest traveler in the world.

He decided, as a result, to go with her on the night-shrimping. That, he thought, would be the clever thing. That would appease her.

They set off the following evening at nine o'clock. The nights were always infinitely beautiful, full of a humid and fragrant softness, under enormous stars. But that night, under dense thickets of hibiscus and breadfruit that overhung the bed of the little stream, the boughs touching overhead in the narrow valley, most of the stars were hidden. He had always thought of the sky, especially that brilliant southern sky, as a companionable place, and that night, under the thick forest leaves, he missed its brightness. As a result he got an increasing sense of uneasiness. There was something uncanny about it all.

Most of the time she walked in her bare feet on the stones of the stream. In her left hand she carried a torch, an ordinary electric battery one, and in her right a thin, two-pronged spear. Soon he was watching her shine the torch into little beds of shrimp eyes: the eyes, he thought, like imploring, guileless little beads, full of wide and dark surprise, as they looked up to their deathblow.

For about an hour he and the girl walked up the narrow valley. During this time he carried the basket and sometimes he could hear the faintest rustle, a mere papery whisper, as the still-alive shrimps stirred among each other in the darkness.

Finally they came out into a break in the thickets. It was a grassy place, with a number of rocks strewn about it, and he sat down on one of the rocks, putting the basket at his side.

A moment later, in a sudden turn, she shone the torch into his face. "Oh! accidentally, of course," he said," but for a moment I was half blinded and I couldn't see. You know how it is — your eyes feel stabbed and they start throbbing up and down."

Then, as his eyes cleared, he saw her standing above him. Whether it was quite accidental again he never quite knew, but he could have sworn the spear was poised. She stood there exactly as if preparing to strike him, just as she struck the shrimps, between his dazzled eyes.

He supposed it must have been accidental, a mere slip of her hand, because a second later she put out the torch and dropped the spear on the ground. She was kneeling in front of him, grasping his hands.

"Please," she started saying. "Please, Rock, don't go away. Please." Her voice had a desperate unnerving break in it. "You won't go, will you? When you said you would go, I thought I would go mad. Quite mad. I couldn't speak about it before, but don't go, Rock, will you? Please don't go."

As she spoke she drew herself up on her knees, until her face was level with his. Her voice was so uncertain that he actually thought she was sobbing. Even in the brilliance of starlight he was not sure whether her enormous eyes were dry or not. He only remembered, with a sudden stab of panic, the night when he had kissed her and had forgotten for a moment how ugly she was.

"Therese," he started saying. "Look—"

"You could like here. I can build a house. I will build a house and live like your *vahine*. It cost nothing. I'll be your *vahine* and work for you. I'll work for you and you can love me—"

He listened, amazed and at first absolutely speechless. Embarrassed too, he actually managed to stand up without seeming to push her away. A moment later she stood up too, suddenly pressing her body against him, her great arms seizing and holding him in a vise.

"Listen to me," he started saying again. "Listen—"

Before he could go on she started kissing him. There was no escaping the big scarred mouth, and she was so violent he could not resist her.

"I might just as well have resisted a buffalo," he said. "And I believe she might have killed me if I had."

He admitted, in fact, an extraordinary thing. He was afraid of her, he said, really quite afraid. He feared her physically.

Then, a moment or so later, a curious change came over her. She seemed to go suddenly limp. She let her hands fall loosely at her sides and she sat down on one of the rocks, quietly.

This quietness of hers was so sudden and so complete that it unnerved him as much as her violence had done. She sat staring heavily into the darkness, and for about five minutes he stood there watching her. All he could hear was the noise of the stream falling away over its stones among the thickets and the small whisper of shrimps as they rustled in the basket.

Then she started speaking.

"Rock—"

That was as far as she got. Her voice was constricted. The one word was almost a cough.

Then after several more minutes she tried speaking

again. By this time her hair had partly fallen over her face and she did not brush it away.

"Rock," she said, "I—"

For the second time she couldn't go on. She put her hands on her knees, gripping them, and her hair fell still further forward over her face, almost hiding it completely.

"What were you going to say?" he said.

She gave a great sigh, more like a sudden gasp for breath, and then violently locked her hands together.

"Nothing," she said. "Nothing, I—"

"What was it?" he said.

"Nothing," she said. "I was thinking—"

She suddenly leapt to her feet, stumbled forward, and started clumsily to walk down the mountainside.

"What were you thinking?" he said. He picked up the basket and started after her. "What was it?"

She didn't answer. It was some moments before he caught up with her, crashing heavily down the mountain path.

"Therese," he said. "What was it? What were you thinking?"

She crashed on through the thickets, making no attempt to stop or look at him. She blundered forward like an animal that had lost its way. But what really disturbed him was not that, he said. What affected him so much was the enormous and helpless sorrow in her voice when she spoke again.

"Thank God," she said, "my thoughts are my own."

He had already made, by that time, the third of his mistakes. He determined not to make another.

"I got the thing taped up," he said. "I found you could pick up the schooner at a village on the other side of the island. In fact on schooner days and on Saturdays there was a bus that would take you there. The bus actually came by the rest-house, used the track along the lagoon, and went round the island by way of the point."

Two or three days before the schooner was due he started to get a few of his things together. He would pack them up a few at a time and then, when the girl was down by the landing stage, gutting fish or getting water or washing her hair, walk along the track to the house in the thicket and leave them there. Fortunately he had only one bag and after two or three journeys most of his things were with the paraqueet, under the truckle bed.

"I know it probably sounds pretty ungrateful and all that. I wanted to do the decent thing but I could see trouble everywhere," he said, "if I didn't get out. Besides, what do you say? If you're going to live with one of these girls you might as well pick a good-looking one. A paraqueet. Not that I wanted to. One way and another I felt I'd had about enough and a bit over."

As he said this he gave me another of those dispirited, rather twisted smiles of his.

"And I was just about as wrong about *that*," he said, "as I could be."

Then, on the morning of the day before the schooner was due to arrive, he began to have something approaching misgivings. He felt very sad. He had not only loved it all. It was, as he was never tired of saying, the most beautiful place on earth. The lagoon alone, sheltered and guarded by these fantastic palm-fledged mountains behind which every evening the sunset opened up like a blast furnace, flaring with every color of flame, was paradise itself.

"They say that the original Garden of Eden was here somewhere in these islands," he said, "and my guess is this was it."

All this, together with his thoughts of how nice the people had been, how tranquil and serenely restful it all was, were enough to explain his sadness.

"I could have wept," he said. "In fact I was so damned miserable that when she suggested, that morning, hav-

123

ing a trip for a few hours to look for tuna, I jumped at it like a shot."

Then, at the last moment, when the boat was ready, he remembered being alone with her twice before, once on the landing stage and once on the mountain, and he didn't fancy it a third time.

"Let the boy come, won't you?" he said. "He loves the boat. He handles it well, too. Go on—let the boy come."

The boy was standing on the landing stage, watching his sister and Rockley prepare the boat. He gave an eager glance at her as Rockley spoke. For a moment she hesitated. Then she gave one of those strong sudden twists of her neck, threw her long hair back from her shoulder, and said an odd thing.

"If he likes to take the risk," she said.

At once the boy clambered down into the boat and in five minutes they were sailing seawards down the lagoon on a light warm breeze. Rockley steered, the boy handled the sail, and Therese squatted in the bows, busying herself with lines and the long white-feathered spinners they were going to use for lures. Rockley noticed that she didn't speak much, though once, when they were almost level with the house where the paraqueet lived, she turned full round, faced him and said:

"Wouldn't you rather be walking instead?"

He didn't pay much attention at the time. No one was moving outside the house. He couldn't help wondering what might have happened if the paraqueet had suddenly come out, recognized him, and waved her hand, but nothing happened and the boat sailed tranquilly past the house and the thicket of breadfruit and hibiscus with their pretty scatterings of fallen flowers.

After a time he became more and more aware of the growing thunder of the reef. At the mouth of the lagoon, still a mile or more from the gap, it was already like the battering surge of an enormous waterfall. He was surprised, even at that distance, by the height of the breaking spray and the strength of the tow pouring in through the gap. Beyond it the Pacific looked calm enough, a brilliant slaty blue without so much as a single white crest across it, but he was to discover only a few minutes later that it was really corrugated by deep, long, and powerful swells.

Meanwhile the boy took in the sail and Therese started to steer, calling to Rockley at the same time to take a paddle. For another twenty minutes he and the boy paddled towards and finally through the gap. It was hard going and once or twice they seemed, he thought, to be making no headway at all against the power of the tow. On both sides the reef rose like rough brown jaws, the coral clear of water, the rust on the wreck glinting scabbily with the color of old dried blood in the iridescent sunshine.

By now he was paddling so hard that he had no time even to brush the sweat from his face. He simply let it pour down over his eyes and lips and into his open mouth, the rivulets of it gathering on his neck and chest and pouring down his body. Then his legs began to feel soggy. He was sucking his breath in short, desperate gasps. Then he felt the boat give a sudden twist, almost a whip to starboard, and he saw the boy ease his rate of paddling.

Less than a minute later the sail was up again and they were well clear of the reef, out in the open sea.

After the exertion of paddling he felt considerably exhausted: so much so that for a time he paid very little attention to either the girl, who was steering now, or her brother, who once again was handling the sail. He thought he heard her occasionally giving directions to the boy about a change in course, but now she spoke in Tahitian and he was not quite sure. He actually shut his eyes for a moment or two. Then he was sharply woken out of himself by a sudden brittleness in her voice, a hard rasping shout, and he opened his eyes to see her hauling on the thick stump rod from the bows, her enormous forearms locked stiff with the pull of the line.

A few minutes later the first tuna was thrashing about in the well of the boat. It wasn't very large and the girl, as if angry or disappointed about its size, suddenly picked up a short stump of wood and started clubbing it to death. She hit it so severely that it actually gave a shocked sort of leap a foot or two in the air and blood spurted everywhere, spattering her bare feet and shins and over her forearms and hair.

Then she whipped out a knife. It was the same knife she had brandished above the giant ray in the lagoon. It was short, thick, and slightly curved.

She bent, a moment later, over the dying fish. She lifted the knife quickly as if she were going to plunge it into the short, iron-smooth body. The boy was at the sail, his back turned.

Rockley waited for the downward cut of the knife. Instead he saw her stand up to her full height. She stood there for a second or two before he realized that her face suddenly looked uglier than ever. He didn't quite grasp it at first. It was evil and dark, and the lip was grossly twisted.

Then she gave a grotesque short yell.

"You go to that house!" she yelled. "You go to that girl. You're going away with her. I saw you take your things. You go to that house, don't you?"

She made a powerful lunge at his face with the knife. He instinctively put up a hand to protect himself, and he felt the knife run in a hot sharp line down his outer forearm. He staggered for a moment and the boat started rocking. He was aware of her making a second lunge. She looked queerly unkempt and wild now, her face frighteningly ugly, her black hair sweeping about her hips, and blood spattering her legs and arms, and she started yelling again, the words incoherent this time.

The boy too stood up, relinquishing his hold on the

sail. He shouted something too, at the same time trying to grab at her arm. She moved so quickly, stabbing air, that he missed her completely, overbalanced, and himself made a grab at air.

A moment later the spar, swinging round, struck the boy full across the mouth. He fell like a boxer, backwards, eyes wide and cast upward, stunned before hitting the water.

In a flash the girl stooped, picked up the bloody, slithering fish in her arms, and hurled it over the stern. A moment later she was swimming.

The boy had already disappeared. And for the space of what seemed to be several minutes, though it could not have been more than a moment or two after she dived, Rockley was alone on the sea.

In the confusion he had fallen on his knees. Now he tried for several seconds to get up again.

His arm was drenched in blood. He tried to clutch the side of the boat with his good arm and then, already fainting, with the other. Then his head fell on his arms and blood started spewing over his face and shirt and body.

He came round to find himself hanging over the side of the boat, down which blood was flowing into the sea. He was too weak to do anything for a moment or two, but presently he managed to heave his legs upward until he was half on his knees again. Then with his good arm he started struggling to drag his shirt over his head.

The shirt was half off when he heard the girl shouting. His head was trapped, as it were, in a crazy sort of bag. From a distance her voice sounded unreal and hoarsely muffled. After a second or so he managed to drag the shirt free of his head and then, his eyes woken suddenly by the dazzle of sunlight, he saw the girl.

She was already hanging on to the side of the boat, holding the boy. She was thrashing water violently with her legs and trying at the same time to heave the boy with her enormous arms and shoulders out of the water. It was as much as Rockley could do to crook his good arm over the side and shout for the boy to clutch it. He was relieved then to see the boy shake his head, quickly shut his eyes, and then as quickly open them again.

A second or two later the girl gave a tremendous heave and the boy fell face forwards into the boat. As he fell over the side he knocked Rockley, too weak even to kneel now, on to his back. Rockley groped there for a moment, blood pouring down his arms and mingling with tuna blood, and then managed to raise himself on one hand, partly supporting himself on one of the paddles.

He was still struggling up when the girl started screaming. The boy yelled, whipped the paddle suddenly from under Rockley's knees, and started madly thrashing water. All the time the girl continued screaming, trying at the same time to heave herself into the boat by her hands.

It was not more than five minutes, Rockley said, at most ten, before he and the boy somehow pulled her aboard. It seemed, he said, like a day. After a time she stopped screaming. Her great scarred mouth folded itself down until the lower lip was invisible and her teeth, clenched far below it, were actually drawing blood.

She still had so much strength that, even then, at the very last moment, she made the final effort of pulling herself aboard. Her entire body seemed to retch itself into the boat with a terrible groan.

She lay there for a minute, perhaps longer, face downwards, before Rockley realized that what he thought was merely the tangled mass of her water-soaked *pareu* folded like a twisted red sheet about the right side of her body was really all that was left, on that side, of her thigh. The teeth of the shark had scoured deep into flesh, so that the bone stared blue.

She somehow turned herself on her back, still conscious. Rockley picked up his shirt, throwing it over her thigh. Faintness started a second wave of blackness across his eyes and by the time he had defeated it he was aware of the boy using his own shirt to bandage his arm.

Some time later the boy had the sail up again and the breeze, blowing crossways towards the reef, began to take them back to shore. All the time the girl lay starkly conscious, her big hands gripping the sides of the boat in stiff agony, her teeth biting lower and lower into the jaw.

For most of the journey back he was simply unaware of the sea. Once or twice he fainted off again and then he was aware, presently, of kneeling beside her, smoothing her hair with his good hand. There was nothing else he could possibly do for her and it was some time before there was even a hint of conscious recognition in the enormous eyes. Then quite quietly, and with a strength of tone that almost fooled him for a moment into thinking that he was, after all, merely on the fringes of a dream of pure ghastliness, she said:

"I'm glad you're with me."

He could find nothing to say in answer. It was actually the first time her mouth had relaxed, allowing the teeth to give up the cruel biting of her jaw. Almost at the same time, as if she had suddenly defeated all pain, her hands relaxed too, unlocked themselves from the side of the boat and folded themselves weakly across the front of her body.

For a long time she held his hand while keeping her eyes fixed on his face. "I'm sorry about the other hand," she said once, and again he could find nothing to say in answer except, so long afterwards that it was merely like an echo that had lost itself across the space of sea and had in some uncanny way floated back again:

"I'm sorry too."

Half an hour later they were running through the gap. All this time he had been so unaware of both time and distance that he actually saw the reef before being aware of the thunder of its roar about him. In the same way he had forgotten the boy, sitting all the time like a strangely aged little statue, all splashed with blood, never speaking, in the stern.

As they drew into the calmness of the lagoon she actually smiled up at him, held his hand a fraction closer and spoke for the first and only time of the paraqueet, the other girl.

"I found out last night," she said. "I saw you go there. Then I knew you had been there before."

It would have been better, he said, if she had stuck the knife into him after all.

"I couldn't sleep last night. Then I came and looked at you while you were asleep," she said. Her voice was proud and without scorn. "And I knew you were going away from me."

Now they were running quite fast into the lagoon. He stared away from her towards the thickets beyond the white strips of beach, hot in the sunshine, and to the rising tiers of palm.

"I said I wouldn't let you go away from me," she said.

He looked back at her face. Its sudden relaxation after pain into calmness made it appear, quite suddenly, not so large as before. The lips were more compact. Even the big snoutlike nostrils seemed to have contracted.

"Now when you go away from me it won't matter."

He could find nothing to say.

"I told you my thoughts were my own," she said. "Do you remember?"

Her voice was very low. He still could not speak or look at her and all his pain and fondness for her dissolved into sudden desolation. He was aware of nothing except a long, profound, tormenting anguish before, for the fifth or sixth time, he fainted away.

When he looked at her again her eyes were staring straight up into glaring sunshine. Her face was no longer placid. In its final moments, no longer ugly, it seemed to have expanded again with remarkable strength, defiantly. With pride she seemed to be glaring back at the flaming sky, handsome and almost contemptuous as she lay there.

A moment later he covered her face. The boat ran past the house in the thickets, where the little paraqueet lived, and all across the lagoon the crowing of jungle cocks was proud and clear.

James Norman Hall

Sing: A Song of Sixpence

Among the authors who have written about the Pacific Islands, one of the most gifted is James Norman Hall (1887-1951). Although known chiefly for the novels written in collaboration with Charles Nordhoff, notably the famous *Bounty* trilogy, he is the author of several books of nonfiction about the South Seas which he wrote alone. Among them are *Mid-Pacific* (1928), *The Tale of a Shipwreck* (1955), *The Forgotten One* (1950), and his autobiographical *My Island Home* (1952). It is in these books especially, Eugene Burdick said, that Hall "caught a time and place so exquisitely that he has given himself a timeless and placeless position" in literature.

At the outbreak of World War I, Hall enlisted as a Canadian in the British Army and served for two years as a machine gunner with "Kitchener's Mob." Later, having trained as a pilot, he joined the Lafayette Flying Corps of the French Foreign Legion and was shot down over Germany, spending the last six months of the war as a prisoner. After the war he and his comrade-in-arms Charles Nordhoff, reacting against the postwar Western "civilization," sailed for the South Seas for what they intended would be a year of freedom and adventure. In Tahiti, however, both men married part-Polynesian girls and decided to settle down there for the rest of their lives. In the eleven books they produced together they became the best-known pair of collaborating writers in modern English literature.

In "Sing: A Song of Sixpence," Hall evidences his most engaging attributes as a writer—his skillful prose, his quiet humor, and his honest sympathy for his materials.

IN THOSE DAYS, while living at the Aina Pare, a hotel on the Papeete waterfront, I had so little success at writing that my funds dwindled to the vanishing point. It seemed the part of wisdom to retire for a time to one of the remote country districts until I could repair my fortunes. On the southern side of the island, thirty-five miles from the town, I found a piece of land, an acre in extent, with a one-room house on it precisely suited to my needs. The veranda overlooked the sea, unbroken by any land as far as the Antarctic Circle, and a mountain stream flowed through my small domain so that I had both fresh-water and sea-water bathing. But a more important feature was the cheapness of the rental — three dollars per month.

The land thereabout was so fertile that I decided to make a vegetable garden. In the tropics gardening would be a delightful occupation, I thought, and it might prove so profitable that I would not need to attempt earning my living at my old trade of authorship. So I set to work hopefully enough, glad of the necessity which had brought me to this decision.

The experience was disillusioning. Millions of ants carried away most of my seed, and if any happened to be overlooked by the ants, the moment they set forth green shoots they were sheared off by the land crabs. After months of patient effort, all that I had to show for my toil were a few ears of sweet corn — or, better, sweet corn cobs, for rats had eaten off the kernels — three small tomatoes, and one squash. Having estimated my time as worth, at a modest figure, twenty cents an hour, and adding expenditures for seed, garden tools, and so on, I found that these vegetables cost me $15.50 each.

Nevertheless, I resolved to try once more and ordered — from America, this time — a small quantity of fresh seeds, for my funds were low indeed, and, furthermore, because of my innumerable enemies I meant to garden on a reduced front. But when I had cleared away the weeds — how marvelously they had flourished meanwhile, without care! — and saw the hosts of ants drawn up in waiting battalions, and the ground perforated like a sieve with the holes of land crabs, with a crab at the entrance of each hole waving his keen-edged nippers in the air, I lost heart. "It is useless," I thought. "I'd better make another attempt at writing." It was not a lucrative profession, but if I practiced it faithfully I should be able to earn at least twenty cents an hour. Therefore, I put away my tools and let Nature plant whatever she would in my garden plot. She chose, as before, lantana and a vicious weed called "false tobacco."

That afternoon as I was oiling and cleaning my typewriter, which had long been rusting in disuse, a Chinese named Hop Sing drove past my door in his dilapidated spring wagon. He lived a quarter of a mile down the lagoon beach from my place, in a house he had built himself from the boards of old packing cases. I knew that he had a vegetable garden of sorts, although he raised only sweet potatoes and a very tough variety of field corn; so I hailed him, thinking he might have use for my dollar's worth of seed. He stopped willingly enough, and I brought out to him a small packet each of beans, sweet corn (Golden Bantam), squash, pumpkin, lettuce, and tomato seed, all of the best varieties. Sing grunted expressions of mild interest while I explained what the various packets contained, and when I had finished, asked "How much?" "Oh, nothing at all," I said. "It's a little present for you." He grasped the back of his seat to steady himself, perhaps, from the shock of receiving a present from a stranger, and his black eyes glittered a trifle more brightly, but these were the only evidences of emotion, if it may be called emotion, that he displayed.

I forgot Hop Sing forthwith. There were other things to think of, chiefly the precarious state of my finances. Having counted upon my garden to furnish food, I had spent my little capital all too freely. I had received in the meantime one check for twelve dollars and another for ten dollars in payment for some newspaper articles I had written earlier. Luckily my rent was paid several months in advance, but I had left only one hundred and twenty-eight francs — a little more than five dollars, American, at the current rate of exchange — and not another penny to be expected until I had written something: story, sketch, whatnot. The manuscript would have to be sent to America, my only market, and even though it should be accepted at once — a remote possibility — I could not hope to receive a check from such a distance for at least three months. How was I to live in the meantime? There were plenty of bananas on my place and about fifty coconut palms; but my landlord, a native, reserved the right to both the fruit and the nuts, which was no more than fair considering the modest rental he asked for house and grounds. He gathered the nuts as they fell and the bananas were picked green to be sent to the Papeete market. I though of fishing, but remembering past experiences I knew it would be foolish to count on that. I had no better luck at fishing than I had at gardening. No, I would have to live, somehow, on my one hundred and twenty-eight francs. That, of course, was impossible, so I resolved not even to try. I kept twenty-eight francs for incidental expenses, spent twenty-five francs for native tobacco, and invested the remainder of my cash in sweet potatoes and tinned beef. When the food was gone — well, I would worry about that when the time came.

Three days later I was on page two of a sketch which I planned to call "Settling Down in Polynesia," a story of some experiences I had had the summer before. It was Sunday, but necessity knows no holy days, and I was doing my utmost to work. But the mere fact of having to work seemed to make accomplishment impossible. I had written and rewritten the two pages of my story, trying with each new draft to blacken page three. I was aroused from a mood of profound dejection by a knock at the door.

It was Hop Sing, and with him were his wife, their

three small children, and a wizened little man shaped like an interrogation point. Hop was dressed in a clean cotton undershirt and a pair of dungaree trousers. His wife wore a pajama suit of black silk, and her hair was elaborately dressed. She carried one child on her arm, led another by the hand, and the third, a baby, rode comfortably in a sling on her back. The children were beautifully dressed, and each of them wore a little skull-cap of blue silk, with flowers and butterflies embroidered on them with gold thread. The ancient wore a robe like a dressing gown. He was very feeble and got down from the wagon with difficulty. It was pathetic to see the effort it cost him to walk. He would advance his staff a few inches and, grasping it with both hands, make a shuffling hop up to it. Then he would rest for a moment whle gathering strength for a new effort. We helped him up the steps, and at length all were seated on my back veranda, Mrs. Sing sitting sidewise in her chair because of the baby in the sling. My unwashed breakfast dishes were on the table, and several slices of fried sweet potatoes on a greasy plate looked anything but appetizing. I was ashamed of the disorder of the place, the more so because this was the first visit I'd ever had from the Sing family. Hop Sing and his wife looked around them in appraising fashion, but I could not judge from their faces what they thought of my housekeeping.

"My fadda-law," said Sing, indicating the old man.

I smiled and nodded.

A rather long silence followed. I felt embarrassed and could think of nothing to say.

"What name, you?" he then asked.

I told him. Another interval of silence. I gave my forefinger to the child on Mrs. Sing's lap. It clasped it gravely and held on. Mrs. Sing smiled. Her father, too, smiled; at least, his face wrinkled suddenly, like a pool into which several pebbles have been thrown. The baby in the sling was asleep, its chubby arms sticking straight out. It looked like a doll rather than a baby. The oldest child, a boy of six or seven, had the curious mature look and the air of precocious wisdom one often sees on the faces of Chinese children.

Sing took from his pocket one of the packets of seeds I had given him.

"What name, this?" he asked.

"In English? . . . Corn, sweet corn. Golden Bantam," I replied. "Very good. Tahiti corn no good—too tough. This corn fine."

"You get from Melica?"

I nodded. He brought forth the other packets. "All this Melican seed?"

He was silent for a moment; then said: "Make fine garden, now. Make plenty big tomato, plenty corn, plenty squash. Bimeby you see."

Thinking of my three tomatoes about the size of pigeon's eggs I was not sanguine about Hop Sing's being plenty big. However, I expressed the hope that they might be. I brought out a seed catalogue and showed him illustrations in color of various kinds of vegetables. The pictures, of course, showed products in their highest imaginative perfection. He was much interested and exchanged remarks in Chinese with his father-in-law. Meanwhile, one of those heavy showers common at Tahiti in the rainy season broke with violence. The thunder of water on my tin roof was deafening. Soon the cloud melted into pure sunlight, the last of it descending in a fine mist shot through with rainbow lights. Sing went out to his wagon and returned with three fine watermelons. He made a second excursion, bringing this time a live fowl, a bottle of Dubonnet *(vin apertif)*, and a basket containing seventeen eggs. All of these articles he placed on my kitchen table.

"Littly plesent, you," he said, with a deprecatory gesture. Mrs. Sing and her father then rose and all three shook my hand, bidding me good-by with smiles and nods. A moment later they drove off, leaving me astonished and genuinely moved at this expression of Chinese friendliness.

It would be difficult to exaggerate the value, to me, of their generous gift. Tinned beef is a nourishing food, but I had lost all relish for it during the First Great War. As for sweet potatoes, I had eaten so many while knocking about the Pacific on trading schooners that I could scarcely endure the sight of them. How welcome, then, was this more palatable food! I thought of having a chicken dinner at once, but on second thought decided to preserve my fowl. Perhaps she would lay, and if I could somehow procure a rooster I might from this small beginning raise enough chickens to provide for all my needs. So I staked the hen out in the dooryard with a string tied to her leg, and having found several coconuts partly eaten by rats, I broke these open and gave her a good meal. Then, having dined on a six-egg omelet with half a watermelon for dessert, I resumed my work with interest and enthusiasm. All the afternoon the bell of my typewriter rang with the steady persistence of an alarm gong at a railway crossing, and pages of manuscript fell on the floor around me like autumn leaves after a heavy frost. By six o'clock that evening I had reached the end of my "Settling Down" story.

I had no time to lose if I was to get it into the northbound mail. The monthly steamer from New Zealand to San Francisco was due at Papeete on Monday. I decided to go into town to post the manuscript myself, not being willing to trust the native mail carrier with so precious a document. A motor bus ran daily between Papeete and Taravao, a village just beyond my place, but the fare for the round trip was twenty-four francs. I would need at least ten francs for stamps and expenses in town, so I decided to walk to Papeete, and if I had money enough left, to ride back. Having fortified myself with another six-egg omelet and a small glass of Dubonnet, I set out.

It was a beautiful night, dewy and still and fresh, with a full moon rising above the palm trees on the Taravao isthmus. The road wound around the shoulders of the hills, now skirting the sea, now crossing the mouths of broad valleys where the land breeze from the mountains blew cool and refreshing. I had glimpses through the trees of lofty precipices festooned with the silvery smoke of waterfalls, and, on the left hand, of the lagoon bordered by the reef, where great combers caught the moonlight in lines of white fire. From native houses along the road came snatches of song, a strange mixture of airs, part French, part Tahitian, to the accompaniment of guitars, accordions, and mouth organs. On verandas here and there women were busy with their ironing, sitting cross-legged on the floor with a lamp beside them, and far out on the lagoon the lights of the fishermen were beginning to appear.

I walked briskly along the road, feeling at peace with the world and with myself. How pleasant, how wise it would be, I thought, really to settle down in this remote island paradise and remain here for the rest of my life. Where else could I find kindlier people, or a life more suited to one of my indolent habits? If it were true that a man's wealth may be estimated in terms of things he can do without, then in that sense I might hope soon to achieve affluence. Material possessions added little to the sum of one's happiness, and I could always earn enough at writing to provide for the simple necessities of life. Whenever the mild-eyed, melancholy tropical wolves came sniffing apologetically at my door, I could write a story of one sort or another, and live on the proceeds of the sale of it until it became necessary to write another.

Musing thus hopefully I proceeded on my way, but toward midnight, when I had covered about half the distance to Papeete, I found myself again thinking of food. The nourishment stored in my second six-egg omelet

139

had already been absorbed and its energy expended. I had a drink of water from a mountain stream and tightened my belt a notch or two. "I'll have a good breakfast when I reach town," I thought. For four francs I could buy a large portion of chop suey at one of the Chinese restaurants. That would suffice until I returned to the country, which I meant to do as soon as I had posted my manuscript.

At a place where the road followed a lonely strip of beach I came to a thatched hut, and sitting near it by a driftwood fire were an old native man and woman. I halted to enjoy the beauty of the scene. The stems of the coconut palms were black against the firelight, which flickered over the faces of the old couple and cast huge shadows behind them. They saw me and called out, "Haere mai ta maa!" ("Come and eat!") This is merely a friendly greeting, and I replied in the customary way, "Paia vau" ("I'm not hungry"), but if my empty stomach could have spoken it would have made indignant denial of the statement. Evidently they really meant that I should partake of their midnight supper. They were roasting over the coals what appeared to be shellfish and some kind of native vegetable, and an appetizing fragrance filled the air.

"Come," said the old woman; "try this. It is very good." And putting several generous portions in a coconut shell, she held it up to me.

Good? I should think it was! The meat of the shellfish was delicately flavored and the vegetable had real substance and a nutlike taste. My hosts were delighted to see the relish with which I ate and urged more food upon me.

"Eat, eat!" said the old man. "We have plenty, enough for a dozen." And he pointed to several buckets filled with uncooked food. So, being very hungry, I ate with a will.

"What kind of shellfish are these?" I asked. "Did you catch them on the reef?"

"These are not shellfish. They're *tupas*," the old man said.

"What!" I exclaimed.

Tupas are land crabs, and those I had been eating with such relish were members of the pestiferous family, countless in numbers, which had assisted the ants in ruining my garden. I hadn't known they were edible, but my hosts told me that Tahitians thought them a great delicacy, which they are, in truth, if one is really hungry. As for the vegetable, it was not a vegetable at all, but a nut, the fruit of the *mape*, the Pacific chestnut tree. These trees flourish on Tahiti. They are found along the banks of streams, and in other moist or swampy places. There was a grove of them on my place and the ground beneath was littered with nuts, which my landlord never disturbed, and which I had not bothered to examine, not knowing they were good to eat.

I was appalled at thought of the time I had wasted trying to make a garden, when all the while there was an inexhaustible supply of food at hand, to be enjoyed without labor, to be had for the mere taking. But no, the taking of land crabs could not be such a simple matter. I remembered the wariness of those than infested my garden. They did all their damage in my absence. The moment they saw me they scurried to their holes and, if I made so much as a move in their direction, dodged down to safety. I had once caught one by digging him out, but that cost me half an hour of hard work.

I asked the old man how he caught them, and he showed me a method so simple and easy that I wondered I had not thought of it. He had a fishpole and a line, but instead of a hook at the end of the line, he tied a bunch of green leaves from the hibiscus tree. These leaves and the blossoms of the hibiscus are the principal food of land crabs when there is no garden stuff at hand. We went a little way from the hut to a spot in full moonlight where there were many crab holes. "Now stand very still," he

141

said. In a moment the crabs, which had vanished at our approach, came warily up again. He then cast his bait much as one does in fly-fishing. The crabs fastened their nippers in the leaves, each of them trying to drag the bundle to his hole. The old man gave the line a deft jerk, and the crabs, not being able to disengage their nippers quickly enough, were dragged to his feet. He pounced upon them and threw them into the bucket with the others.

I then tried my hand, with such success that I was tempted to return home at once and begin fishing in my garden. But more prudent counsels prevailed. One's appetite for food so plentiful and so easily procured might become jaded in time. Furthermore I would need a certain amount of money for paper, typewriter ribbons, shaving materials, and such. So I bade farewell to my friendly hosts and proceeded on my way, reaching Papeete at dawn, just as the steamer which was to carry my manuscript to America was entering the harbor. Stamps for the parcel cost three francs. I breathed over it a silent prayer and slipped it into the letter chute.

I have heard travelers call Papeete a tropical slum, and it must be admitted that it does leave something to be desired in the way of cleanliness and sanitation. Nevertheless it is a colorful town, particularly in the early morning, when the people are going to and from the market place. Everyone is abroad at that hour, and the French and Chinese restaurants are filled with folk exchanging gossip over their morning coffee. I had a good breakfast at the cost of four francs, then strolled along the waterfront, doubly enjoying the gaiety of the scene after my long sojourn in the country. I was walking along the Quai de Commerce looking at the shipping when someone touched my shoulder. It was a bald, fat little Chinese who had evidently been running after me. He was so out of breath that he could not speak for a moment. Then he began talking in Chinese-Tahitian, a sort of *biche-la-mer* I don't understand. I shook my head. He renewed his efforts, speaking earnestly and rapidly, and I caught the name Hop Sing.

"Hop Sing?" I said.

"E! E!" ("Yes! Yes!") he replied, and of a sudden found some English words.

"You know Hop Sing? Hop Sing flen, you?"

Yes, I said, I knew him. "Hop Sing live close me, Papeari."

Papeari was the name of the district where I was living. The face of the Chinese glowed with pleasure.

"*Maitai, maitai!* ("Good!") Hop Sing send me letta. I know name, you! You give seed, put in gloun, make garden. Maitai! Maitai! Hop Sing glad. Me glad. Hop Sing brudda-law, me."

"What name, you?" I asked.

"Lee Fat. Keep store, over there." And he pointed down the street. "When you go back Papeari?"

"Go this morning, on motor bus," I replied.

"Goo-by," said the Chinese, and rushed away without another word. I was surprised at the abrupt leave-taking and stood looking after him, touched at the thought of this odd little man chasing me down the street to thank me for the trifling favor I had done his brother-in-law.

I sat on the bench near the post office to wait for the motor bus. "The beachcombers' bench," it was called, for it was usually occupied on steamer day with waifs and strays from various parts of the world who sit there waiting for the distribution of the monthly mail, always expecting letters containing money and nearly always disappointed. "I'm in the same boat now," I thought. "Three months hence I'll be sitting here nursing the same forlorn hope." It was possible, of course, that my manuscript would sell at once, but repeated past experience warned me that it would be foolish to count on it. Well, I still had twenty-one francs and would have nine left after paying my bus fare. Certainly, I would not starve, with land crabs and mape nuts to eat. Meanwhile I would work as never before, sending out manuscripts as long as I could find money for postage. Having made this resolve I put my worries aside.

It was nearly midday when I arrived at Papeari. While paying the driver my fare, the boy who attended to the distribution of parcels put a box down beside me.

"You've made a mistake," I said. "That isn't mine."

"Yes, it is," he replied.

"No, no. I didn't have a box and I've ordered nothing from town."

He insisted, however, that it was mine. A Chinese had brought it just before the bus left the market, he said, and had paid for its carriage to my place. I still thought there was some mistake, but upon prying off the lid I found a card with "Lee Fat. No. 118" printed on it. Every Chinese on Tahiti has a number, for identification purposes. Under the name was written, in pencil: "Mr. Hall, for you."

The parcel contained the following articles: a two-pound box of New Zealand chocolates, a paper bag of litchi nuts, one quart of champagne (Louis Roederer), and a Chinese lacquered box with a gold dragon on the lid. In the box were two silk handkerchiefs and a silk pajama suit.

I was tempted to open the champagne at once that I might drink long life and abundant health to Hop Sing and his brother-in-law, Lee Fat, No. 118; but I had no ice, and I knew that I could not drink a quart of champagne without having a headache afterward. So I tied a string to the bottle and lowered it into the cistern to cool. Then I went out to attend to my hen.

She was gone. The string was still tied to the stake, but she had worked her foot out of the noose and vanished. After a long search I found her under the back steps. She had laid an egg and was sitting on it. Evidently she was

144

ready to set when Hop Sing brought her to me. The egg under her was probably unfertilized, so I took that out. Then I made her a nest of the excelsior which had been packed around the articles in Lee Fat's gift box, and placed in it the five eggs remaining from Hop Sing's gift. The hen settled down upon them with contented cluckings, and when comfortable closed her eyes as much to say: "Now then, all I ask is to be left alone, and twenty-one days hence we shall see what we shall see."

It seems to me now that the definite upward trend in the graph of my fortunes began that afternoon when I started landcrab fishing. I could not eat a tenth of the crabs I caught, so I made a pen of stakes set closely together and driven deeply into the ground, and turned the surplus loose inside it. They immediately dug new holes for themselves, but this did not disturb me, for I knew that I could easily catch them again. It occurred to me that by feeding them regularly on hibiscus leaves and blossoms I might add to their size and increase the delicacy of their flavor. The experiment was highly successful. The crabs throve upon regular and abundant food, and I throve upon them. At the time of Hop Sing's visit, what with worry and an uncongenial diet, I was very thin, but within six weeks I had gained fourteen pounds.

Meanwhile, promptly upon the appointed day, my hen stepped out of her nest followed by four chicks. I was quite as proud of them as she was and doubtless took more credit to myself on the occasion than the facts warranted. I fed the hen and her brood on a mixture of roasted land crabs and ground mape nuts, and never have I seen baby chicks grow more rapidly.

It may seem incredible that my bottle of champagne should have remained unbroached during this time, but such is the case. In my interest in crab-and-chicken farming I had quite forgotton it; but one day when my landlord was gathering coconuts in a nearby grove I invited him in to share it with me. He was more than willing, and his somewhat reserved attitude toward me altered with the first glass. I then learned the reason for his coolness. He told me that his last tenant had not only eaten bananas and coconuts to which he had no right, but had gone away without paying his rent, three months in arrears at that time. Gathering, from the simplicity of my way of life, that I too had little money, he feared that I might play him the same trick. I reassured him on this point and we drank confusion to his former tenant, wherever he might be. Several of my landlord's children had accompanied him to the house and I shared among them the box of chocolates. It was a merry little party, and after much pleasant talk my landlord left me with repeated expressions of good will.

The next morning I found on my back veranda a bunch of bananas and a copra sack half filled with mangos and oranges, gifts from my landlord and his family. Not infrequently, thereafter, Mata, his wife, would send me baked fish, breadfruit, and mountain plantain fresh from her native oven, and I remembered with deep gratitude that I really owed these benefits to Hop Sing.

Meanwhile, I worked steadily at writing, and Hop Sing's garden was flourishing. All the seeds I had given him had sprouted and gave promise of a rich harvest under his patient, ceaseless care. He was always at work, and so too was Mrs. Sing, despite the demands on her time made by three small children. Sometimes of a late afternoon I walked down to their place. They always greeted me in the most friendly way, but never for a moment did they leave off working. "Surely," I would think, "the Chinese deserve to inherit the earth, and doubtless will inherit it if industry and patience count for anything." Even the ancient, not Mrs. Sing's father but her grandfather, as I was to learn, was far from being useless, despite his little strength; and the oldest child, although only a baby himself, took care of his smaller brother. Mrs. Sing was usually to be found in a little back shed sorting and cleaning vegetables for the Papeete market. All of her members were busy at once. She rocked the smallest baby, which lay in a little cradle hanging from a rafter, by means of a cord attached to her foot. Now and then she pulled another cord which hung just over her head. This one ran by a system of pulleys to the garden where there was a sort of jumping-jack scarecrow to frighten away those robbers, the mynah birds. Meanwhile, the vegetables got themselves cleaned and deftly packed in little baskets.

The ancient was a baker, and twice a week, after his long day's toil in the garden, Hop Sing made the rounds of the district in his spring wagon, selling crisp loaves of bread and pineapple tarts to the native population. During these excursions he often left something at my gate, either a tart or a loaf of bread. No protest on my part served to dry up his fountain of gratitude for my wretched little gift of seed.

Under these circumstances the weeks passed so pleasantly that steamer day—the third since the posting of my manuscript—was at hand before I realized it. I walked into town once more and waited on the familiar bench till the mail should be distributed. I waited through the latter part of the afternoon until everybody in Papeete and its environs had called for their letters. I waited until the sun was sinking behind the mountains of Moorea and the post office was about to close. Then, summoning all my resolution, I mounted the steps and walked to the delivery window, saying inwardly: "It's useless to ask. I'm quite certain to be disappointed." The girl who presided there went hastily through a small number of letters from the "H" box.

"No, there's nothing for you," she said, with a smile so typical of post-office clerks who preside at General Delivery windows.

I made a ghastly attempt to smile in return and was going toward the door when she called after me:

147

"Oh! Just a moment! What name did you say?"

I repeated it, enunciating the words with the utmost care.

"Yes, there is one letter," she said. "Fifty centimes postage due."

Having paid this I had left only a twenty-five-centime piece, the smallest coin used in French Oceania. But little that mattered. The letter contained a gracious note accepting my manuscript, and a check for five hundred dollars.

To those living luxurious lives in the high latitudes, five hundred dollars may seem a trifling sum, but it was a fortune to me. I had never before received even half of that amount for anything I had written. With the half of it, plus two dollars, I could pay the rental for my house and grounds for a period of seven years, and the two hundred and fifty remaining would suffice for other expenses for a time nearly as long, provided that I lived as modestly in the future as I had in the immediate past. But now, with bright vistas of ease and plenty and peace of mind opening out before me, I found myself perversely considering the idea of leaving Tahiti. The northbound steamer to San Francisco would be due shortly, and I fell to considering the varied experience I might now have by virtue of movement and my five hundred dollars. Remembering past fortunes in authorship, I knew that it was the part of wisdom to remain on Tahiti, where living was, for the first time, within my means. And yet, if I did not go now, I might have to wait long before I should again have enough money for a steamboat ticket. I walked the streets of Papeete until a late hour, anxiously considering this matter. The clock in the cathedral was striking two before the decision—to go—was made.

Hop Sing was in town on the day of my departure. He had come with garden produce, and both he and Lee Fat came to see me off. Fat insisted on my accepting a pair of Russia-leather bedroom slippers and a Chinese fan of blue silk embellished with gold butterflies hovering over a fantasy of flowers. Sing's parting gift was a basket of tomatoes as large as oranges, and a dozen ears of sweet corn (Golden Bantam). They smiled good-bys as the steamer backed away from the wharf and headed for the passage to the open sea. I then went to my cabin, in order that departure from that most beautiful of islands might be a little less poignant. While I was unpacking my bag, a steward looked in.

"You've been assigned to the doctor's table, sir," he said. "It's a table for four, but this trip there's only one other gentleman there beside yourself. Is that satisfactory?"

"Quite," I replied. "By the way, will you please have this corn prepared and served at luncheon? Take a couple of ears for yourself if you care to."

"Thank you, sir. I hope the other gentleman at your table likes sweet corn. He's done nothing but complain about the food ever since we left Wellington, and to tell you the truth, it's not what it might be."

The doctor did not come down for luncheon. I had just seated myself when the other passenger at his table came in. He was a tall, spare man with a drooping mustache and a bilious complexion. He was dressed in a baggy linen coat and knickerbockers and low white shoes. He sat down without even a nod in my direction and adjusted a pair of nose glasses, picking up the menu card, puffing out his cheeks as he examined it, letting the air escape dejectedly through his lips. He struck me as being a man who would be extremely hard to please in the matter of food or anything else. He was partaking gloomily of a dish of creamed tinned salmon when the steward brought in a platter with eight splendid ears of Golden Bantam corn steaming on it. He gazed at it in astonishment.

"Take this away," he said to the steward, pushing the dish of salmon to one side, "and bring me another dinner plate."

Never before had I seen a man give himself up to the enjoyment of food with such purely physical abandon. One would have thought he had not eaten for days. When he had finished his second ear, he said: "Steward, where does this corn come from? It's not on the card."

"No, sir, it's not on the regular bill. It's a gift to the table from the gentleman sitting opposite you."

He gave me a grudging glance as though he had just become aware of my presence.

"Consider yourself thanked, sir," he said, brusquely.

I nodded.

"Is this corn of your own growing?"

"Well, yes, in a sense," I replied.

He plowed a hasty furrow along his third ear before speaking again. Then he said: "What do you mean by 'in a sense'? You either raised it or you didn't, I should think."

He had a waspish, peppery way of speaking as though he had been long accustomed to asking whomever whatever he chose, with the certainty of a deferential reply. In view of the fact that he was eating my — or rather, Hop Sing's — corn, I felt that he might have made an effort, at least, to be gracious. Therefore I merely said, as coldly as possible, "Oh, you'd have to live on Tahiti to understand that." Having finished my luncheon I rose and left him there, still eating corn.

Half an hour later I was standing at the rail, aft, watching the peak of Orohena, the highest mountain on Tahiti, slowly sinking into the sea. A hand was laid on my arm, and, turning, I found my table companion.

"Well, sir," he said, "one would think that you were about to jump overboard."

"I have been considering it," I replied; "but it's too far to swim back, now."

"You like Tahiti as much as that? Well, I don't wonder. An island whre they grow such delicious corn must be a good place to live. I ate six of those ears — finished the lot, in fact."

"I'm glad you enjoyed it," I replied.

"See here! You mustn't mind my grumpiness. I'm afraid I was a little brusque at luncheon. I've got dyspepsia, and a wayward liver and an enlarged spleen—Lord knows what all else is the matter with me. Gives me a sort of jaundiced outlook on life. But I want you to know that I'm grateful. Sweet corn is one of the few things I can eat without suffering afterward. Now, then, tell me something about your island. I didn't go ashore. Useless trying to see even a small island in six hours. It's only an aggravation."

I scarcely know how it came about, but within a few minutes I was talking as freely as though to an old friend. I told him of the beauty of the islands in the eastern Pacific, of the changing life, of the mingling races; of the strange outcroppings of savage beliefs and customs through the shale of what in those parts is called civilization. Presently I halted, thinking he might be bored.

"Not at all," he said. "Well, you've had an interesting time, evidently, and you seem to have made good use of your eyes and ears. You're an American, aren't you? What do you do for a living—besides raising sweet corn, 'in a sense'?" he added, with a smile.

I told him that I was an itinerant journalist.

"Is that so?" he said, looking amazed. "Got any of your stuff with you?"

"A few sketches of various sorts," I replied.

"Would you mind letting me see them?"

"Not in the least." And so, at his suggestion, I brought out a small sheaf of manuscript, six slight papers on various island subjects, each of them about two thousand words long. He settled himself in his deck chair and adjusted his glasses.

"Come back an hour from now," he said, "and I'll tell you what I think of them."

He thought two of them worthless, and, strangely enough, they were the ones I thought best.

"But these four are not bad. What do you want for them?"

"You—you mean you would like to buy them?" I asked.

"Yes, of course. But I forgot to tell you: I'm a director of a newspaper syndicate in the U.S.A. We can use these sketches. Tropical island stuff is always popular. Interest in the South Seas never wanes, and it never will as long as life is what it is in America .... Well, what do you want for them?"

"Oh, I don't know . . . ." I said. I was about to add: "Would one hundred dollars be too much?" meaning one hundred for the four. He interrupted me.

"Give you one hundred and fifty each for them. Is that agreeable?"

I admitted that it was.

That evening I set down on paper, for my own amusement, a list as complete as I could make it of all the benefits, direct and indirect, accruing to me from my trifling gift to Hop Sing. With this before me I came to the conclusion that Adam himself, the first husbandman, even under the exceptionally favorable conditions prevailing in the Garden of Eden before the Fall, could not have reaped such a rich and varied harvest as I did from my garden at Tahiti. And it all came from a dollar's worth of seed.

William S. Stone

Chez Quinn

Anyone desirous of the title of "old Tahiti hand" must be able to recall stories of days and nights at "Quinn's Bar," the ramshackle cabaret that never recovered fully from a disastrous waterfront fire a generation ago. In its prime, no visit to Papeete would be complete without at least a quick drink in the relaxed, if not somnolent, atmosphere of polyglot pleasure.

One of the best accounts is given by a long-time resident of the island. William Standish Stone (1907-1970), born in Santa Barbara, California, of New England parentage, entered Harvard University in 1926. He became in 1929 a licensed airline transport pilot and instructor in a flying school in the Southwest. He had early begun the practice of law in Arizona, and in 1936 made his home in Tahiti, where he was able to continue counseling on legal affairs. He was stricken with polio at the age of thirty, but enjoyed swimming off the island shores.

Stone began publishing his writing in 1935, and in Tahiti turned out eight books, dealing mainly with the South Seas. One of the best non-fiction volumes about his adopted island is *Tahiti Landfall* (1946), from which the following selection is taken. He also published three books for young people. The novel *Two Came by Sea* (1953) describes the conflict on the little Society Island of Atea between Pierre Lestrade, former member of the French resistance who comes to teach the gentle people there, and Alexandre Tissot, a man of Vichy who comes to rule over them. Stone was deeply concerned with the myths and legends of Polynesia, and perhaps his best book is *The Ship of Flame: A Saga of the South Seas* (1945). Tetua, the bard of Tahiti, sits in his thatched house at Matavai Bay and tells of the foremost of island kings, named Rata, who achieves many victories as he sails with his warrior crew of *Vaa-i-ama*, the Ship of Flame. Tetua is also the narrator of Stone's last book, *Idylls of the South Seas* (1970), a series of tales drawn from the legendary past of French Oceania.

IT HAD seemed hardly worth while to enter Fati's car to cover the few blocks we had to go, and so he was allowed to drive ahead while we followed afoot through the unlighted streets. We walked, waving only moderately, with arms locked, Miri on my right, Tavae on the left.

"*Aue,*" Miri sighed as she breathed the cool air which drifted around us in the narrow lanes, "how I love this place!" And then, for the twentieth time that evening she assured me that never, never would she go away again—not to America, or France, or Poland, or to any of the many other lands in which she had sung and danced and been much feted and adored. She meant it at the moment, but though it did not strike me as a notion in the least strange, I knew better than to imagine her days of wandering to be over. As long as Miri's beauty lasts, and as long as men of means and imagination pass through Tahiti on their ways across the world, there can be no certainty that the next week will not find her en route for Paris or Prague or Saigon or whatever alluring spot you will. And yet never again, I think, will she be gone for long.

"Is it not too bad," she said suddenly, "that all people cannot live here?"

Sometimes I have thought that such appears to be almost everyone's eventual intention. "Perhaps it is as well that they cannot," I told her. "We should be a bit crowded. And besides, there are many who would not like it in the least."

"Are there?"

"Yes."

"Surely they would like Quinn's?"

"Most reasonable sane people would abhor it."

"But you are no more than a little crazy. *You* like it. Why?"

Why indeed? Whether Miri realized it or not, she had

posed a difficult question and I searched for an answer as we went along.

No street lamps burned overhead, but here and there the open doorways of Chinese shops were faintly outlined by dim lights guttering somewhere far within. Into each of these I peered as if expecting to find a reply that might satisfy the girl. But all that I could see was an occasional naked babe creeping on the floor, a black-pajamed woman, a gaunt dog, a man silently cutting shoe soles from a worn-out tire. We passed a darkened patisserie, a native blacksmith's, a Hindu restaurant through whose swinging doors there came a subdued mumble of voices and a bar of light to fall across the unpaved way. Behind us I could hear the faint scuffing of bare feet where the rest of our party followed. Except for a periodic and regrettable announcement from Punau, no one spoke and the quiet melody that Timi plucked from a single string of his guitar seemed only to accentuate the welcome hush. Perhaps it was the encircling Tahitian night which thus succeeded in momentarily subduing our so recently noisy company, the night which by nearly obliterating the disorderly little town brought near the brooding mountains at our backs and the silent sea toward which we walked. More probably Teuru and Tavae and all the others merely rested, gathering their forces in order to burst with the greater eclat into the cabaret. But regardless of its reason, the transient peace was palpable and real. High above, the under surfaces of scattered clouds were touched by the light of a moon that still hung low over the island's central crags, yet neither the moon itself nor the vaguely reflecting clouds served to lessen the thick, friendly darkness where Papeete hid. The jumbled tin roofs, the unlovely, close-compacted clutter of frame buildings with their peeling walls of yellow or white or blue, all were swimming shadows that mingled with the night. Now and then bicycle riders passed, indistinct ghosts with tinkling bells, briefly seen, then lost again. At an intersection a pair of bonito fishermen loomed before us with the day's catching swinging between them on a long, shoulder-borne pole.

"There was luck?" Timi inquired.

"Luck enough, thank you," one of them replied quietly, and in the next instant both were swallowed by the blackness that lay still more intense in the direction of the market.

But we had come to a place from which it was possible to see the end of the street where it met the water's edge, and there, in a sharply defined area, night did not exist. There, bathed in the brilliance of high-swung arc lights, *Wairuna* lay squat and ungainly and serviceable against the wharf. Huge gnarled trees stood out in bold relief between us and the ship, yet we could see her clearly. We could hear faintly the rattle of her steam winches and see the loading nets swing from the dockside to drop within her waiting holds. *Wairuna* was our bond with all other Pacific lands and peoples — with Suva and Noumea, Christchurch, Wellington and San Francisco. But for all her faithful and stubborn regularity, what a fragile tie it seemed. For some reason the sight of her, the stolid emissary of a world of steel and power and machines, the sole busied, wakeful thing in a harbor of furled and sleeping sails, served only to bring home the more strongly our remoteness and detachment, our disinterest in, and our unimportance to, all that lay beyond the seas. Yes, ours still remains a lonely island, far from the paths that most ships ply, yet for *Wairuna*'s visits we are grateful. Each time she brings to port an echo of the cities into which she's put her bows and stirs memories of the sort of life they hold. Any land, however fair, would begin to pall, I suppose, if it were long enough taken quite for granted, and this danger the old freighter helps one to avoid. Often I have been obliged to step aboard to let her carry me from south to north, and for each safe passage I am duly thankful. But what pleasure it is, when she has

come to anchor, to be able to eye her with calm uncon-
cern and to think, "Not this time, my friend; go your way
and let me be."

I turned to Miri. "Why do you go to Quinn's yourself?"
I asked.

Miri had probably forgotten that it was she who
brought the matter up in the first place. She smiled
quickly. "I just like. No reason." It was the correct, the
only possible answer.

We rounded a corner into the harbor-front drive, and
in so doing left behind all that part of Papeete which was
somnolent or decorous. Little more than a block away,
glaring light spilled from the open doors of the famous
cabaret to show a large crowd milling in the street. From
the same doors there also issued a volume of sound so
grand that it may appear strange that it had not sooner
come to our ears. But, most mercifully for those of the
town interested in sleep, the shape and situation of this
palace of joy is such that its strident clamor is funneled
out to sea, where it disperses itself harmlessly in infinite
space. I wish it were possible to describe the raucous
composite voice in which Quinn's shouts down the endless halls of night, striving, so it seems, with brave and
puny defiance to make an impression upon the insen-
tient darkened sky and the darker waters. One may iso-
late and identify certain sections of the weird cacophony,
but the ebbing and swelling chorus of them all is not to
be imagined. There is the blare and bleat which thick
Tahitian lips and strong Tahitian lungs wring from various horns of wood and brass; there is the infernal,
earsplitting metallic rattle produced by beating lustily
with sticks upon cans that once held Crown or Union
gas; there is the roaring and the high falsettos of vocal-
ists possessed. Good for dancing? Only see the effect it
has upon the mob who jostle on the barnlike floor and
you'll know it is the best there ever was. But the music
comes from the efforts of no more than a dozen earnest

men. There are hundreds more to swell the orchestra of the whole and no single patron fails to add his quota. They are all inspired and each one will make his presence known. They stamp and shout and laugh and bang their fists upon the tables. Yet more insistent than all else is a rhythmic background of sound in which the tooting, the singing and yelling, the intermittent clatter of broken glass or the splintering crash of a faulty chair are blended, and it comes from the scrape of countless pairs of feet on thin-worn boards, from feet of sailors in their heavy shoes, of island whites in thong-tied sandals, of natives with naked calloused soles.

Arrived on the outskirts of the throng, we began energetically to elbow our way through the compressed bodies, intent on entering where we might add, to the best of our abilities, to the general tumult. There are several reasons for the congestion in the street about the doors. One of these is that the bamboo-sided bar is a two-way affair built to cater to those on the outside as well as to those who have managed to force themselves in. Like a long and narrow house within a house, it has a separate roof of its own and it stretches the entire width of the building between the two flanking entrances. Here the jam is always fearful, and there can be no question that if the bar were solidly constructed it would fall before the massed assaults. But native materials, like native characters, are elastic; they bend resignedly before a storm and then, once the pressure is released, assume again their former shape. So, depending upon which way the tide of beseigers chances momentarily to flow the strongest, Quinn's fascinating bar lists inward or streetward like a ship doing valiant battle on the sea, and the rows of colored Christmas-tree lights strung along the eaves nod and sway most charmingly. Not everyone who remains outside in the night's fresh air is, however, fighting for a drink. Some have been ejected from the close interior because of an infringement of the management's rules. (The only rule that comes to mind is one forbidding women to pull each other's hair.) Some, happening to be without francs, are free to take the music that overflows for dancing and use the hard-packed ground of the street on which to do it. Still others are patronizing the many Chinese pushcarts from whose canvas awnings dimly smoking lanterns hang. The perambulating shops are clustered beneath the protecting, heavily massed leaves of ancient trees and on their counters, in cases made of window glass, are candies and cakes, mangoes and oranges, French cigarettes, ready-husked coconuts to slake the thirst which other beverages produce. Generally, too, a pair of busy ice-cream venders are to be found taking advantage of the lodestone that is Quinn's, but on the night of Miri's party the cry of only a single one was to be heard.

"*Pape toetoe, pape toetoe!*" he called incessantly while he slowly pedaled the tricycle on which the freezer was supported. What had become of his partner was suddenly explained when we had nearly gained the portals of the cabaret.

"Take care!" someone shouted in quick alarm. "Take care—it is Madame Telephone!"

I looked and did not at first see the lady in question, but in the next instant the missing second ice-cream outfit shot from the gloom farther down the street. It came into the more brightly lighted area in front of Quinn's at an amazingly rapid rate of speed, yet in fashion most erratic. It careened to graze the curb on the right, tacked and bore away abruptly for the left, then back again. Mrs. Telephone, I soon saw, was in command and the unfortunate owner raced along behind her futilely screaming shrill Chinese.

"Save yourselves!" a man cried hoarsely. "She is *uaoti roa!*" (Meaning that she was three sheets in the wind or, more exactly, "very finished.")

Past experience had taught the danger, and there was

a concerted rush for the safety of the sidewalks, from which point of vantage they quickly turned to shout encouragement and advice at the intrepid young cyclist and her luckless pursuer.

"Faster, madame, faster!"

"Run, little Chinaman, run!"

"It is the *mousseu,*" Miri exclaimed, delightedly clapping her hands. "I am so happy — nothing is changed. Always when she drinks *mousseu* it is the same. *Allez, cherie,*" she cried, *"vite, vite, vite!"*

Having gained the spotlight, so to speak, Mrs. Telephone went into a series of breathtaking loops and turns and figure eights, through all of which the puffing Chinese followed with a precision so admirable that he had the air of being drawn after her by an invisible cord. The shout of appreciation which greeted these intricate maneuvers was so loud that it was heard throughout the length of Quinn's. The band stopped playing and threw down their instruments, the drinkers stopped their drinks, the dancers broke apart and all made a dash for the street.

Interruptions of this sort were frequent in the course of an evening in Tahiti's principal night club, for in a land where the days have all a certain sameness everyone is concerned to miss no happening that may be even slightly out of the ordinary. The sound of two taxis tangling fenders, voices raised in anger or lamentation — or the mere rumor that something excitable or laughable is about to happen — is sufficient to empty Quinn's in a trice. At first I used to join in each pell-mell exodus as eagerly as the rest, but the alarms proved so often false that the time came when I no longer bothered. Today I remained seated in the empty place, content to wait for the patrons to straggle back and inform me of what has been going on. It is a satisfactory procedure in view of energy saved, and also because the report is almost certain to be far superior to the event itself.

160

I should have been disappointed, nevertheless, not to have witnessed Mrs. Telephone with my own eyes, hers being a performance to which not even the highly colored and imaginative words of Tahitians could have done justice. As the mob of spectators increased, so did her skill and daring. Dressed in white shorts and a Hawaiian print shirt, her small feet tucked into green sandals, she whirled about the arena bounded on one side by Ah You's store and on the other by Quinn's. Her very blond hair streamed out behind, her slim white legs flashed on the pedals, and, guiding the freezer-burdened velocipede with one hand, she raised the other to the enthusiastic throng, saluting them with the careless and slightly condescending grace of a circus rider. But unlike a silently smiling queen of the big top, Mrs. Telephone opened every few seconds her pretty red lips and with head tilted back proclaimed to the heavens, "*Pape toetoe! Who will buy? Toss me your francs for pape toetoe!*"

Miri lifted her voice to be heard above the peals of delighted laughter. "I will! I will buy!" She threw a coin.

"And I!" Timi exclaimed, following it with another.

"*Et moi!*" Teuru shrilled, happily flinging, not one, but several of the francs I'd given her for the morrow's marketing.

Apparently it was contagious. Of what use is money anyway? What can it be meant for if not for sport? With a merry tinkling the metal disks flew from every hand. "Me too!" they all cried, and the money showered down like darkly tarnished rain.

In consequence the show came to an end, yet I think it was more likely sheer exhaustion than avarice which caused the little Chinaman abruptly to abandon the hopeless pursuit and to drop to his knees. That he then began methodically gathering up the coins which strewed the ground all above him was probably a simple afterthought, and a sensible one besides. Perceiving that the game was over, Mrs. Telephone allowed her steed to coast, and then, catching sight of Miri's face among the many, came to a stop before us and jumped lightly off.

"Miri darling!" she exclaimed in glad surprise. "You're back again!" They embraced affectionately and then Mrs. Telephone (whose name was Marjorie before she came to Tahiti with a man who wore an ear trumpet) held the girl at arm's length. "But you look younger than ever! How do you do it?"

"Men and absinthe," Miri acknowledged.

"Aren't you awful. We don't change a bit, do we?" She looked about vaguely as if she had forgotten something and her eyes lighted upon the Chinaman, who had come to take possession of his machine. She went to him, placed a dollar bill in his hand, and after kissing him lightly on each of his thin, parchment-colored cheeks returned to us. "Now let's go in before all the tables are taken and Bill will find us some *mousseu*, won't you, *cheri?*"

I followed them, idly wondering if it was really nothing more than sparkling wine which caused Marjorie to put on such outrageous scenes on Quinn's doorstep. I had a suspicion that, far from spontaneous, her weird exhibitions were carefully, cold-bloodedly preconceived. She came to the cabaret. Every seat was filled. What to do? Why, empty the place and then slip in before the slower-witted among the sidewalk crowd have discovered that the curtain's down. Unconscious or planned, it was fine strategy and it worked: we found a vacant table, a low circular one about which were scattered a number of luxuriously comfortable frame and canvas easychairs. We had, for the time being at least, become separated from the captain and the other recruits gathered at the Tiare, and after seeing that drinks were brought for Timi and Tavae, Teuru, Miri, and Marjorie, I leaned back prepared to allow matters to take their usual unpredictable course.

Tavae manipulated the cork of the bottle of *mousseu*, pushing it this way and that with his thumb till it burst out with a resounding pop and sailed bullet-straight to strike the red neck of one of *Wairuna*'s stokers, who sat around the next table in undershirts and dungarees.

He turned belligerently. "What the bloody . . .?"

"Pardon, m'sieu," said Tavae. "I am desolated; it is like that the *mousseu*, you know."

The fellow got up and came toward us threateningly. "Don't give me any of your parlez-vous."

He was big and fair and very young. Mrs. Telephone's clear blue eyes surveyed him speculatively, taking in the full chest, the hard midriff, the long wrestler's arms, and she put a hand to her hair to assure herself that it properly framed her pretty face.

The seaman bent and brought his sunburned nose close to Tavae's. "Maybe somebody is lookin' to have his bloody block knocked off." These words Tavae did not, of course, literally understand but the tone in which they were uttered made translation quite unnecessary. My yard boy is not of warlike disposition; he prefers to be everyone's friend, and he glanced to me for help.

"It was an accident," I said. "No offense. You'd better have a drink and then go and sit down."

"And who might *you* be?"

A simple enough question, one would think. But no answer came to me at the minute and we appeared to have reached something of an impasse when the young man's glance fell upon Miri and Teuru, both of whom were gazing at him very sweetly. Almost instantly his expression changed. He ceased to frown, the muscles about his jaw relaxed, he smiled, flushed, stammered.

"I say. What have we got here?"

"Tahitian women," said Timi, pouring a glass of wine and handing it to him.

"A little bit of all right, that's what." He emptied the glass, replaced it on the table, hesitated while he looked from one to the other of us, and then asked, "They belong to you blokes?"

"Nope," said Timi who always tends to wax needlessly loquacious whenever he has the opportunity to speak English. "They're free, brown, and twenty-one; they got no permanent attachments."

"Blimey," remarked the young giant. And then, with charming diffidence, "Mind if I speak to 'em?"

Timi waved a hand airily. "Go ahead, Jack; this is a free country."

How free it is, Jack had already learned in a bare six hours ashore, and he soon made it clear that in the same short while he had also grasped the essentials of the local languages. He went to Miri's side.

"Haere taoto?" he inquired genially.

Miri shook her head, but smiled at the same time in so affable a manner that the sailor was obviously perplexed to know whether the sum total signified acceptance or rejection. He moved on to Teuru and repeated his question, giving it a try this time in French.

"Faire l'amour, mam'selle?"

Teuru did not shake her head but turned to Timi and began to speak rapidly and with apparent indignation in her own tongue. *"Aue,* Timi—how crazy they all are, these *popaas!* 'Make love, make love.' Do they think of nothing else? Whether they are little or fat or ugly or, like this one, handsome, big and tall, it is always the same. When is one to have any pleasure? We come to Quinn's to laugh and dance and drink and be gay, and before we can begin to do any of these things it is here again: *'Haere taoto? Faire l'amour?'* Tell him, Timi, that I am *fiu, fiu, FIU!"* she concluded dramatically, meaning that she was respectively "bored," "very bored," and "bored something awful." Well pleased with her little oration, she then regarded the importunate young man from beneath long, demurely lowered lashes—a procedure having the effect of heightening, rather than hiding, the softly caressive quality of her eyes.

"What does she say?" he asked eagerly of Timi.

"She says later, maybe. It's early yet. Come back later on," Timi advised.

"Right you are."

"A good deal later."

"Righto."

"Along toward morning sometime."

"Right." He turned away. "Cheerio," he said over his shoulder, and in a now happy frame of mind went to join his fellow Aussies.

"Very nicely handled, Timi," I observed as we all relaxed. "He'll forget within the hour."

"It is possible," Teuru murmured with a faint smile of the sort that should be accompanied by a purr. "But I do not think he goes to forget."

Mrs. Telephone laughed. "Did you see? He didn't so much as look as me. What chance has a girl with these dark-eyed vahines?"

"None," I said. "You ought to take that milky white skin back to a country where it belongs." It was advice that, most fortunately, has never been accepted. Tahiti would be the loser if Marjorie should take her blond prettiness away. And, despite the competition, she gets on very well.

The orchestra had pulled themselves together and, taking note who made up our party, began the dreamy melody named for another Miri, but equally appropriate to ours. "*Miri itie, here vau ia oe . . .*" Yes, as the lyric repeated, we all loved Miri, and for the moment the blatant racket of Quinn's was stilled. Though the music that rose in its stead was composed of many Polynesian voices, they were voices temporarily subdued, softened in keeping with the haunting air they sang. It was necessary only to close the eyes to be lifted from the shabby cabaret and transported to Tahiti's borders close to the sea, for Miri's song evokes as no other the spirit of her island. In it one hears the rhythmic swishing patter of warm rain, the ocean's slow and measured breathing, the whispered conversation of the palms — soothing, Lethean sounds in which I had quite lost myself when I was aroused by a determined pulling on my trouser leg.

Teuru was trying to direct my attention to three elderly dames who had come to stand beside us, their outstretched arms loaded with a marvelous variety of flower wreaths. "*Heis* are required," she stated.

This I had no need of being told, and as soon as I had nodded agreement Teuru rose to begin unburdening the three venders of their fragrant, dew-wet wares. She tossed a *hei* to each of us, and about Miri's throat carefully arranged first a long red and yellow wreath of *purau* and hibiscus blossoms, next a smaller one of delicate creamy jasmine, then crowned the raven hair with a circlet of Tahitian gardenias, purest white. She decorated herself as generously and paid the smiling flower sellers. "Thank you, old mother," she said to each, and took her place as the last notes of Miri's song faded in a diminuendo that left Quinn's cabaret in rarely experienced silence. The hush was brief and it was broken when friends by the many score rushed with glad cries to embrace the girl so recently returned. Because no one else ever thinks of such matters, I wrapped both arms about the table, hoping to prevent it, and the various glasses upon it, from being overturned.

When the crowd had thinned a little Miri turned to me with eyes that glistened brightly. "Ah, Beel, it make me so happy and so sad!"

"Dance, Miri!" someone called, and immediately the excited demands arose upon all sides. "*A-ori*, Miri, *a-ori!*"

Teuru jumped up, ran to the bar, dove behind it and came back waving a grass skirt which she thrust in Miri's lap. "Put it on, *cherie!* Quickly, quickly!"

Miri turned the soft, whitely bleached mass of thinshredded *purau* bark in her hands, fondling it, pressing it to her face, running her fingers over the brilliantly dyed tassels and the belt of beaded shells.

166

Teuru drew her by the hand. "Come, my little one. None of us has seen the true dance of Tahiti since you went away. Come!"

Miri allowed herself to be pulled to her feet. "But of course I shall dance. I think I shall dance as never before. How can one help it when he is all full of happiness?"

Timi looked at her dubiously. "You are a little full of the things you have drunk, no?"

"*Mamu,*" she told him pleasantly. "Shut up."

"Go ahead, then. But not *a poil,* eh?"

She held up the grass skirt. "How shall I be naked if I wear the *ahu-more?*"

"Yes, yes. But the little pants underneath—the little *piripo* there is no need to remove."

"*Aue!* I am *fiu* with *piripo.* Of what use can they be in Tahiti?" and with Teuru to help her don what little is required for the *ori* she skipped off to a room at the back.

"Well, *mon vieux,*" Timi sighed when they had gone, "what would you? With the women one can do nothing. Let us drink."

Content though I was that nothing could be done, we clinked glasses and nodded at each other in solemn masculine understanding.

The floor was cleared. A dog that had curled up comfortably in the center of the place was kicked out yelping; a few stray drunks who wandered aimlessly were led to the sidelines. The band exploded into hurrying, feverish rhythm little short of demented. It was no puling Hawaiian music made of slithering steel guitars, but the solid, rapid-thudding, rump-shaking, blood-firing stuff that gives quick and joyous birth to a dance beside which the northern hula seems the epitome of sedateness and reserve. There is no withstanding the excitement that it breathes and it will not permit one to remain a calm bystander. It reaches out and grips each hearer roughly, relentlessly. It sets the heart swift-beating, feet will not stay still, without volition hands begin to clap. Every man and woman in the cabaret—and the scattering of tots who were always underfoot as well—was swept up in the same delirious contagion and fused into a single riotously enthusiastic percussive orchestra. Fortunately, Quinn's is far more sturdy than the venerable Tiare and well accustomed to such madly concentrated effort. Even so, the barnlike structure did not remain impassive but responded to the temper of its inmates with a sympathetic shimmying vibration that reached from top to bottom.

"There she is!" someone shouted. *"La voila, la voila!"* All eyes swerved to where Teuru was determinedly shoving people aside to make a path for her darling friend. A tremendous cheer went up as Miri burst out onto the floor.

Probably it is no wonder that music capable of stirring into something resembling life even a man like myself, whose forebears spent their days in chilly New England, should do far more for a girl whose roots go down in warmer soil. Miri was transfigured. It goes without saying that even in repose she seemed animated in comparison with the dull apathy in which so many a Northener appears permanently, leadenly sunk. But now, suddenly, she was become an utterly different girl beside which her more customary lightly gay self was tame and domesticated indeed. Doubtless it was the real Miri that the frenzied pagan drumming called forth, the Miri who at other times slumbered just below the surface and who now shone through the golden-glowing skin, savage, wild and free, clear for all to see. It was as if she reached back into the island's heathen past, drawing up its reckless fecund power, its untrammeled passions, its joyous lust for living, giving it all glad rebirth in her supple, weaving body, flinging it all prodigally before us so that each one who watched might breathe of, share in and take to himself a part of her boundless, overflowing vitality.

In the theaters of Europe and America, on the sets of

Hollywood, Miri's dancing caused a furor and it is unlikely that many of those who saw her suspected that what they witnessed was a pale adulteration, a mere shadowy suggestion of the true *ori-Tahiti*. But on the impromptu stage of Quinn's there was nothing to dampen or inhibit, nothing to impose restraint, nothing to hide or dim the ardor and the intoxicating happiness which filled the girl that night. Like a high priestess of the love-worshipping sect called Arioi, she gave jubilant expression to the ancient mating rite remembered from a distant past, imbuing each sinuous, provocative movement with unabashed and forthright meaning that no onlooker might fail to comprehend.

The native language contains one word alone capable of expressing emotions deep seated as those which Miri's splendidly primitive and simple magic roused. From the lips of some it fell like an ecstatic whisper, from others like an anguished moan, and from still others as a shout of exuberant joy; but always the word was one. "*Aue!*— *aue*, Miri-e!"

Marjorie had gripped my wrist. "If only I could dance like that!" she exclaimed.

"To do so you would have to be Tahitian."

"How I wish I were!"

Our exotic Mrs. Telephone was far from the first to have such a fleeting wish. No foreigner could follow Miri as she began to circle the cleared space in the center of the crowded cabaret without a twinge of envy. Yet envy of things one cannot hope to attain is waste of time. And who of those not born upon Tahiti is capable of feeling so intense, of transport so complete as that which guided Miri's legs and arms through the swift patterns of her dance? Others may guess the sensations which run tingling through her, flowing from her finger tips and nimbly weaving feet—and that is all. But everyone— white, brown, yellow, or black—can clap and cheer and sing. And so they do. Everyone can watch each move and gesture, imagining that she dances for him alone. And so, for each in turn, she does, hovering before this man or that while with eyes and lips and her whole self she makes him briefly partner in her siren game, then quickly, tantalizingly breaking away and moving on to seduce as merrily and wantonly the next.

Quinn's boasts no spotlight to train upon a performer who chances to take the floor, and in Miri's case, at least, none was needed. Since all eyes were fastened upon her with a fixity equal to my own, others must have been subject to the same illusion: Miri, one felt, sent forth a brilliance of her own. It was light which left the rest of the cabaret in shadow, illuminating only the girl herself and the features of those nearest her on whom it fell. But "illusions" is hardly the word. Too much was real. Though she had gained the far end of the building, I could see plainly the effect of the curious electrical magic that she spread. From the blur of the crowd the faces of those to whom she momentarily called became suddenly detached and distinct; they lightened, awakened, identified themselves clearly, shone for a few seconds in the reflection of her radiance, then slipped back into anonymity when she moved on to bring others into transient prominence. In this way Miri unrolled the cyclorama that was Quinn's, disclosing one after another the faces of the devotees of that temple of indecorum. And as in her dance itself, there was rhythm as repetitive and definite in the succession of portraits that she so displayed. Four or five or six brown skins swam into focus, to be followed by one of contrasting, punctuating white, then by brown again. Always the color of Tahiti predominated and always at regular intervals it was interrupted by the pale cast of the north with here and there an abrupt offbeat—a sort of accidental, syncopated note of yellow or of black. Many of those in the passing parade were familiar or well known: dusky boys and girls from the district of Hitiaa, where suns and rains are fiercest; fishermen from Haapape; the proudly mustached chief of Punaauia; a thin, effete Dutchman of vast wealth and his fragile Austrian wife; a buxom Tahitian princess and a handsome, gray-haired, hopelessly infatuated French surgeon; a group of French sailors surrounding the native mistress of a temporarily absent Chilian millionaire; a German painter with childlike blue eyes and fair beard who loves to draw Tahitians with enormously exaggerated feet and rears; a direct descendant of Fletcher Christian of the good ship *Bounty*; a New Yorker who—disliking the island—doggedly stays on to write an unpleasant book about it; a retired American chemist and native mistress; a retired British consul and native mistress; the owner of an Australian radio station and native mistress; an Italian sculptor who spends most of his time on the little island of Maupiti, where men are strangely feminine. If there are elsewhere four walls that hold humanity so diverse as those of Quinn's I have never discovered them. Most numerous are the people of Tahiti itself. There are also tall, statuesque men and women of Rapa, where formerly the greatest warriors grew. There are darker-skinned, tougher-fibered folk come from the atolls, where life has always called for struggle. There are others from Mangareva, the Marquesas, the Australs, and forgotten Huahine, and in one thing only were they all quite the same. That was their enraptured submission to the spell of Miri's dance.

She had come near the place we were sitting when Fati, who had come unnoticed to stand behind us, could contain himself no longer. With a tremendous, exultant whoop he plunged past us, overturning the table, sending its freight of bottles and long-stemmed glasses merrily crashing. A deluge of shouted advice, much of it of a none too delicate nature, met him as he burst onto the floor. He threw himself into the dance and set out in pursuit of Miri with his great mass of blubber trembling like brown jelly. Miri's smile broadened, an added sparkle appeared in her eyes, the circlets of flowers which Teuru had bound about wrists and ankled moved with a new life, her firm slim legs flashed still more swiftly through the strands of the *ahu-more* which whirled about her as if caught by a playful breeze. So she drew Fati on, luring him, provoking him, promising unbelievable delights. And he was right after her, fitting his movements to hers, replying to each abandoned invitation with proper male aggression. The musicians, the perspiring spectators, everyone soared to fresh heights of delirium.

Timi alone among the many appeared to watch with anything approaching calm. He leaned over and spoke in my ear. "You see," he remarked resignedly, "she is indeed completely *a poil*."

I was about to comfort him with the suggestion that it was all in the interests of Miri's art when, suddenly, he grinned broadly, let out a yell rivaling Fati's own, jumped from his chair, and rushed out to bear down, madly dancing, upon Miri from the other side. It was the signal for half a dozen bucks to spring onto the floor, where they leaped into the frantic tempo set by the girl and then began implacably to converge upon her. Miri was trapped. There was no escape from the circle of ardent *tanes* whose eloquent contortions brought them ever nearer, confining her movements to a smaller and smaller area. But the *ori-Tahiti* was never devised with thought for evasion. Rather, of course, its whole purpose was to give rise to hot pursuit and insure the final desired surrender and captivation. The drumming rose to a climax. With knees far bent so that Miri seemed tall beside them, the men pressed in, closer, closer till they formed a solid, pelvis-rolling ring about her, till at the final beat of the music she was unable to move to right or left, forward or back, and stood with arms above her head, body all aquiver. There was a second's silence when the music stopped, a second in which the dancers remained motionless, frozen in the postures the last note

172

had cut short. Then they broke. Quinn's dissolved into a pandemonium of applause. Timi caught up his sister and, carrying her back to us, deposited her in the chair beside me.

"Soon as you get your breath," he advised, "go put on some clothes. To sit around when you're covered with sweat is to catch cold."

Miri laughed at him. "You know a funny thing, Marjorie?" she said to Mrs. Telephone. "When I dance in Hollywood or Warsaw or Vienna I finish dry and cool. And the dance is — what you think? — like breadfruit that is stale. But here, here where is my home, I take fire, I burn up, I am drenched like in heated rain. And the dance . . ."

"Is thrilling!" Marjorie gushed.

"Is formidable," Tavae agreed.

"Is *numero hoe*," Teuru added, "number one."

"Is *nave-nave*," Fati stated, wiping his brow and clinching the matter by that word describing the moment of greatest joy which man and woman can experience.

W. Somerset Maugham

My South Sea Island

One of the most versatile and widely read English authors of this century, W. Somerset Maugham (1874-1965), while serving as a British secret agent during World War I, spent several months in 1916 and 1917 visiting various islands of Polynesia. He stopped first at Hawaii and then went on to Samoa and Tahiti. These islands provided him with material for two of his best books of fiction: *The Moon and Sixpence* (1919), a novel based on the life of Paul Gauguin; and *The Trembling of a Leaf* (1921), a collection of six stories, including "Red," which he regarded as his most successful short story, and "Rain," the one that is best known.

In the brief tale that follows, Maugham tells of a curious experience he had while living on a small coral island near Tahiti.

I HAVE always thought it must be the most delightful thing in the world to own an island; not Ireland, of course, or Borneo— that would really be too much of a good thing—but an island that you could walk round without hurrying yourself in a couple of hours; and now and then I have been offered one, if not for a song, at least for no more than I shall get for this article. But it was always at least a thousand miles from where I happened to be, and that seemed a considerable distance to go (especially as there was no means of getting there) in order to inspect an island which, after all, might not be exactly the sort of island I wanted. Besides, if I were not living on it, I should always be worried about it; I should awake in the night in London and wonder anxiously whether anyone had run away with it. You have to be so careful with portable property in the South Seas.

But in Tahiti I met a man who owned an island, and when I told him that I envied him he offered to lend it to me. There was something so casual about the suggestion, like a man in a railway carriage who asks you if you would like his *Punch*, that I accepted at once.

The island happened to be no more than a hundred miles away from anywhere else (that in the Pacific is cheek by jowl, no farther than Piccadilly Circus from Trafalgar Square), so that it was a wonderful chance to enjoy the satisfaction of proprietorship.

I found a small cutter with a gasoline engine to take me over; I had a native servant whose extraordinary incompetence was only equaled by his unfailing good nature, and I engaged a Chinese cook — for I thought this was an occasion to do things in style.

I bought a bag of rice, a quantity of tinned goods, a certain amount of whisky, and a great many bottles of soda, for the owner had warned me that there was no water on the island.

I set my foot on the beach. The island was mine for as long as I chose to inhabit it. The beach really had the silver whiteness that you read of in descriptions of the South Sea islands, and when I walked along in the sunshine it was so dazzling that I could hardly bear to look at it. Here and there were the white shells of dead crabs and the skeletons of sea birds.

I walked up through the coconuts and came upon a grove of enormous, old, and leafy trees; they gave coolness and a grateful shade. It was among these that the tiny settlement was built. There was the headman's hut and another for the workman, two more to store the copra, and a somewhat larger one, trim and clean, which the owner of the island used when he visited it and in which I was to dwell.

I unloaded my stores and bedding and proceeded to make myself at home. But I had not reckoned with the mosquitoes. There were swarms of them; I have never seen so many; and they were bold and fierce and pitiless. I rigged up a net in the veranda of my hut and placed a table and a chair beneath it, but the mosquitoes were ingenious to enter, and I had to kill twenty at least before I could sit down in peace.

Here I took my frugal meals, but when a dish was hurriedly passed between the curtains a dozen mosquitoes dashed in and I had to kill them one by one before I could eat.

I set about exploring the island. It had evidently been raised from the sea at a comparatively recent date, and much of the interior was barren and almost swampy, so that I sank in as I walked. I suppose what was now dry land had not very long ago been brackish lake. Beside the coconuts nothing much seemed to grow but rank grass and a shrub something like a broom.

There were no animals on the island but rats, perhaps, and though throughout the Pacific you find everywhere the mynah bird, noisy and quarrelsome, to this lonely spot he had never found his way; and the wild fowl I saw were great black gulls with long beaks. They had a piercing, almost a human, whistle. I thought that in them abode, restless and menacing, the souls of dead seamen drowned at sea. They gave something sinister to the smiling sunlit island.

But it was not till I had been on the island for several days that I discovered they were not the only sinister things there. I thought I had explored every inch of it, and I was surprised one evening to catch through the coconuts a glimpse of a little grass hut. I saw a moving shape, and I wondered if it was possible that anyone lived there.

I strolled toward the hut and I saw what was certainly a man, but as I approached he vanished. I supposed that I had startled him and he had slunk away among the brush-wood. But I wondered why he had chosen this lonely dwelling, who he was, and how he lived.

The Polynesians are a friendly and sociable race, and I was intrigued to find anyone in that tiny island who needed solitude so much that he must live away even from the half-dozen persons who formed the island's entire population. I puzzled my brains. It could not be a watchman, for among the coconuts there was nothing to watch and no danger to guard against.

When I returned to my own house I told the headman what I had seen and asked him who this solitary creature was; but he would not, or could not, understand me. It was not till I was once more in Papeete that I found out. I thanked the owner of the island for the loan of it and then I asked him who was the mysterious man who seemed to shun the approach of his fellows.

"Oh, that's my leper," he said. "I thought he'd amuse you."

"He tickled me to death," I answered. "But haven't you rather a peculiar sense of humor?"

Rupert Brooke

Tiare Tahiti

No other poet who drew inspiration from the Pacific islands had the genius of Rupert Brooke (1887-1915). Born at Rugby, Warwickshire, he went to school there and in 1906 entered Kings College, Cambridge, where he was a brilliant student in classics and English literature. With the publication of his first book, *Poems* (1911), he was recognized as one of the most talented young writers in England. In the spring of 1913 he set out for a year of travel, first visiting the United States and Canada and then going on to Hawaii, Samoa, Fiji, New Zealand, and Tahiti. Soon after he returned to England, in June, 1914, the World War broke out. He was commissioned in the Royal Naval Division, took part in the Belgian campaign, and early in 1915 sailed with his division for the Dardanelles. On the way he contracted blood poisoning, and within two days he was dead. He was buried at Skyros in the Aegean. His book *1914 and Other Poems*, published posthumously, contains the poems written in the South Seas, among them "Tiare Tahiti," "The Great Lover," "Clouds," "Waikiki," and other examples of his finest work. In the following section, "Pupure" was Brooke himself; the Tahitian name was given him because of his fair hair.

Tiare Tahiti

Mamua, when our laughter ends,
And hearts and bodies, brown as white
Are dust about the doors of friends,
Or scent a-blowing down the night,
Then, oh! then, the wise agree,
Comes our immortality.

Mamua, there waits a land
Hard for us to understand.
Out of time, beyond the sun,
All are one in Paradise,
You and Pupure are one,
And Tau, and the ungainly wise.
There the Eternals are, and there
The Good, the Lovely, and the True
And Types, whose earthly copies were
The foolish broken things we knew;
There is the face, whose ghosts we are;
The real, the never-setting Star;
And the Flower, of which we love
Faint and fading shadows here
Never a tear, but only Grief;
Dance, but not the limbs that move;
Songs in Song shall disappear;
Instead of lovers, Love shall be;
For hearts, Immutability;
And there, on the Ideal Reef,
Thunders the Everlasting Sea!

     And my laughter, and my pain,
Shall home to the Eternal Brain.
And all the lovely things, they say,
Meet in Loveliness again;
Miri's laugh, Teipo's feet,
And the hands of Matua,
Stars and sunlight there shall meet,
Coral's hues and rainbows there,
And Teura's braided hair;
And with the starred *tiare's* white,
And white birds in the dark ravine,
And flamboyants ablaze at night,
And jewels and evening's after-green,
And dawns of pearl and gold and red,
Mamua, your lovelier head!

And there'll no more be one who dreams
Under the ferns, of crumbling stuff,
Eyes of illusion, mouth that seems,
All time-entangled human love.
And you'll no longer swing and sway
Divinely down the scented shade,
Where feet to Ambulation fade,
And moons are lost in endless Day.
How shall we wind these wreaths of ours,
Where there are neither heads nor flowers?
Oh, Heaven's Heaven!—but we'll be missing
The palms, and sunlight, and the south;
And there's an end, I think, of kissing,
When our mouths are one with Mouth . . .

    Tau here, Mamua,
Crown the hair, and come away!
Hear the calling of the moon,
And the whispering scents that stray
About the idle warm lagoon.
Hasten, hand in human hand,
Down the dark, the flowered way,
Along the whiteness of the sand,
And in the water's soft caress,
Was the mind of foolishness,
Mamua, until the day.
Spend the glittering moonlight there
Pursuing down the soundless deep
Limbs that gleam and shadowy hair,
Or floating lazy, half-asleep.
Dive and double and follow after,
Snare in flowers, and kiss, and call,
With lips that fade, and human laughter
And faces individual,
Well this side of Paradise! . . .
There's little comfort in the wise.

II. The Travelers

Jack London

Darling, the Nature Man

Jack London (1876-1916) set out with his second wife, Charmian, and a small crew aboard his ketch *Snark* from San Francisco in the spring of 1907 on a two-year cruise of Hawaii, the Marquesas, the Society group, Samoa, Fiji, the "terrible Solomons," and other islands. After a rough traverse from Hawaii via the Marquesas group, the yacht moored in December with others along the main street of Papeete. Although he had earned thousands of dollars from his writing during the year, London learned that his balance in the California bank was no more than $66, and he was forced to make a quick trip by steamer to disentangle his financial affairs. His irritation when held up for more than three months in the small port while the yacht ran up large expenses accounts in part for his low opinion of the people of the colony. However, he did obtain material there for several of his best stories, such as "The House of Mapuhi." He also renewed acquaintance with Ernest Darling, the "Nature Man," forerunner early in our century of movements seeking to return to styles of living closer to the elements of healthful human existence.

Some years after London gave his account of Ernest Darling's adventures in Tahiti, Frederic O'Brien left San Francisco for Papeete and observed a commotion at departure, which turned out to be the forceful eviction of Darling from the steamer. He had evidently tried to return to Tahiti by stowing away on the vessel. O'Brien became curious about the "Nature Man," and when he landed he made inquiries about him. He learned that Darling had attracted a group of fellow nature worshippers to his plantation, who shared his ecological beliefs and worked hard growing fruits and vegetables for the market. But their unconventional behavior caused the authorities to deport these lunatics, who were setting a bad example to the native people because they did not always wear sarongs on the road. As O'Brien reported in his *Mystic Isles of the South Seas*, a police officer told him fiercely: "Is the French Republic to permit here in its colony the whites who enjoy its hospitality to shame the nation before the Tahitians by their nakedness?"

"Ernest Darling died in Fiji at the age of fifty-two," according to Wilmon Menard, "during the devastating influenza epidemic." In later years, Tahiti was no longer a refuge for such eccentric Americans.

I FIRST met him on Market Street in San Francisco. It was a wet and drizzly afternoon, and he was striding along, clad solely in a pair of abbreviated knee-trousers and an abbreviated shirt, his bare feet going slick-slick through the pavement slush. At his heels trooped a score of excited gamins. Every head—and there were thousands—turned to glance curiously at him as he went by. And I turned, too. Never had I seen such a lovely sunburn. He was all sunburn, of the sort a blond takes on when his skin does not peel. His long yellow hair was burnt, so was his beard, which sprang from a soil unplowed by any razor. He was a tawny man, a golden-tawny man, all glowing and radiant with the sun. Another prophet, thought I, come up to town with a message that will save the world.

A few weeks later I was with some friends in their bungalow in the Piedmont hills overlooking San Francisco Bay. "We've got him, we've got him," they barked. "We caught him up a tree; but he's all right now, he'll feed from the hand. Come on and see him." So I accompanied them up a dizzy hill, and in a rickety shack in the midst of a eucalyptus grove found my sunburned prophet of the city pavement.

He hastened to meet us, arriving in the whirl and blur of a handspring. He did not shake hands with us; instead, his greeting took the form of stunts. He turned more handsprings. He twisted his body sinuously, like a snake, until, having sufficiently limbered up, he bent from the hips and, with legs straight and knees touching, beat a tattoo on the ground with the palms of his hands. He whirligigged and pirouetted, dancing and cavorting round like an inebriated ape. All the sun-warmth of his ardent life beamed in his face. "I am so happy" was the song without words he sang.

He sang it all evening, ringing the changes on it with an endless variety of stunts. "A fool! a fool! I met a fool in the forest!" thought I. And a worthy fool he proved. Between handsprings and whirligigs he delivered his message that would save the world. It was twofold. First, let suffering humanity strip off its clothing and run wild in the mountains and valleys; and, second, let the very miserable world adopt phonetic spelling. I caught a glimpse of the great social problems being settled by the city populations swarming naked over the landscape, to the popping of shotguns, the barking of ranch dogs, and countless assaults with pitchforks wielded by irate farmers.

The years passed, and, one sunny morning, the *Snark* poked her nose into a narrow opening in a reef that smoked with the crashing impact of the trade-wind swell, and beat slowly up Papeete harbor. Coming off to us was a boat flying a yellow flag. We knew it contained the port doctor. But quite a distance off, in its wake, was a tiny outrigger canoe that puzzled us. It was flying a red flag. I studied it through the glasses, fearing that it marked some hidden danger to navigation, some recent wreck or some buoy or beacon that had been swept away. Then the doctor came on board. After he had examined the state of our health and been assured that we had no live rats hidden away in the *Snark*, I asked him the meaning of the red flag. "Oh, that is Darling," was the answer.

And then Darling, Ernest Darling, flying the red flag that is indicative of the brotherhood of man, hailed us. "Hello, Jack!" he called. "Hello, Charmian!" He paddled swiftly nearer, and I saw that he was the tawny prophet of the Piedmont hills. He came over the side, a sun-god clad in a scarlet loincloth, with presents of Arcady and greeting in both his hands — a bottle of golden honey and a leaf-basket filled with great golden mangoes, golden bananas specked with freckles of deeper gold, golden pineapples and golden limes, and juicy oranges minted from the same precious ore of sun and soil. And in this fashion, under the southern sky, I met once more Darling, the Nature Man.

Tahiti is one of the most beautiful spots in the world, inhabited by thieves and robbers and liars, also by several honest and truthful men and women. Wherefore, because of the blight cast upon Tahiti's wonderful beauty by the spidery human vermin that infest it, I am minded to write, not of Tahiti, but of the Nature Man. He, at least, is refreshing and wholesome. The spirit that emanates from him is so gentle and sweet that it would harm nothing, hurt nobody's feelings save the feelings of a predatory and plutocratic capitalist.

"What does this red flag mean?" I asked.

"Socialism, of course."

"Yes, yes, I know that," I went on; "but what does it mean in your hands?"

"Why, that I've found my message."

"And that you are delivering it to Tahiti?" I demanded incredulously.

"Sure," he answered simply; and later on I found that he was, too.

When we dropped anchor, lowered a small boat into the water, and started ashore, the Nature Man joined us. Now, thought I, I shall be pestered to death by this crank. Waking or sleeping I shall never be quit of him until I sail away from here.

But never in my life was I more mistaken. I took a house and went to live and work in it, and the Nature Man never came near me. He was waiting for the invitation. In the meantime he went aboard the *Snark* and took possession of her library, delighted by the quantity of scientific books, and shocked, as I learned afterward, by the inordinate amount of fiction. The Nature Man never wastes time on fiction.

After a week or so, my conscience smote me, and I invited him to dinner at a downtown hotel. He arrived looking unwontedly stiff and uncomfortable in his cotton jacket. When invited to peel it off, he beamed his gratitude and joy, and did so, revealing his sun-gold skin, from waist to shoulder, covered only by a piece of fish net of coarse twine and large of mesh. A scarlet loincloth completed his costume. I began my acquaintance with him from that night, and during my long stay in Tahiti that acquaintance ripened into friendship.

"So you write books," he said, one day when, tired and sweaty, I finished my morning's work.

"I, too, write books," he announced.

Alas, thought I, now at last he is going to pester me with his literary efforts. My soul was in revolt. I had not come all the way to the South Seas to be a literary bureau.

"This is the book I write," he explained, smashing himself a resounding blow on the chest with his clenched fist. "The gorilla in the African jungle pounds his chest till the noise of it can be heard half a mile away."

"A pretty good chest," quoth I, admiringly; "it would even make a gorilla envious."

And then, and later, I learned the details of the marvelous book Ernest Darling had written. Twelve years ago he lay close to death. He weighed but ninety pounds, and was too weak to speak. The doctors had given him up. His father, a practicing physician, had given him up. Consultations with other physicians had been held upon him. There was no hope for him. Overstudy (as a schoolteacher and as a university student) and two successive attacks of pneumonia were responsible for his breakdown. Day by day he was losing strength. He could extract no nutrition from the heavy foods they gave him;

187

nor could pellets and powders help his stomach to do the work of digestion. Not only was he a physical wreck, but he was a mental wreck. His mind was overwrought. He was sick and tired of medicine, and he was sick and tired of persons. Human speech jarred upon him. Human attentions drove him frantic. The thought came to him that since he was going to die, he might as well die in the open, away from all the bother and irritation. And behind this idea lurked a sneaking idea that perhaps he would not die after all if only he could escape from the heavy foods, the medicines, and the well-intentioned persons who made him frantic.

So Ernest Darling, a bag of bones and a death's-head, a perambulating corpse, with just the dimmest flutter of life in it to make it perambulate, turned his back upon men and the habitations of men and dragged himself for five miles through the brush, away from the city of Portland, Oregon. Of course he was crazy. Only a lunatic would drag himself out of his deathbed.

But in the brush, Darling found what he was looking for—rest. Nobody bothered him with beefsteaks and pork. No physicians lacerated his tired nerves by feeling his pulse, nor tormented his tired stomach with pellets and powders. He began to feel soothed. The sun was shining warm, and he basked in it. He had the feeling that the sunshine was an elixir of health. Then it seemed to him that his whole wasted wreck of a body was crying for the sun. He stripped off his clothes and bathed in the sunshine. He felt better. It had done him good—the first relief in weary months of pain.

As he grew better, he sat up and began to take notice. All about him were the birds fluttering and chirping, the squirrels chattering and playing. He envied them their health and spirits, their happy, carefree existence. That he should contrast their condition with his was inevitable; and that he should question why they were splendidly vigorous while he was a feeble, dying wraith of a man, was likewise inevitable. His conclusion was the very obvious one, namely, that they lived naturally, while he lived most unnaturally; therefore, if he intended to live, he must return to nature.

Alone, there in the brush, he worked out his problem and began to apply it. He stripped off his clothing and leaped and gamboled about, running on all fours, climbing trees; in short, doing physical stunts—and all the time soaking in the sunshine. He imitated the animals. He built a nest of dry leaves and grasses in which to sleep at night, covering it over with bark as a protection against the early fall rains. "Here is a beautiful exercise," he told me once, flapping his arms mightily against his sides: "I learned it from watching the roosters crow." Another time I remarked the loud, sucking intake with which he drank coconut milk. He explained that he had noticed the cows drinking that way and concluded there must be something in it. He tried it and found it good, and thereafter he drank only in that fashion.

He noted that the squirrels lived on fruits and nuts. He started on a fruit-and-nut diet, helped out by bread, and he grew stronger and put on weight. For three months he continued his primordial existence in the brush, and then the heavy Oregon rains drove him back to the habitations of men. Not in three months could a ninety-pound survivor of two attacks of pneumonia develop sufficient ruggedness to live through an Oregon winter in the open.

He had accomplished much, but he had been driven in. There was no place to go but back to his father's house, and there, living in close rooms with lungs that panted for all the air of the open sky, he was brought down by a third attack of pneumonia. He grew weaker than before. In that tottering tabernacle of flesh, his brain collapsed. He lay like a corpse, too weak to stand the fatigue of speaking, too irritated and tired in his miserable brain to care to listen to the speech of others. The only act of will of which he was capable was to stick his fingers in his ears and resolutely to refuse to hear a single word that was spoken to him. They sent for the insanity experts. He was adjuged insane, and also the verdict was given that he would not live a month.

By one such mental expert he was carted off to a sanitarium on Mt. Tabor. Here, when they learned that he was harmless, they gave him his own way. They no longer dictated as to the food he ate, so he resumed his fruits and nuts—olive oil, peanut butter, and bananas the chief articles of his diet. As he regained his strength he made up his mind to live thenceforth his own life. If he lived like others, he would surely die. The fear of death was one of the strongest factors in the genesis of the Nature Man. To live, he must have a natural diet, the open air, and the blessed sunshine.

Now an Oregon winter has no inducements for those who wish to return to nature, so Darling started out in search of a climate. He mounted a bicycle and headed south for the sunlands. Stanford University claimed him for a year. Here he studied and worked his way, attending lectures in as scant garb as the authorities would allow and applying as much as possible the principles of living that he had learned in squirrel-town. His favorite method of study was to go off in the hills back of the university and there to strip off his clothes and lie on the grass, soaking in sunshine and health at the same time that he soaked in knowledge.

But Central California has her winters, and the quest for a Nature Man's climate drew him on. He tried Los Angeles and Southern California, being arrested a few times and brought before the insanity commissions because, forsooth, his mode of life was not modeled after the mode of life of his fellowmen. He tried Hawaii, where, unable to prove him insane, the authorities deported him. It was not exactly a deportation. He could have remained by serving a year in prison. They gave him his choice. Now prison is death to the Nature Man, who thrives only in the open air and in God's sunshine. The authorities of Hawaii are not to be blamed. Darling was an undesirable citizen. Any man is undesirable who disagrees with one. And that any man should disagree to the extent Darling did in his philosophy of the simple life is ample vindication of the Hawaiian authorities' verdict of his undesirableness.

So Darling went thence in search of a climate which would not only be desirable, but wherein he would not be undesirable. And he found it, in Tahiti, the garden spot of garden spots. And so it was, according to the narrative as given, that he wrote the pages of his book. He wears only a loincloth and a sleeveless fish-net shirt. His stripped weight is one hundred and sixty-five pounds. His health is perfect. His eyesight, that at one time was considered ruined, is excellent. The lungs that were practically destroyed by three attacks of pneumonia have not only recovered, but are stronger than ever before.

I shall never forget the first time, while talking to me, that he squashed a mosquito. The stinging pest had settled in the middle of his back between his shoulders. Without interrupting the flow of conversation, without dropping even a syllable, his clenched fist shot up in the air, curved backward and smote his back between the shoulders, killing the mosquito and making his frame resound like a bass drum. It reminded me of nothing so much as of horses kicking the woodwork in their stalls.

"The gorilla in the African jungle pounds his chest until the noise of it can be heard half a mile away," he will announce suddenly, and thereat beat a hair-raising, devil's tattoo on his own chest.

One day he noticed a set of boxing gloves hanging on the wall, and promptly his eyes brightened.

"Do you box?" I asked.

"I used to give lessons in boxing when I was at Stanford," was the reply.

And there and then we stripped and put on the gloves. Bang! a long, gorilla arm flashed out, landing the gloved end on my nose. Biff! he caught me, in a duck, on the side of the head, nearly knocking me over sidewise. I carried the lump raised by that blow for a week. I ducked under a straight left, and landed a straight right on his stomach. It was a fearful blow. The whole weight of my body was behind it, and his body had been met as it lunged forward. I looked for him to crumple up and go down. Instead of which his face beamed approval, and he said, "That was beautiful." The next instant I was covering up and striving to protect myself from a hurricane of hooks, jolts, and uppercuts. Then I watched my chance and drove in for the solar plexus. I hit the mark. The Nature Man dropped his arms, gasped, and sat down suddenly.

"I'll be all right," he said. "Just wait a moment."

And inside thirty seconds he was on his feet — ay, and returning the compliment, for he hooked me in the solar plexus, and I gasped, dropped my hands, and sat down just a trifle more suddenly than he had.

All of which I submit as evidence that the man I boxed with was a totally different man from the poor, ninety-pound wight of eight years before, who, given up by physicians and alienists, lay gasping his life away in a closed room in Portland, Oregon. The book that Ernest Darling has written is a good book, and the binding is good, too.

Hawaii has wailed for years her need for desirable immigrants. She has spent much time, and thought, and money, in importing desirable citizens, and she has, as yet, nothing much to show for it. Yet Hawaii deported the Nature Man. She refused to give him a chance. So it is, to chasten Hawaii's proud spirit, that I take this opportunity to show her what she has lost in the Nature Man. When he arrived in Tahiti, he proceeded to seek out a piece of land on which to grow the food he ate. But land was difficult to find — that is, inexpensive land. The Na-

192

ture Man was not rolling in wealth. He spent weeks in wandering over the steep hills, until, high up the mountain, where clustered several tiny canyons, he found eighty acres of brush-jungle which were apparently unrecorded as the property of anyone. The government officials told him that if he could clear the land and till it for thirty years he would be given a title for it.

Immediately he set to work. And never was there such work. Nobody farmed that high up. The land was covered with matted jungle and overrun by wild pigs and countless rats. The view of Papeete and the sea was magnificent, but the outlook was not encouraging. He spent weeks in building a road in order to make the plantation accessible. The pigs and the rats ate up whatever he planted as fast as it sprouted. He shot the pigs and trapped the rats. Of the latter, in two weeks he caught fifteen hundred. Everything had to be carried up on his back. He usually did his packhorse work at night.

Gradually he began to win out. A grass-walled house was built. On the fertile, volcanic soil he had wrested from the jungle and jungle beasts were growing five hundred coconut trees, five hundred papaya trees, three hundred mango trees, many breadfruit trees and alligator-pear trees, to say nothing of vines, bushes, and vegetables. He developed the drip of the hills in the canyons and worked out an efficient irrigation scheme, ditching the water from canyon to canyon and paralleling the ditches at different altitudes. His narrow canyons became botanical gardens. The arid shoulders of the hills, where formerly the blazing sun had parched the jungle and beaten it close to earth, blossomed into trees and shrubs and flowers. Not only had the Nature Man become self-supporting, but he was now a prosperous agriculturist with produce to sell to the city dwellers of Papeete.

Then it was discovered that his land, which the government officials had informed him was without an owner, really had an owner, and that deeds, descriptions, etc., were on record. All his work bade fair to be lost. The land had been valueless when he took it up, and the owner, a large landholder, was unaware of the extent to which the Nature Man had developed it. A just price was agreed upon, and Darling's deed was officially filed.

Next came a more crushing blow. Darling's access to market was destroyed. The road he had built was fenced across by triple barb-wire fences. It was one of those jumbles in human affairs that is so common in this absurdest of social systems. Behind it was the fine hand of the same conservative element that haled the Nature Man before the Insanity Commission in Los Angeles and that deported him from Hawaii. It is so hard for self-satisfied men to understand any man whose satisfactions are fundamentally different. It seems clear that the officials have connived with the conservative element, for to this day the road the Nature Man built is closed; nothing has been done about it, while an adamant unwillingness to do anything about it is evidenced on every hand. But the Nature Man dances and sings along his way. He does not sit up nights thinking about the wrong which has been done him; he leaves the worrying to the doers of the wrong. He has no time for bitterness. He believes he is in the world for the purpose of being happy, and he has not a moment to waste in any other pursuit.

The road to his plantation is blocked. He cannot build a new road, for there is no ground on which he can build it. The government has restricted him to a wild-pig trail which runs precipitously up the mountain. I climbed the trail with him, and we had to climb with hands and feet in order to get up. Nor can that wild-pig trail be made into a road by any amount of toil less than that of an engineer, a steam engine, and a steel cable. But what does the Nature Man care? In his gentle ethics the evil men do him he requites with goodness. And who shall say he is not happier than they?

"Never mind their pesky road," he said to me as we dragged ourselves up a shelf of rock and sat down, panting, to rest. "I'll get an air machine soon and foil them. I'm clearing a level space for a landing stage for the airships, and next time you come to Tahiti you will alight right at my door."

Yes, the Nature Man has some strange ideas besides that of the gorilla pounding his chest in the African jungle. The Nature Man has ideas about levitation. "Yes, sir," he said to me, "levitation is not impossible. And think of the glory of it—lifting one's self from the ground by an act of will. Think of it! The astronomers tell us that our whole solar system is dying; that, barring accidents, it will all be so cold that no life can live upon it. Very well. In that day all men will be accomplished levitationists, and they will leave this perishing planet and seek more hospitable worlds. How can levitation be accomplished? By progressive fasts. Yes, I have tried them, and toward the end I could feel myself actually getting lighter."

The man is a maniac, thought I.

"Of course," he added, "these are only theories of mine. I like to speculate upon the glorious future of man. Levitation may not be possible, but I like to think of it as possible."

One evening, when he yawned, I asked him how much sleep he allowed himself.

"Seven hours," was the answer. "But in ten years I'll be sleeping only six hours, and in twenty years only five hours. You see, I shall cut off an hour's sleep every ten years."

"Then when you are a hundred you won't be sleeping at all," I interjected.

"Just that. Exactly that. When I am a hundred I shall not require sleep. Also, I shall be living on air. There are plants that live on air, you know."

"But has any man every succeeded in doing it?"

He shook his head.

195

"I never heard of him if he did. But it is only a theory of mine, this living on air. It would be fine, wouldn't it? Of course it may be impossible—most likely it is. You see, I am not unpractical. I never forget the present. When I soar ahead into the future, I always leave a string by which to find my way back again."

I fear me the Nature Man is a joker. At any rate he lives the simple life. His laundry bill cannot be large. Up on his plantation he lives on fruit, the labor cost of which, in cash, he estimates at five cents a day. At present, because of his obstructed road and because he is head over heels in the propaganda of socialism, he is living in town, where his expenses, including rent, are twenty-five cents a day. In order to pay those expenses he is running a night school for Chinese.

The Nature Man is not bigoted. When there is nothing better to eat than meat, he eats meat, as, for instance, when in jail or on shipboard and the nuts and fruit give out. Nor does he seem to crystallize into anything except sunburn.

"Drop anchor anywhere and the anchor will drag— that is, if your soul is a limitless, fathomless sea, and not a dog-pound," he quoted to me, then added: "You see, my anchor is always dragging. I live for human health and progress, and I strive to drag my anchor always in that direction. To me, the two are identical. Dragging anchor is what has saved me. My anchor did not hold me to my deathbed. I dragged anchor into the brush and fooled the doctors. When I recovered health and strength, I started, by preaching and by example, to teach the people to become nature men and nature women. But they had deaf ears. Then, on the steamer coming to Tahiti, a quartermaster expounded socialism to me. He showed me that an economic square deal was necessary before men and women could live more naturally. So I dragged anchor once more, and now I am working for the co-operative commonwealth. When that arrives, it will be easy to bring about nature living.

"I had a dream last night," he went on thoughtfully, his face slowly breaking into a glow. "It seemed that twenty-five nature men and nature women had just arrived on the steamer from California, and that I was starting to go with them up the wild-pig trail to the plantation."

Ah, me, Ernest Darling, sun-worshipper and nature man, there are times when I am compelled to envy you and your carefree existence. I see you now, dancing up the steps and cutting antics on the veranda; your hair dripping from a plunge into the salt sea, your eyes sparkling, your sun-gilded body flashing, your chest resounding to the devil's own tattoo as you chant: "The gorilla in the African jungle pounds his chest until the noise of it can be heard half a mile away." And I shall see you always as I saw you that last day, when the *Snark* poked her nose once more through the passage in the smoking reef, outward bound, and I waved goodby to those on shore. Not least in goodwill and affection was the wave I gave to the golden sun-god in the scarlet loincloth, standing upright in his tiny outrigger canoe.

Paul Gauguin

Fishing Season

A French artist best known for his paintings of Tahiti, Paul Gauguin (1848-1903) was born in Paris but spent part of his childhood in Peru. He was educated at the lycee at Orleans and for several years was a sailor in the merchant marine and the French Navy. At twenty-three he entered a firm of exchange brokers in Paris, soon married, and, succeeding rapidly in business, settled down to what seemed a comfortable bourgeois life. In 1875 he began to paint in his spare time, and five years later, giving up his secure position, he began to devote himself entirely to painting. Unable to sell his paintings, destitute and separated from his wife and children, he went to Martinique in search of refuge and new subjects for his art. Then after bitter years in France, still unsuccessful, he obtained some money by selling his pictures at auction, and in 1891 sailed for Tahiti. There he found the colorful scene and primitive people he wanted as subjects for his work, as well as a mode of life that gave him longed-for freedom and simplicity. The experiences and impressions of his first year on the island appear in *Noa Noa*, the only book he published. Gauguin moved to the Marquesas Group, settling down on the island of Hiva-Oa. Here he lived the last two years of his life, poor and in wretched health, but still painting brilliantly; at odds with the white officials, but friendly with the natives, who had always accepted him like one of their own race. A few years after his death, his reputation as an artist rose rapidly and the islands were searched for any scrap of his work that chanced to remain there. W. Somerset Maugham based a novel upon his life, *The Moon and Sixpence* (1919). In 1985, Gauguin's 38-page manuscript of *Noa Noa* sold at auction for the record sum of $132,000.

SINCE about a fortnight there have been swarms of flies, which are rare at other times, and they have become insupportable.

But the Maoris rejoice. The bonitoes and tunny fish are coming to the surface. The flies proclaim that the season for fishing is at hand, the season of labor. But let us not forget that on Tahiti work itself is pleasure.

Everyone was testing the strength of his lines and hooks. Women and children with unusual activity busied themselves in dragging nets, or rather long grates of coconut leaves, upon the seashore, and the corals which occupied the sea bottom between the land and the reefs. By this method certain small bait fish of which the tunny fish are very fond are caught.

After the preparations have been completed, which takes not less than three weeks, two large pirogues are tied together and launched upon the sea. They are furnished at the prow with a very long rod, which can be quickly raised by means of two lines fixed behind. The rod is supplied with a hook and bait. As soon as a fish has bitten, it is drawn from the water and stored in the boat.

We set out upon the sea on a beautiful morning— naturally I participated in the festival— and soon were beyond the line of reefs. We ventured quite a distance out into the open sea. I still see a turtle with the head above the water, watching us pass.

The fishermen were in a joyful mood, and rowed lustily.

We came to a spot which they called "tunny hole," where the sea is very deep, opposite the grottoes of Mara.

There, it is said, the tunny fish sleep during the night at a depth inaccessible to the sharks.

A cloud of sea birds hovered above the hole on the alert for tunnies. When one of the fish appeared, the birds dashed down with unbelievable rapidity, and then rose again with a ribbon of flesh in the beak.

Thus everywhere in the sea and in the air, and even in our pirogues, carnage is contemplated or carried out.

When I ask my companions why they do not let a long line down to the bottom of the "tunny hole," they reply to me that it is impossible since it is a sacred place.

"The god of the sea dwells there."

I suspect that there is a legend behind this, and without difficulty I succeed in getting them to tell it to me.

Roiia Hatou, a kind of Tahitian Neptune, slept here at the bottom of the sea.

A Maori was once foolhardy enough to fish here, and his hook caught in the hair of the god, and the god awoke.

Filled with wrath he rose to the surface to see who had the temerity to disturb his sleep. When he saw that the guilty one was a man, he decided that all the human race must perish to expiate the impiety of one.

By some mysterious indulgence, however, the author himself of the crime escaped punishment.

The god ordered him to go with all his family upon Toa Marama, which according to some is an island or mountain, and according to others a pirogue or an "ark."

When the fisher and his family had gone to the designated place, the waters of the ocean began to rise. Slowly they covered even the highest mountains and all the living perished except those who had taken flight upon (or in) Toa Marama.

Later they repeopled the islands.

We left the "tunny hole" behind us, and the master of the pirogue designated a man to extend the rod over the sea and cast out the hook.

We waited long minutes, but not a bite came.

It was now the turn of another oarsman; this time a magnificent tunny fish bit and made the rod bend downward. Four powerful arms raised it by pulling at the ropes behind, and the tunny appeared on the surface. But simultaneously a huge shark leaped across the waves. He struck a few times with his terrible teeth, and nothing was left on the hook except the head.

The master gave a signal. I cast out the hook.

In a very short time we caught an enormous tunny. Without paying much attention to it, I heard my companions laughing and whispering among themselves. Killed by blows on the head, the animal quivered in its death agony in the bottom of the boat. Its body was transformed into a gleaming many-faceted mirror, sending out the lights of a thousand fires.

The second time I was lucky again.

Decidedly, the Frenchman brought good luck. My companions joyously congratulated me, insisted that I was a lucky fellow, and I, quite proud of myself, did not make denial.

But amid all this unanimity of praise, I distinguished, as at the time of my first exploit, an unexplained whispering and laughter.

The fishing continued until evening.

When the store of small bait fish was exhausted, the sun lighted red flames on the horizon, and our pirogue was laden with ten magnificent tunny fish.

They were preparing to return.

While things were being put in order, I asked one of the young fellows as to the meaning of the exchange of whispered words and the laughter which had accompanied my two captures. He refused to reply. But I was insistent, knowing very well how little power of resistance a Maori has and how quickly he gives in to energetic pressure.

Finally he confided to me. If the fish is caught with the hook in the lower jaw — and both my tunnies were thus caught — it signifies that the *vahina* is unfaithful during the *tane's* absence.

I smiled incredulously.

And we returned.

Night falls quickly in the tropics. It is important to forestall it. Twenty-two alert oars dipped and redipped simultaneously into the sea, and to stimulate themselves the rowers uttered cries in rhythm with their strokes. Our pirogues left a phosphorescent wake behind.

I had the sensation of a mad flight. The angry masters of the ocean were pursuing us. Around us the frightened and curious fish leaped like fantastic troupes of indefinite figures.

In two hours we were approaching the outermost reefs.

The sea beats furiously here, and the passage is dangerous on account of the surf. It is not an easy maneuver to steer the pirogue correctly. But the natives are skillful. Much interested and not entirely without fear I followed the operation, which was executed perfectly.

The land ahead of us was illumined with moving fires. They were enormous torches made of the dry branches of the coconut trees. It was a magnificent picture. The families of the fishermen were awaiting us on the sand on the edge of the illumined water. Some of the figures remained seated and motionless; others ran along the shore waving torches; the children leapt hither and thither and their shrill cries could be heard from afar.

With powerful movement the pirogue ran up on the sand.

Immediately they proceeded to the division of the booty.

All the fish were laid on the ground, and the master divided them into as many equal parts as there were persons — men, women, and children — who had taken part in the fishing for the tunnies or in the catching of the little fish used for bait.

There were thirty-seven parts.

Without loss of time, my *vahine* took the hatchet, split some wood, and lighted the fire while I was changing clothes and putting on some wraps on account of the evening chill.

One of our two parts was cooked; her own Tehura put away raw.

Then she asked me fully about the various happenings of the day, and I willingly satisfied her curiosity. With childlike contentment she took pleasure in everything, and I watched her without letting her suspect the secret thoughts which were occupying me. Deep down within me, without any plausible cause, a feeling of disquietude had awakened which it was no longer possible to calm. I was burning to put a certain question to Tehura, a certain question . . . and it was vain for me to ask myself, "to what good?" I, myself, replied, "Who knows?"

The hour of going to bed had come, and, when we were both stretched out side by side, I suddenly asked.

"Have you been sensible?"

"Yes."

"And your lover today, was he to your liking?"

"I have no lover."

"You lie. The fish has spoken."

Tehura raised herself and looked fixedly at me. Her face had imprinted upon it an extraordinary expression of mysticism and majesty and strange grandeur with which I was unfamiliar and which I would never have expected to see in her naturally joyous and still almost childlike face.

The atmosphere in our little hut was transformed. I felt that *something sublime* had risen up between us. In spite of myself I yielded to the influence of Faith, and I was waiting for a message from above. I did not doubt that this message would come; but the sterile vanity of our skepticism still had its influence over me, in spite of the glowing sureness of a faith like this rooted though it was in some superstition or other.

Tehura softly crept to our door to make sure that it was tightly shut, and having come back as far as the center of the room she spoke aloud this prayer:

Save me! Save me!
It is evening, it is evening of the Gods!
Watch close over me, O my God!
Watch over me, O my Lord!
Preserve me from enchantments and evil counsels.
Preserve me from sudden death,
And from those who send evil and curses;
Guard me from quarrels over the division of the lands,
That peace may reign about us!
O my God, protect me from raging warriors!
Protect me from him who in erring threatens me,
Who takes pleasure in making me tremble,
Against him whose hairs are always bristling!
To the end that I and my soul may live,
O my God!

That evening, I verily joined in prayer with Tehura.

When she had finished her prayer, she came over to me and said with her eyes full of tears,

"You must strike me, strike me many, many times."

In the profound expression of this face and in the perfect beauty of this statue of living flesh, I had a vision of the divinity herself who had been conjured up by Tehura.

Let my hands be eternally cursed if they will raise themselves against a masterpiece of nature!

Thus naked, the eyes tranquil in the tears, she seemed to me robed in a mantle of orange-yellow purity, in the orange-yellow mantle of Bhixu.

She repeated,

"You must strike me, strike me many, many times; otherwise you will be angry for a long time and you will be sick."

I kissed her.

And now that I love without suspicion and love her as much as I admire her, I murmur these words of Buddha to myself,

"By kindness you must conquer anger; by goodness evil; and by the truth lies."

That night was divine, more than any of the others—
and the day rose radiant.

Early in the morning her mother brought us some
fresh coconuts.

With a glance she questioned Tehura. She knew.

With a fine play of expression she said to me,

"You went fishing yesterday. Did all go well?"

I replied,

"I hope soon to go again."

Pierre Loti

A Concert at the Palace

Louis Marie Julien Viaud (1850-1923), better known by his pen name Pierre Loti, was born in Rochefort, France. After preliminary education he entered the French Navy in 1870 as a midshipman. Although only moderately successful as a naval officer, he made a brilliant reputation as a writer of exotic novels based on experiences and impressions gained from visits to many strange ports all over the world. His books include *Aziyade* (1879), *Le Mariage de Loti*, originally titled *Rarahu* (1880), *Pecheur d'Islande* (1886), *Madame Chrysantheme* (1887), *Au Maroc* (1890), *Un Pelerin d' Ankor* (1912), and many others. None is better known that *Le Mariage de Loti*, a semi-autobiographical novel describing a young midshipman's sojourn in Tahiti in 1872 and his love affair with Rarahu, a native girl attached to the court of Pomare, the old Tahitian queen. In this book he caught the sensuous luxuriance of tropical nature and the spirit of a primitive people when their way of life, under the impact of western civilization, was inevitably changing. No book published since has had more influence in determining the tone and viewpoint of South Sea fiction and travel literature.

———————————

THE scene took place at Queen Pomare's palace in November, 1872.

The court, which commonly goes barefoot, lying on the fresh grass or on mats of pandanus fiber, was in full dress that evening, keeping high festival.

I was at the piano; before me was the score of the *Africaine*. This piano, which had only that morning arrived, was a novelty at the court of Tahiti; it was a costly instrument with a soft, rich tone, like the notes of an organ or of distant bells, and Meyerbeer's music was to be heard for the first time in the halls of Pomare. Standing by me was my shipmate Randle, who subsequently left the sea to become a leading tenor in the American opera houses; he enjoyed a brief spell of fame under the name of Randetti, until, having taken to drink, he died in abject poverty.

He was just now in full possession of his voice and gifts, and never have I heard a man's voice more touching or more exquisite. He and I together charmed many Tahitian ears, for in that land music is instinctively understood by all, even by the most savage natives.

At the upper end of the room, under a full-length portrait of herself — painted by a clever artist some thirty years before, and representing her as handsome and idealized — sat the old queen on her gilt throne, which was covered with red brocade. In her arms was her now dying grandchild, little Pomare V, who fixed her large black eyes, glittering with fever, on my face. The old woman's ungraceful bulk filled the whole breadth of her seat. She was dressed in a loose gown of crimson velvet, a stockingless ankle was laced in slipshod fashion into a satin boot. By the side of the throne was a tray full of pandanus cigarettes.

An interpreter in evening dress stood close at hand, for this woman, who understood French as well as any Parisian, never in her life would utter a single word of it.

The admiral, the governor, and the consuls had seats near Her Majesty.

There still was dignity in that face, brown, wrinkled, set and hard as it was; above all else it was sad, infinitely sad — with watching as death snatched from her all her children, one after another, all stricken with the same incurable malady; with seeing her kingdom invaded by civilization and fast breaking up, her lovely island degraded to a scene of debauchery.

The windows were open to the gardens, and outside

heads could be seen crowned with flowers, and moving to and fro as they came closer to hear. All the women in attendance on the queen; Faimana, wreathed like a naiad with water plants and reeds; Tehamana with a crown of datura, Teria, Raourea, Tapou, Erere, Tairea, Tiahoui and Rarahu.

The side of the room opposite to where I sat was all open; there was no wall, only a colonnade of timber, and beyond it the Tahitian landscape under a star-sown sky.

At the feet of the columns, against that dark, remote background, rose a whole row of figures seated on a bench; the ladies of rank these, princesses of chiefs in their own right. Four gilt candelabra of Pompadour style, astonished at finding themselves amid such surroundings, lighted them fully and showed off their dresses, which were really very elegant and handsome. Their feet, naturally small, were neatly shod in irreproachable satin boots.

Here was the splendid Ariinoore, in a tunic of cherry-colored satin and a garland of *peia*—Ariinoore, who refused to marry Lieutenant M—, of the French Navy, though he had ruined himself in buying her a *corbeille,*— and who had also rejected Kamehameha V, king of the Sandwich Islands.

By her side sat Paura, her inseparable friend, a fasinating type of savage with her singular ugliness—or beauty? A head that would eat raw fish or human flesh —a strange creature, dwelling in the forest wilds of a remote district, with the education of an English Miss —waltzing, too, like a Spaniard.

Then Titaua, who charmed Prince Alfred of England, the only Tahitian who ever preserved any beauty in her riper years; she was a constellation of splendid pearls and crowned with fluttering *revareva.* Her two daughters, just come home from a school in London, were as handsome as their mother. They wore European ball dresses, half-disguised, out of regard for the queen's prejudices, under Tahitian tapas of white gauze.

Princess Ariitea, Pomare's daughter-in-law, with her sweet, innocent, dreamy face, faithful to her own head-dress of China roses caught here and there in her flowing hair.

The queen of Bora-Bora, a thorough old savage with pointed teeth, in a velvet dress.

Queen Moe (*moe* meaning sleep or mystery) in a dark robe; regular features and a mystical type of face, with strange eyes half-shut, and an expression of introspection, like some old-fashioned portraits.

Behind these groups, in broad candlelight, rose the mountain peaks, dark in the transparent atmosphere of the Oceanian night, sharply outlined against the starry sky; and in the foreground the picturesque mass of a clump of bananas with their enormous leaves and bunches of fruit, looking like colossal candelabra ending in great black flowers. As a background to these trees the nebulae of the southern hemisphere spread a sheet of blue light, and in the middle blazed the Southern Cross. Nothing could be more ideally tropical than this faraway perspective.

The air was full of that exquisite fragrance of orange blossom and gardenia which is distilled by night under the thick foliage; there was a great silence, accentuated by the bustle of insects in the grass, and that sonorous quality, peculiar to night in Tahiti, which predisposes the listener to feel the enchanting power of music.

The piece we chose was Vasco's song when he walks alone in the island he has just discovered, intoxicated with admiration for its strange new aspect — a passage in which the composer has perfectly represented all he knew by intuition of the remote glories of these lands of light and verdure. And Randle, with a glance at the scene around him, began in his lovely voice:

"Land of wondrous beauty, gardens of delight
. . . .

O Paradise! — risen from the waters!"

The shade of Meyerbeer must have felt a thrill of pleasure that evening, at hearing his music thus rendered at the other side of the world.

Herman Melville

At the Calabooza Beretanee

No other American writer who told of the sea and the islands
of the Pacific has so high a place as Herman Melville (1819-
1891). He was born in New York, spent a few years in school,
tried such occupations as clerking in a bank and teaching, and at
seventeen shipped as a cabin boy on a voyage to Liverpool. In
1841, restless and again hankering for the sea, he sailed on the
whaleship *Acushnet*, bound for the Pacific.

After eighteen months of whale hunting, weary of life in the
forecastle, he deserted the ship with a friend at Nukuhiva, one
of the Marquesas Islands. Here he remained for four or five
weeks, living with the natives and experiencing Polynesian life
as narrated in his first novel, *Typee* (1846).

Melville was rescued by the crew of an Australian whaler,
Lucy Ann, which in his novel *Omoo* (1847) is called *Julia*. The vessel had a bad record, and when a rebellion broke out the spine-
less captain put in at Papeete on September 20, 1842. Melville's
account of the mutiny is dramatized in his novel. He was ailing
from a leg injury incurred at Typee and held a medical certifi-
cate, but voluntarily joined his fellow crewmen who, under the
orders of the acting British consul, Charles B. Wilson, were
condemned to the stocks to await the arrival of a British warship. Melville's closest friend was the former steward of the
Lucy Ann, John B. Troy, who appears in the novel under the
nickname of "Doctor Long Ghost." The view they enjoyed
from the roadside "Calabooza Beretanee" or British jail enabled
Melville to present a picturesque portrayal of Tahiti around the
mid-century.

THE examination over, Wilson and his friends advanced
to the doorway; when the former, assuming a severe

expression, pronounced our perverseness, infatuation in the extreme. Nor was there any hope left: our last chance for pardon was gone. Even were we to become contrite, and crave permission to return to duty, it would not now be permitted.

"Oh! get along with your gammon, *counselor*," exclaimed Black Dan, absolutely indignant that his understanding should be thus insulted.

Quite enraged, Wilson bade him hold his peace; and then, summoning a fat native to his side, addressed him in Tahitian, giving directions for leading us away to a place of safekeeping.

Hereupon, being marshaled in order, with the old man at our head, we were put in motion, with loud shouts, along a fine pathway, running far on, through wide groves of the coconut and breadfruit.

The rest of our escort trotted on beside us in high good humor; jabbering broken English, and in a hundred ways giving us to understand that Wilson was no favorite of theirs, and that we were prime, good fellows for holding out as we did. They seemed to know our whole history.

The scenery around was delightful. The tropical day was fast drawing to a close; and from where we were, the sun looked like a vast red fire burning in the woodlands — its rays falling aslant through the endless ranks of trees, and every leaf fringed with flame. Escaped from the confined desks of the frigate, the air breathed spices to us; streams were heard flowing; green boughs were rocking; and far inland, all sunset flushed, rose the still, steep peaks of the island.

As we proceeded, I was more and more struck by the picturesqueness of the wide, shaded road. In several places, durable bridges of wood were thrown over large watercourses; others were spanned by a single arch of stone. In any part of the road, three horsemen might have ridden abreast.

This beautiful avenue — by far the best thing which

civilization has done for the island — is called by foreigners "the Broom Road," though for what reason I do not know. Originally planned for the convenience of the missionaries journeying from one station to another, it almost completely encompasses the larger peninsula; skirting for a distance of at least sixty miles along the low, fertile lands bordering the sea. But on the side next to the Taiarboo, or the lesser peninsula, it sweeps through a narrow, secluded valley, and thus crosses the island in that direction.

The uninhabited interior, being almost impenetrable from the densely wooded glens, frightful precipices, and sharp mountain ridges absolutely inaccessible, is but little known, even to the natives themselves; and so, instead of striking directly across from one village to another, they follow the Broom Road round and round.

It is by no means, however, altogether traveled on foot; horses being now quite plentiful. They were introduced from Chile; and possessing all gaiety, fleetness, and docility of the Spanish breed, are admirably adapted to the tastes of the higher classes, who as equestrians have become very expert. The missionaries and chiefs never think of journeying except in the saddle; and at all hours of the day, you see the latter galloping along at full speed. Like the Sandwich Islanders, they ride like Pawnee-Loups.

For miles and miles I have traveled the Broom Road, and never wearied of the continual change of scenery. But wherever it leads you — whether through level woods, across grassy glens, or over hills waving with palms — the bright blue sea on one side, and the green mountain pinnacles on the other, are always in sight.

About a mile from the village we came to a halt.

It was a beautiful spot. A mountain stream here flowed at the foot of a verdant slope; on one hand, it murmured along until the waters, spreading themselves upon a beach of small, sparkling shells, trickled into the sea; on the other was a long defile, where the eye pursued a gleaming, sinuous thread, lost in shade and verdure.

The ground next the road was walled in by a low, rude parapet of stones; and, upon the summit of the slope beyond, was a large, native house, the thatch dazzling white and, in shape, an oval.

"Calabooza! Calabooza Beretanee!" (the English Jail), cried our conductor, pointing to the building.

For a few months past, having been used by the consul as a house of confinement for his refractory sailors, it was thus styled to distinguish it from similar places in and about Papeetee.

Though extremely romantic in appearance, on a near approach it proved but ill adapted to domestic comfort. In short, it was a mere shell, recently built, and still unfinished. It was open all round, and tufts of grass were growing here and there under the very roof. The only piece of furniture was the "stocks," a clumsy machine for keeping people in one place, which, I believe, is pretty much out of date in most countries. It is still in use, however, among the Spaniards in South America; from whom, it seems, the Tahitians have borrowed the contrivance, as well as the name by which all places of confinement are known among them.

The stocks were nothing more than two stout timbers, about twenty feet in length, and precisely alike. One was placed edgeways on the ground, and the other resting on top, left, at regular intervals along the seam, several round holes, the object of which was evident at a glance.

By this time, our guide had informed us that he went by the name of "*Capin Bob*" (Captain Bob); and a hearty old Bob he proved. It was just the name for him. From the first, so pleased were we with the old man that we cheerfully acquiesced in his authority.

Entering the building, he set us about fetching heaps of dry leaves to spread behind the stocks for a couch. A

214

trunk of a small coconut tree was then placed for a bolster—rather a hard one, but the natives are used to it. For a pillow they use a little billet of wood, scooped out and standing on four short legs—a sort of head-stool.

These arrangements completed, Captain Bob proceeded to "hannapar," or secure us, for the night. The upper timber of the machine being lifted at one end, and our ankles placed in the semicircular spheres of the lower one, the other beam was then dropped; both being finally secured together by an old iron hoop at either extremity. This initiation was performed to the boisterous mirth of the natives, and diverted ourselves not a little.

Captain Bob now bustled about, like an old woman seeing the children to bed. A basket of baked taro, or Indian turnip, was brought in, and we were given a piece all round. Then a great counterpane, of coarse, brown "tappa," was stretched over the whole party; and, after sundry injunctions to "moee-moee," and be "maitai"—in other words, to go to sleep and be good boys—we were left to ourselves, fairly put to bed and tucked in.

Much talk was now had concerning our prospects in life; but the doctor and I, who lay side by side, thinking the occasion better adapted to meditation, kept pretty silent; and, before long, the rest ceased conversing and, wearied with loss of rest on board the frigate, were soon sound asleep.

After sliding from one revery into another, I started, and gave the doctor a pinch. He was dreaming, however; and, resolved to follow his example, I troubled him no more.

How the rest managed I know not; but for my own part I found it very hard to get asleep. The consciousness of having one's foot *pinned*, and the impossibility of getting it anywhere else than just where it was, was most distressing.

But this was not all: there was no way of lying but straight on your back; unless, to be sure, one's limb went round and round in the ankle, like a swivel. Upon getting into a sort of doze, it was no wonder this uneasy posture gave me the nightmare. Under the delusion that I was about some gymnastics or other, I gave my unfortunate member such a twitch that I started up with the idea that someone was dragging the stocks away.

Captain Bob and his friends lived in a little hamlet hard by; and when morning showed in the east the old gentleman came forth from that direction likewise, emerging from a grove and saluting us loudly as he approached.

Finding everybody awake, he set us at liberty; and, leading us down to the stream, ordered every man to strip and bathe.

"All han's, my boy, hanna-hanna, wash!" he cried. Bob was a linguist, and had been to sea in his day, as he many a time afterward told us.

At this moment, we were all alone with him; and it would have been the easiest thing in the world to have given him the slip; but he seemed to have no idea of such a thing; treating us so frankly and cordially, indeed, that even had we thought of running we would have been ashamed of attempting it. He very well knew, nevertheless (as we ourselves were not slow in finding out), that, for various reasons, any attempt of the kind, without some previously arranged plan for leaving the island, would be certain to fail.

As Bob was a rare one every way, I must give some account of him. There was a good deal of "personal appearance" about him; in short, he was a corpulent giant, over six feet in height, and literally as big round as a hogshead. The enormous bulk of some of the Tahitians has been frequently spoken of by voyagers.

Beside being the English consul's jailer, as it were, he carried on a little Tahitian farming; that is to say, he owned several groves of the breadfruit and palm and never hindered their growing. Close by was a taro patch of his, which he occasionally visited.

216

Bob seldom disposed of the produce of his lands; it was all needed for domestic consumption. Indeed, for gormandizing, I would have matched him against any three common-council men at a civic feast.

A friend of Bob's told me that, owing to his voraciousness, his visits to other parts of the island were much dreaded; for, according to Tahitian customs, hospitality without charge is enjoined upon every one; and though it is reciprocal in most cases, in Bob's it was almost out of the question. The damage done to a native larder in one of his morning calls was more than could be made good by his entertainer's spending the holydays with him.

The old man, as I have hinted, had, once upon a time, been a cruise or two in a whaling vessel; and, therefore, he prided himself upon his English. Having acquired what he knew of it in the forecastle, he talked little else than sailor phrases, which sounded whimsically enough.

I asked him one day how old he was. "Olee?" he exclaimed, looking very profound in consequence of thoroughly undertanding so subtle a question—"Oh! very olee—'tousand 'ear—more—big man when Capin Tootee (Captain Cook) heavey in sight." (In sea parlance, come into view.)

This was a thing impossible; but adapting my discourse to the man, I rejoined—"Ah! you see Capin Tootee— well, how you like him?"

"Oh! he maitai (good) friend of me, and know my wife."

On my assuring him strongly, that he could not have born at the time, he explained himself by saying, that he was speaking of his father all the while. This, indeed, might very well have been.

It is a curious fact that all these people, young and old, will tell you that they have enjoyed the honor of a personal acquaintance with the great navigator; and if you listen to them, they will go on and tell anecdotes without end. This springs from nothing but their great desire to please; well knowing that a more agreeable topic for a white man could not be selected. As for the anachronism of the thing, they seem to have no idea of it: days and years are all the same to them.

After our sunrise bath, Bob once more placed us in the stocks, almost moved to tears at subjecting us to so great a hardship; but he could not treat us otherwise, he said, on pain of the consul's displeasure. How long we were to be confined, he did not know; nor what was to be done with us in the end.

As noon advanced, and no signs of a meal were visible, someone inquired whether we were to be boarded, as well as lodged, at the Hotel de Calabooza?

"Vast heavey" (avast heaving, or wait a bit) — said Bob — "kow-kow" (food) "come ship by by."

And, sure enough, along comes Rope Yarn with a wooden bucket of the *Julia*'s villainous biscuit. With a grin, he said it was a present from Wilson; it was all we were to get that day. A great cry was now raised; and well was it for the landlubber that he had a pair of legs, and the men could not use theirs. One and all, we resolved not to touch the bread, come what might; and so we told the natives.

Being extravagantly fond of ship biscuit — the harder the better — they were quite overjoyed; and offered to give us every day a small quantity of baked breadfruit and Indian turnip in exchange for the bread. This we agreed to; and every morning afterward, when the bucket came, its contents were at once handed over to Bob and his friends, who never ceased munching until nightfall.

Our exceedingly frugal meal of breadfruit over, Captain Bob waddled up to us with a couple of long poles hooked at one end, and several large baskets of woven coconut branches.

Not far off was an extensive grove of orange trees in full bearing; and myself and another were selected to go with him and gather a supply for the party. When we

218

went in among the trees, the sumptuousness of the orchard was unlike anything I had ever seen; while the fragrance shaken from the gently waving boughs regaled our senses most delightfully.

In many places the trees formed a dense shade, spreading overhead a dark, rustling vault, groined with boughs, and studded here and there with the ripened spheres, like gilded balls. In several places, the overladen branches were borne to the earth, hiding the trunk in a tent of foliage. Once fairly in the grove, we could see nothing else; it was oranges all round.

To preserve the fruit from bruising, Bob, hooking the twigs with his pole, let them fall into his basket. But this would not do for us. Seizing hold of a bough, we brought such a shower to the ground that our old friend was fain to run from under. Heedless of remonstrance, we then reclined in the shade, and feasted to our heart's content. Heaping up the baskets afterward, we returned to our comrades, by whom our arrival was hailed with loud plaudits; and in a marvelously short time nothing was left of the oranges we brought but the rinds.

While inmates of the Calabooza, we had as much of the fruit as we wanted; and to this cause, and others that might be mentioned, may be ascribed the speedy restoration of our sick to comparative health.

The orange of Tahiti is delicious—small and sweet, with a thin, dry rind. Though now abounding, it was unknown before Cook's time, to whom the natives are indebted for so great a blessing. He likewise introduced several other kinds of fruit; among these were the fig, pineapple, and lemon, now seldom met with. The lime still grows, and some of the poorer natives express the juice to sell to the shipping. It is highly valued as an antiscorbutic. Nor was the variety of foreign fruits and vegetables which were introduced the only benefit conferred by the first visitors to the Society group. Cattle and sheep were left at various places. More of them anon.

Thus, after all that of late years has been done for these islanders, Cook and Vancouver may, in one sense at least, be considered their greatest benefactors.

Our place of confinement being open all round, and so near the Broom Road, of course we were in plain sight of everybody passing; and, therefore, we had no lack of visitors among such an idle, inquisitive set as the Tahitians. For a few days, they were coming and going continually; while thus ignobly fast by the foot we were fain to give passive audience.

During this period, we were the lions of the neighborhood; and, no doubt, strangers from the distant villages were taken to see the "Karhowrees" (white men), in the same way that countrymen, in a city, are gallanted to the Zoological Gardens.

All this gave us a fine opportunity of making observations. I was painfully struck by the considerable number of sickly or deformed persons; undoubtedly made so by a virulent complaint which, under native treatment, almost invariably affects, in the end, the muscles and bones of the body. In particular, there is a distortion of the back, most unsightly to behold, originating in a horrible form of the malady.

Although this, and other bodily afflictions, were unknown before the discovery of the islands by the whites, there are several cases found of the fa-fa, or elephantiasis — a native disease, which seems to have prevailed among them from the earliest antiquity. Affecting the legs and feet alone, it swells them, in some instances, to the girth of a man's body, covering the skin with scales. It might be supposed that one thus afflicted would be incapable of walking; but to all appearance, they seem to be nearly as active as anybody; apparently suffering no pain and bearing the calamity with a degree of cheerfulness truly marvelous.

The fa-fa is very gradual in its approaches and years

elapse before the limb is fully swollen. Its origin is ascribed by the natives to various causes; but the general impression seems to be that it arises, in most cases, from the eating of unripe breadfruit and Indian turnip. So far as I could find out, it is not hereditary. In no stage do they attempt a cure; the complaint being held incurable.

Speaking of the fa-fa reminds me of a poor fellow, a sailor, whom I afterward saw at Roorootoo, a lone island, some two days' sail from Tahiti.

The island is very small, and its inhabitants nearly extinct. We sent a boat off to see whether any yams were to be had, as formerly the yams of Roorootoo were as famous among the islands round about as Sicily oranges in the Mediterranean. Going shore, to my surprise, I was accosted, near a little shanty of a church, by a white man, who limped forth from a wretched hut. His hair and beard were unshorn, his face deadly pale and haggard, and one limb swelled with the fa-fa to an incredible bigness. This was the first instance of a foreigner suffering from it that I had ever seen, or heard of; and the spectacle shocked me accordingly.

He had been there for years. From the first symptoms, he could not believe his complaint to be what it really was, and trusted it would soon disappear. But when it became plain that his only chance for recovery was a speedy change of climate, no ship would receive him as a sailor: to think of being taken as a passenger was idle. This speaks little for the humanity of sea captains; but the truth is that those in the Pacific have little enough of the virtue; and, nowadays, when so many charitable appeals are made to them, they have become callous.

I pitied the poor fellow from the bottom of my heart; but nothing could I do, as our captain was inexorable. "Why," said he, "here we are—started on a six months' cruise—I can't put back; and he is better off on the island than at sea. So on Roorootoo he must die." And probably he did.

I afterward heard of this melancholy object from two seamen. His attempts to leave were still unavailing and his fate was fast closing in.

Notwithstanding the physical degeneracy of the Tahitians as a people, among the chief individuals of personable figures are still frequently met with; and, occasionally, majestic-looking men, and diminutive women as lovely as the nymphs who, nearly a century ago, swam round the ships of Wallis. In these instances, Tahitian beauty is quite as seducing as it proved to the crew of the *Bounty*; the young girls being just such creatures as a poet would picture in the tropics — soft, plump, and dreamy-eyed.

The natural complexion of both sexes is quite light; but the males appear much darker from their exposure to the sun. A dark complexion, however, in a man is highly esteemed, as indicating strength of both body and soul. Hence there is a saying, of great antiquity among them,

> "If dark the cheek of the mother,
> The son will sound the war-conch;
> If strong her fame, he will give laws."

With this idea of manliness, no wonder the Tahitians regard all pale and tepid-looking Europeans as weak and feminine; whereas a sailor, with a cheek like the breast of a roast turkey, is held a lad of brawn: to use their own phrase, a "taata tona," or man of bones.

Speaking of bones recalls an ugly custom of theirs, now obsolete — that of making fish-hooks and gimblets out of those of their enemies. This beats the Scandinavians turning people's skulls into cups and saucers.

But to return to the Calabooza Beretanee. Immense was the interest among the throngs that called there; they would stand talking about us by the hour, growing most unnecessarily excited too, dancing up and down with all the vivacity of their race. They invariably sided with us; flying out against the consul and denouncing him as "Ita maitai nuee," or very bad exceedingly. They must have borne him some grudge or other.

Nor were the women, sweet souls, at all backward in visiting. Indeed, they manifested even more interest than the men; gazing at us with eyes full of a thousand meanings and conversing with marvelous rapidity. But, alas! inquisitive though they were and, doubtless, taking some passing compassion on us, there was little real feeling in them after all, and still less sentimental sympathy. Many of them laughed outright at us, noting only what was ridiculous in our plight.

I think it was the second day of our confinement that a wild, beautiful girl burst into the Calabooza and, throwing herself into an arch attitude, stood afar off and gazed at us. She was a heartless one:— tickled to death with Black Dan's nursing his chafed ankle and indulging in certain moral reflections on the consul and Captain Guy. After laughing her fill at him, she condescended to notice the rest; glancing from one to another in the most methodical and provoking manner imaginable. Whenever anything struck her comically, you saw it like a flash — her finger leveled instantaneously and, flinging herself back, she gave loose to strange, hollow little notes of laughter that sounded like the bass of a music box, playing a lively air with the lid down.

Now, I knew not that there was anything in my own experience calculated to disarm ridicule; and, indeed, to have looked at all heroic, under the circumstances, would have been rather difficult. Still, I could not but feel exceedingly annoyed at the prospect of being screamed at in turn by this mischievous young witch, even though she were but an islander. And, to tell a secret, her beauty had something to do with this sort of feeling; and, pinioned as I was to a log and clad most unbecomingly, I began to grow sentimental.

Ere her glance fell upon me, I had, unconsciously, thrown myself into the most graceful attitude I could assume, leaned my head upon my hand, and summoned up as abstracted an expression as possible. Though my face was averted, I soon felt it flush and knew that the glance was on me: deeper and deeper grew the flush, and not a sound of laughter.

Delicious thought! she was moved at the sight of me. I could stand it no longer, but started up. Lo! there she was; her great hazel eyes rounding and rounding in her head like two stars, her whole frame in a merry quiver, and an expression about the mouth that was sudden and violent death to anything like sentiment.

The next moment she spun round and, bursting from peal to peal of laughter, went racing out of the Calabooza; and, in mercy to me, never returned.

A few days passed; and, at last, our docility was rewarded by some indulgence on the part of Captain Bob.

He allowed the entire party to be at large during the day; only enjoining upon us always to keep within hail. This, to be sure, was in positive disobedience to Wilson's orders; and so care had to be taken that he should not hear of it. There was little fear of the natives telling him; but strangers traveling the Broom Road might. By way of precaution, boys were stationed as scouts along the road. At sight of a white man, they sounded the alarm; when we all made for our respective holes (the stocks being purposely left open): the beam then descended and we were prisoners. As soon as the traveler was out of sight, of course, we were liberated.

Notwithstanding the regular supply of food which we obtained from Captain Bob and his friends, it was so small that we often felt most intolerably hungry. We could not blame them for not bringing us more, for we soon became aware that they had to pinch themselves in order to give us what they did; beside, they received nothing for their kindness but the daily bucket of bread.

Among a people like the Tahitians, what we call "hard

times" can only be experienced in a scarcity of edibles; yet, so destitute are many of the common people that this most distressing consequence of civilization may be said, with them, to be ever present. To be sure, the natives about the Calabooza had abundance of limes and oranges; but what were *these* good for, except to impart a keener edge to appetites which there was so little else to gratify? During the height of the breadfruit season, they fare better; but, at other times, the demands of the shipping exhaust the uncultivated resources of the island; and the lands being mostly owned by the chiefs, the inferior orders have to suffer for their cupidity. Deprived of their nets, many of them would starve.

As Captain Bob insensibly remitted his watchfulness and we began to stroll farther and farther from the Calabooza, we managed, by a systematic foraging upon the country round about, to make up for some of our deficiencies. And fortunate it was that the houses of the wealthier natives were just as open to us as those of the most destitute; we were treated as kindly in one as the other.

Once in a while, we came in at the death of a chief's pig; the noise of whose slaughtering was generally to be heard at a great distance. An occasion like this gathers the neighbors together and they have a bit of a feast, where a stranger is always welcome. A good loud squeal, therefore, was music in our ears. It showed something going on in that direction.

Breaking in upon the party tumultuously, as we did, we always created a sensation. Sometimes we found the animal still alive and struggling; in which case it was generally dropped at our approach. To provide for these emergencies, Flash Jack generally repaired to the scene of operations with a sheath knife between his teeth and a club in his hand. Others were exceedingly officious in singeing off the bristles and disemboweling. Doctor Long Ghost and myself, however, never meddled with these preliminaries, but came to the feast itself with un-impaired energies.

Like all lank men, my long friend had an appetite of his own. Others occasionally went about seeking what they might devour but *he* was always on the alert.

He had an ingenious way of obviating an inconvenience which we all experienced at times. The islanders seldom use salt with their food; so he begged Rope Yarn to bring him some from the ship, also a little pepper, if he could; which, accordingly, was done. This he placed in a small leather wallet—a "monkey bag" (so called by sailors)—usually worn as a purse about the neck.

"In my poor opinion," said Long Ghost, as he tucked the wallet out of sight, "it behooves a stranger, in Tahiti, to have his knife in readiness and his caster slung."

The ship out of the way, we were quite anxious to know what was going to be done with us. On this head, Captain Bob could tell us nothing; no further at least than that he still considered himself responsible for our safekeeping. However, he never put us to bed any more; and we had everything our own way.

The day after the *Julia* left, the old man came up to us in great tribulation, saying that the bucket of bread was no longer forthcoming, and that Wilson had refused to send anything in its place. One and all, we took this for a hint to disperse quietly and go about our business. Nevertheless, we were not to be shaken off so easily; and taking a malicious pleasure in annoying our old enemy we resolved, for the present, to stay where we were. For the part he had been acting, we learned that the consul was the laughingstock of all the foreigners ashore, who frequently twitted him upon his hopeful protegees of the Calabooza Beretanee.

As we were wholly without resources, so long as we remained on the island no better place than Captain Bob's could be selected for an abiding place. Besides, we heartily loved the old gentleman and could not think of leaving him; so, telling him to give no thought as to wherewithal we should be clothed and fed, we resolved, by extending and systematizing our foraging operations, to provide for ourselves.

We were greatly assisted by a parting legacy of Jermin's. To him we were indebted for having all our chests sent ashore and everything left therein. They were placed in the custody of a petty chief living nearby, who was instructed by the consul not to allow them to be taken away; but we might call and make our toilets whenever we pleased.

We went to see Mahinee, the old chief; Captain Bob going along, and stoutly insisting upon having the chattels delivered up. At last this was done; and in solemn procession the chests were borne by the natives to the Calabooza. Here we disposed them about quite tastefully; and made such a figure that in the eyes of old Bob and his friends the Calabooza Beretanee was by far the most sumptuously furnished saloon in Tahiti.

Indeed, so long as it remained thus furnished, the native courts of the district were held there; the judge, Mahinee, and his associates, sitting upon one of the chests, and the culprits and spectators thrown at full length upon the ground, both inside of the building, and under the shade of the trees without; while, leaning over the stocks as from a gallery, the worshipful crew of the *Julia* looked on and canvassed the proceedings.

I should have mentioned before that, previous to the vessel's departure, the men had bartered away all the clothing they could possibly spare; but now it was resolved to be more provident.

The contents of the chest were of the most miscellaneous description: — sewing utensils, marlinspikes, strips of calico, bits of rope, jackknives; nearly everything, in short, that a seaman could think of. But of wearing apparel there was little but old frocks, remnants of jackets, and legs of trousers, with now and then the foot of a stocking. These, however, were far from being valueless; for, among the poorer Tahitians, everything European is highly esteemed. They come from "Beretanee, Fenooa Pararee" (Britain, Land of Wonders) and that is enough.

The chests themselves were deemed exceedingly precious, especially those with unfractured locks, which would absolutely click and enable the owner to walk off with the key. Scars, however, and bruises were considered great blemishes. One old fellow, smitten with the doctor's large mahogany chest (a well filled one, by the by) and finding infinite satisfaction in merely sitting thereon, was detected in the act of applying a healing ointment to a shocking scratch which impaired the beauty of the lid.

There is no telling the love of a Tahitian for a sailor's trunk. So ornamental is it held as an article of furniture in his hut that the women are incessantly tormenting their husbands to bestir themselves and make them a present of one. When obtained, no pier table just placed in a drawing room is regarded with half the delight. For these reasons, then, our coming into possession of our estate at this time was an important event.

The islanders are much like the rest of the world; and the news of our good fortune brought us troops of "tayos" or friends, eager to form an alliance after the national custom and do our slightest bidding.

The really curious way in which all the Polynesians are in the habit of making bosom friends at the shortest possible notice is deserving of remark. Although, among a people like the Tahitians, vitiated as they are by sophisticating influences, this custom has in most cases degenerated into a mere mercenary relation, it nevertheless had its origin in a fine, and in some instances, heroic sentiment, formerly entertained by their fathers.

In the annals of the island are examples of extravagant

friendships, unsurpassed by the story of Damon and Pythias: in truth, much more wonderful; for, notwithstanding the devotion—even of life in some cases—to which they led, they were frequently entertained at first sight for some stranger from another island.

Filled with love and admiration for the first whites who came among them, the Polynesians could not testify the warmth of their emotions more strongly than by instantaneously making their abrupt proffer of friendship. Hence, in old voyages we read of chiefs coming off from the shore in their canoes and going through with strange antics expressive of this desire. In the same way, their inferiors accosted the seamen; and thus the practice has continued in some islands down to the present day.

There is a small place, not many days' sail from Tahiti, and seldom visited by shipping, where the vessel touched to which I then happened to belong.

Of course, among the simple-hearted natives, we had a friend all round. Mine was Poky, a handsome youth, who never could do enough for me. Every morning at sunrise, his canoe came alongside loaded with fruits of all kinds; upon being emptied, it was secured by a line to the bowsprit, under which it lay all day long, ready at any time to carry its owner ashore on an errand.

Seeing him so indefatigable, I told Poky one day that I was a virtuoso in shells and curiosities of all kinds. That was enough; away he paddled for the head of the bay and I never saw him again for twenty-four hours. The next morning, his canoe came gliding slowly along the shore, with the full-leaved bough of a tree for a sail. For the purpose of keeping the things dry, he had also built a sort of platform just behind the prow, railed in with green wicker work; and here was a head of yellow bananas and cowree shells; young coconuts and antlers of red coral; two or three pieces of carved wood; a little pocket idol, black as jet, and rolls of printed tappa.

We were given a holyday; and upon going ashore Poky,

of course, was my companion and guide. For this, no mortal could be better qualified; his native country was not large and he knew every inch of it. Gallanting me about, everyone was stopped and ceremoniously introduced to Poky's "tayo karhowree nuee" or his particular white friend.

He showed me all the lions; but more than all, he took me to see a charming lioness—a young damsel—the daughter of a chief—the reputation of whose charms had spread to the neighboring islands, and even brought suitors therefrom. Among these was Tooboi, the heir of Tamatoy, King of Raiatair, one of the Society Isles. The girl was certainly fair to look upon. Many heavens were in her sunny eyes; and the outline of that arm of hers, peeping forth from a capricious tappa robe, was the very curve of beauty.

Though there was no end to Poky's attentions, not a syllable did he ever breathe of reward; but sometimes he looked very knowing. At last the day came for sailing and with it, also, his canoe, loaded down to the gunwale with a sea stock of fruits. Giving him all I could spare from my chest, I went on deck to take my place at the windlass; for the anchor was weighing. Poky followed and heaved with me at the same handspike.

The anchor was soon up; and away we went out of the bay with more than twenty shallops towing astern. At last they left us; but long as I could see him at all there was Poky, standing alone and motionless in the bow of his canoe.

On Sundays I always attended the principal native church on the outskirts of the village of Papeete and not far from the Calabooza Beretanee. It was esteemed the best specimen of architecture in Tahiti.

Of late they have built their places of worship with more reference to durability than formerly. At one time, there were no less than thirty-six on the island—mere barns, tied together with thongs, which went to destruction in a very few years.

One, built many years ago in this style, was a most remarkable structure. It was erected by Pomaree II who, on this occasion, showed all the zeal of a royal proselyte. The building was over seven hundred feet in length, and of a proportionate width; the vast ridgepole was at intervals supported by a row of thirty-six cylindrical trunks of breadfruit tree; and, all round, the wall plates rested on shafts of the palm. The roof — steeply inclining to within a man's height of the ground — was thatched with leaves and the sides of the edifice were open. Thus spacious was the Royal Mission Chapel of Papoar.

At its dedication, three distinct sermons were, from different pulpits, preached to an immense concourse gathered from all parts of the island.

As the chapel was built by the king's command, nearly as great a multitude was employed in its construction as swarmed over the scaffolding of the great temple of the Jews. Much less time, however, was expended. In less than three weeks from planting the first post, the last tier of palmetto leaves drooped from the eaves and the work was done.

Apportioned to the several chiefs and their dependents, the labor, though immense, was greatly facilitated by everyone's bringing his post, or his rafter, or his pole strung with thatching ready for instant use. The materials thus prepared being afterward secured together by thongs, there was literally "neither hammer, nor axe, nor any tool of iron head in the house while it was building."

But the most singular circumstance connected with this South Sea cathedral remains to be related. As well for the beauty as the advantages of such a site, the islanders love to dwell near the mountain streams; and so a considerable brook, after descending from the hills and watering the valley, was bridged over in three places

231

and swept clean through the chapel.

Flowing waters! what an accompaniment to the songs of the sanctuary; mingling with them, the praises and thanksgivings of the green solitudes inland.

But the chapel of the Polynesian Solomon has long since been deserted. Its thousand rafters of hibiscus have decayed and fallen to the ground; and now the stream murmurs over them in its bed.

The present metropolitan church of Tahiti is very unlike the one just described. It is of moderate dimensions, boarded over, and painted white. It is furnished also with blinds but no sashes; indeed, were it not for the rustic thatch, it would remind one of a plain chapel at home.

The woodwork was all done by foreign carpenters, of whom there are always several about Papeetee.

Within, its aspect is unique and cannot fail to interest a stranger. The rafters overhead are bound round with fine matting of variegated dyes; and all along the ridge pole these trappings hang pendent, in alternate bunches of tassels and deep fringes of stained glass. The floor is composed of rude planks. Regular aisles run between ranges of native settees, bottomed with crossed braids of the coconut fiber and furnished with backs.

But the pulpit, made of a dark, lustrous wood and standing at one end is by far the most striking object. It is preposterously lofty; indeed, a capital bird's-eye view of the congregation ought to be had from its summit.

Nor does the church lack a gallery, which runs round on three sides and is supported by columns of the coconut tree.

Its facings are here and there daubed over with a tawdry blue, and in other places (without the slightest regard to uniformity) patches of the same color may be seen. In their ardor to decorate the sanctuary the converts must have borrowed each a brush full of paint and zealously daubed away at the first surface that offered.

As hinted, the general impression is extremely curious. Little light being admitted, and everything being of a dark color, there is an indefinable Indian aspect of duskiness throughout. A strange, woody smell, also—more or less pervading every considerable edifice in Polynesia—is at once perceptible. It suggests the idea of worm-eaten idols packed away in some old lumber room at hand.

For the most part, the congregation attending this church is composed of the better and wealthier orders—the chiefs and their retainers; in short, the rank and fashion of the island. This class is infinitely superior in personal beauty and general healthfulness to the "maren-hoar," or common people; the latter having been more exposed to the worst and most debasing evils of foreign intercourse. On Sundays, the former are invariably arrayed in their finery; and thus appear to the best advantage. Nor are they driven to the chapel, as some of their inferiors are to other places of worship; on the contrary, capable of maintaining a handsome exterior and possessing greater intelligence, they go voluntarily.

In respect of the woodland colonnade supporting its galleries, I called this chapel the Church of the Coconuts.

It was the first place for Christian worship in Polynesia that I had seen; and the impression upon entering during service was all the stronger. Majestic-looking chiefs, whose fathers had hurled the battle club, and old men who had seen sacrifices smoking upon the altars of Oro were there. And hark! hanging from the boughs of a breadfruit tree without, a bell is being struck with a bar of iron by a native lad. In the same spot, the blast of the war conch had often resounded. But to the proceedings within.

The place is well filled. Everywhere meets the eye the gay calico draperies worn on great occasions by the higher classes and forming a strange contrast of patterns and colors. In some instances, these are so fashioned as to resemble, as much as possible, European garments. This is in excessively bad taste. Coats and pantaloons, too, are here and there seen; but they look awkwardly enough and take away from the general effect.

But it is the array of countenances that most strikes you. Each is suffused with the peculiar animation of the Polynesians when thus collected in large numbers. Every robe is rustling, every limb in motion, and an incessant buzzing going on throughout the assembly. The tumult is so great that the voice of the placid old missionary, who now rises, is almost inaudible. Some degree of silence is at length obtained through the exertions of half-a-dozen strapping fellows in white shirts and no pantaloons. Running in among the settees, they are at great pains to inculcate the impropriety of making a noise by creating a most unnecessary racket themselves. This part of the service was quite comical.

There is a most interesting Sabbath School connected with the church, and the scholars, a vivacious, mischievous set, were in one part of the gallery. I was amused by a party in a corner. The teacher sat at one end of the bench with a meek little fellow by his side. When the others were disorderly, this young martyr received a rap; intended, probably, as a sample of what the rest might expect if they didn't amend.

Standing in the body of the church and leaning against a pillar was an old man, in appearance very different from others of his countrymen. He wore nothing but a coarse, scant mantle, of faded tappa; and from his staring, bewildered manner, I set him down as an aged bumpkin from the interior, unaccustomed to the strange sights and sounds of the metropolis. This old worthy was sharply reprimanded for standing up, and thus intercepting the view of those behind; but not comprehending exactly what was said to him, one of the white-liveried gentry made no ceremony of grasping him by the shoulders and fairly crushing him down into a seat.

During all this the old missionary in the pulpit, as well

as his associates beneath, never ventured to interfere—leaving everything to native management. With South Sea islanders, assembled in any numbers, there is no other way of getting along.

A worthy young man, formerly a friend of mine (I speak of Kooloo with all possible courtesy, since after our intimacy there would be an impropriety in doing otherwise)—this worthy youth, having some genteel notions of retirement, dwelt in a "maroo boro," or breadfruit shade, a pretty nook in a wood, midway between the Calabooza Beretanee and the Church of Coconuts. Hence, at the latter place, he was one of the most regular worshippers.

Kooloo was a blade. Standing up in the congregation in all the bravery of a striped calico shirt, with the skirts rakishly adjusted over a pair of white sailor trousers, and hair well anointed with coconut oil, he ogled the ladies with an air of supreme satisfaction. Nor were his glances unreturned.

But such looks as the Tahitian belles cast at each other: frequently turning up their noses at the advent of a new cotton mantle recently imported in the chest of some amorous sailor. Upon one occasion, I observed a group of young girls, in tunics of coarse, soiled sheeting, disdainfully pointing at a damsel in a flaming red one. "Oee tootai owree!" said they with ineffable scorn, "itai maitai!" (you are a good-for-nothing hussy, no better than you should be).

Now, Kooloo communed with the church; so did all these censorious young ladies. Yet after eating breadfruit at the Eucharist I knew several of them, the same night, to be guilty of some sad derelictions.

Puzzled by these things, I resolved to find out, if possible, what ideas, if any, they entertained of religion; but as one's spiritual concerns are rather delicate for a stranger to meddle with, I went to work as adroitly as I could.

Farnow, an old native who had recently retired from

active pursuits, having thrown up the business of being a sort of running footman to the queen, had settled down in a snug little retreat, not fifty rods from Captain Bob's. His selecting our vicinity for his residence may have been with some view to the advantages it afforded for introducing his three daughters into polite circles. At any rate, not averse to receiving the attentions of so devoted a gallant as the doctor, the sisters (communicants, be it remembered) kindly extended to him free permission to visit them sociably whenever he pleased.

We dropped in one evening and found the ladies at home. My long friend engaged his favorites, the two younger girls, at the game of "Now," or hunting a stone under three piles of tappa. For myself, I lounged on a mat with Ideea the eldest, dallying with her grass fan, and improving my knowledge of Tahitian.

The occasion was well adapted to my purpose, and I began.

"Ah, Ideea, mickonaree oee?" the same as drawling out —"By the by, Miss Ideea, do you belong to the church?"

"Yes, me mickonaree," was the reply.

But the assertion was at once qualified by certain reservations, so curious that I cannot forbear their relation.

"Mickonaree *ena*" (church member *here*), exclaimed she, laying her hand upon her mouth and a strong emphasis on the adverb. In the same way, and with similar exclamations, she touched her eyes and hands. This done, her whole air changed in an instant; and she gave me to understand, by unmistakable gestures, that in certain other respects she was not exactly a "mickonaree." In short, Ideea was

> "A sad good Christian at the heart—
> A very heathen in the carnal part."

The exclamation terminated in a burst of laughter, in which all three sisters joined; and, for fear of looking silly, the doctor and myself. As soon as good breeding would permit we took leave.

The hypocrisy in matters of religion, so apparent in all Polynesian converts, is most injudiciously nourished in Tahiti by a zealous, and in many cases a coercive superintendence over their spiritual well-being. But it is only manifested with respect to the common people, their superiors being exempted.

On Sunday mornings, when the prospect is rather small for a full house in the minor churches, a parcel of fellows are actually sent out with rattans into the highways and byways as whippers-in of the congregation. This is a sober fact.

These worthies constitute a religious police; and you always know them by the great white diapers they wear. On week days they are quite as busy as on Sundays; to the great terror of the inhabitants going all over the island and spying out the wickedness thereof.

Moreover, they are the collectors of fines — levied generally in grass mats — for obstinate non-attendance upon divine worship and other offenses amenable to the ecclesiastical judicature of the missionaries.

Old Bob called these fellows "kannakippers," a corruption, I fancy, of our word constable.

He bore them a bitter grudge; and one day, drawing near home, and learning that two of them were just then making a domiciliary visit at his house, he ran behind a bush; and as they came forth two green breadfruit from a hand unseen, took them each between the shoulders. The sailors in the Calabooza were witnesses to this, as well as several natives; who, when the intruders were out of sight, applauded Captain Bob's spirit in no measured terms; the ladies present vehemently joining in. Indeed, the kannakippers have no greater enemies than the latter. And no wonder: the impertinent varlets, popping into their houses at all hours, are forever prying into their peccadilloes.

Kooloo, who at times was patriotic and pensive, and mourned the evils under which his country was groaning, frequently inveighed against the statute which thus authorized an utter stranger to interfere with domestic arrangements. He himself — quite a ladies' man — had often been annoyed thereby. He considered the kannakippers a bore.

Besides their confounded inquisitiveness they add insult to injury by making a point of dining out everyday at some hut within the limits of their jurisdiction. As for the gentleman of the house, his meek endurance of these things is amazing. But "good easy man," there is nothing for him but to be as hospitable as possible.

These gentry are indefatigable. At the dead of night prowling round the houses, and in the daytime hunting amorous couples in the groves. Yet in one instance, the chase completely baffled them.

It was thus.

Several weeks previous to our arrival at the island, someone's husband and another person's wife, having taken a mutual fancy for each other, went out for a walk. The alarm was raised, and with hue and cry they were pursued; but nothing was seen of them again until the lapse of some ninety days, when we were called out from the Calabooza to behold a great mob inclosing the lovers and escorting them for trial to the village.

Their appearance was most singular. The girdle excepted, they were quite naked; their hair was long, burned yellow at the ends, and entangled with burrs; and their bodies scratched and scarred in all directions. It seems that acting upon the "love in a cottage" principle they had gone right into the interior, and throwing up a hut in an uninhabited valley had lived there until, in an unlucky stroll, they were observed and captured.

They were subsequently condemned to make one hundred fathoms of Broom Road — a six months' work, if not more.

Often, when seated in a house, conversing quietly with its inmates, I have known them betray the greatest confusion at the sudden announcement of a kannakipper's being in sight. To be reported by one of these officials as a "tootai owree" (in general, signifying a bad person or disbeliever in Christianity), is as much dreaded as the forefinger of Titus Oates was, leveled at an alleged papist.

But the islanders take a sly revenge upon them. Upon entering a dwelling, the kannakippers oftentimes volunteer a pharisaical prayer meeting: hence, they go in secret by the name of "Boora-Artuas," literally, "Pray-to-Gods."

Except where the employment of making "tappa" is inflicted as a punishment, the echoes of the cloth mallet have long since died away in the listless valleys of Tahiti. Formerly, the girls spent their mornings like ladies at their tambour frames; *now*, they are lounged away in almost utter indolence. True, most of them make their own garments, but this comprises but a stitch or two; the ladies of the mission, by the by, being entitled to the credit of teaching them to sew.

The "kihee whihenee," or petticoat, is a mere breadth of white cotton or calico, loosely enveloping the person from the waist to the feet. Fastened simply, by a single tuck or by twisting the upper corners together, this garment frequently becomes disordered; thus affording an opportunity of being coquettishly adjusted. Over the "kihee," they wear a sort of gown, open in front, very loose, and as negligent as you please. The ladies here never dress for dinner.

But what shall be said of those horrid hats! Fancy a bunch of straw, plaited into the shape of a coal scuttle and stuck, bolt upright, on the crown, with a yard or two of red ribbon flying about like kite strings. Milliners of Paris, what would ye say to them! Though made by the natives, they are said to have been first contrived and recommended by the missionaries' wives; a report which, I really trust, is nothing but scandal.

Curious to relate, these things for the head are esteemed exceedingly becoming. The braiding of the straw is one of the few employments of the higher classes; all of which but minister to the silliest vanity. The young girls, however, wholly eschew the hats, leaving those dowdy old souls, their mothers, to make frights of themselves.

As for the men, those who aspire to European garments seem to have no perception of the relation subsisting between the various parts of a gentleman's costume. To the wearer of a coat, for instance, pantaloons are by no means indispensable; and, a bell-crowned hat and a girdle are full dress. The young sailor for whom Kooloo deserted me presented him with a shaggy old pea jacket; and, with this buttoned up to his chin, under a tropical sun, he promenaded the Broom Road quite elated. Doctor Long Ghost, who saw him thus, ran away with the idea that he was under medical treatment at the time — in the act of taking, what the quacks call, a "sweat."

A bachelor friend of Captain Bob rejoiced in the possession of a full European suit, in which he often stormed the ladies' hearts. Having a military leaning, he ornamented the coat with a great scarlet patch on the breast, and mounted it also, here and there, with several regimental buttons, slyly cut from the uniform of a parcel of drunken marines sent ashore on a holyday from a man-of-war. But, in spite of the ornaments, the dress was not exactly the thing. From the tightness of the cloth across the shoulders, his elbows projected from his sides like an ungainly rider's; and his ponderous legs were jammed so hard into his slim, nether garments that the threads of every seam showed; and, at every step, you looked for a catastrophe.

In general, there seems to be no settled style of dressing among the males: they wear anything they can get;

in some cases awkwardly modifying the fashions of their fathers so as to accord with their own altered views of what is becoming.

But ridiculous as many of them now appear, in foreign habiliments, the Tahitians presented a far different appearance in the original national costume, which was graceful in the extreme, modest to all but the prudish, and peculiarly adapted to the climate. But the short kilts of dyed tappa, the tasseled maroes, and other articles formerly worn are, at the present day, prohibited by law as indecorous. For what reason necklaces and garlands of flowers, among the women, are also forbidden, I could never learn; but, it is said that they were associated, in some way, with a forgotten heathen observance.

Many pleasant and, seemingly, innocent sports and pastimes are likewise interdicted. In old times, there were several athletic games practiced, such as wrestling, foot-racing, throwing the javelin, and archery. In all these they greatly excelled; and, for some, splended festivals were instituted. Among their everyday amusements were dancing, tossing the football, kite flying, flute playing, and singing traditional ballads; *now*, all punishable offenses; though most of them have been so long in disuse that they are nearly forgotten.

In the same way, the "Opio," or festive harvest home of the breadfruit, has been suppressed; though, as described to me by Captain Bob, it seemed wholly free from any immoral tendency. Against tattooing, of any kind, there is a severe law.

That this abolition of their national amusements and customs was not willingly acquiesced in is shown in the frequent violation of many of the statutes inhibiting them; and, especially, in the frequency with which their "hevars," or dances, are practiced in secret.

Doubtless, in thus denationalizing the Tahitians, as it were, the missionaries were prompted by a sincere desire for good; but the effect has been lamentable. Supplied with no amusements, in place of those forbidden, the Tahitians, who require more recreation than other people, have sunk into a listlessness, or indulge in sensualities, a hundred times more pernicious than all the games ever celebrated in the Temple of Tanee.

Charles Darwin

Darwin Climbs the Mountain

Charles Robert Darwin (1809-1882), the greatest English naturalist, was born in Shrewsbury. Studying for the ministry at Cambridge University, he met geologists and botanists who awakened his interest in the physical world, and he sailed as naturalist on H.M.S. *Beagle* on a surveying expedition that lasted from December, 1831, to October, 1836. This voyage to South America and the South Pacific Ocean gave him much material on the fauna, flora, and geology of many lands, upon which he later based his theory of natural selection; and it may be significant that the two greatest British biologists of the nineteenth century, Darwin and Thomas Henry Huxley, both served apprenticeships as naturalists on official exploring vessels in the Pacific. In his autobiography, Darwin remarks: "The voyage of the *Beagle* has been by far the most important event in my life, and has determined my whole career .... Everything about which I thought or read was made to bear directly on what I had seen or was likely to see; and this habit of mind was continued during the five years of the voyage. I feel sure that it was this training which has enabled me to do whatever I have done in science."

Darwin spent only a dozen days in Tahiti in November, 1835, but his journal records a surprising number of valuable comments, ranging from scientific notes to remarks on the morality of the women of the island. This selection is taken from his classic *Journal of Researches into the Natural History and Geology of the Countries Visited during the Voyage of H.M.S.* Beagle (1839). Later, Darwin upset the thinking of his time by publishing *The Origin of Species* (1859) and *The Descent of Man* (1871).

OCTOBER 20th [1835]. The survey of the Galapagos Archipelago being concluded, we steered towards Tahiti and commenced our long passage of 3,200 miles. In the course of a few days we sailed out of the gloomy and clouded ocean-district which extends during the winter far from the coast of South America. We then enjoyed bright and clear weather, while running pleasantly along at the rate of 150 or 160 miles a day before the steady trade wind. The temperature in this more central part of the Pacific is higher than near the American shore. The thermometer in the poop cabin, by night and day, ranged between 80° and 83°, which feels very pleasant; but with one degree or two higher, the heat becomes oppressive. We passed through the Low or Dangerous Archipelago, and saw several of those most curious rings of coral land, just rising above the water's edge, which have been called Lagoon Islands. A long and brilliantly white beach is capped by a margin of green vegetation; and the strip, looking either way, rapidly narrows away in the distance and sinks beneath the horizon. From the masthead a wide expanse of smooth water can be seen within the ring. These low hollow coral islands bear no proportion to the vast ocean out of which they abruptly rise; and it seems wonderful that such weak invaders are not overwhelmed by the all-powerful and never-tiring waves of the great sea, miscalled the Pacific.

November 15th. At daylight, Tahiti, an island which must for ever remain classical to the voyager in the South Sea, was in view. At a distance the appearance was not attractive. The luxuriant vegetation of the lower part could not yet be seen, and as the clouds rolled past, the wildest and most precipitous peaks showed themselves towards the center of the island. As soon as we anchored in Matavai Bay, we were surrounded by canoes. This was our Sunday, but the Monday of Tahiti: if the case had been reversed, we should not have received a single visit, for the injunction not to launch a canoe on

244

the sabbath is rigidly obeyed. After dinner we landed to enjoy all the delights produced by the first impressions of a new country, and that country the charming Tahiti. A crowd of men, women, and children was collected on the memorable Point Venus, ready to receive us with laughing, merry faces. They marshalled us towards the house of Mr. Wilson, the missonary of the district, who met us on the road and gave us a very friendly reception. After sitting a short time in his house, we separated to walk about, but returned there in the evening.

The land capable of cultivation is scarcely in any part more than a fringe of low alluvial soil, accumulated round the base of the mountains and protected from the waves of the sea by a coral reef, which encircles the entire line of coast. Within the reef there is an expanse of smooth water, like that of a lake, where the canoes of the natives can ply with safety and where ships anchor. The low land which comes down to the beach of coral-sand is covered by the most beautiful productions of the intertropical regions. In the midst of bananas, orange, coconut, and breadfruit trees spots are cleared where yams, sweet potatoes, the sugar cane, and pineapples are cultivated. Even the brushwood is an imported fruit tree, namely, the guava, which from its abundance has become as noxious as a weed. In Brazil I have often admired the varied beauty of the bananas, palms, and orange trees contrasted together; and here we also have the breadfruit, conspicuous from its large, glossy, and deeply digitated leaf. It is admirable to behold groves of a tree, sending forth its branches with the vigor of an English oak, loaded with large and most nutritious fruit. However seldom the usefulness of an object can account for the pleasure of beholding it, in the case of these beautiful woods the knowledge of their high productiveness no doubt enters largely into the feeling of admiration. The little winding paths, cool from the surrounding shade, led to the scattered houses, the owners of which everywhere gave us a cheerful and most hospitable reception.

I was pleased with nothing so much as with the inhabitants. There is a mildness in the expression of their countenances which at once banishes the idea of a savage, and an intelligence which shows that they are advancing in civilizaton. The common people, when working, keep the upper part of their bodies quite naked, and it is then that the Tahitians are seen to advantage. They are very tall, broad-shouldered, athletic, and well-proportioned. It has been remarked that it requires little habit to make a dark skin more pleasing and natural to the eye of an European than his own color. A white man bathing by the side of a Tahitian was like a plant bleached by the gardener's art compared with a fine dark green one growing vigorously in the open fields. Most of the men are tattooed, and the ornaments follow the curvature of the body so gracefully that they have a very elegant effect. One common pattern, varying in its details, is somewhat like the crown of a palm tree. It springs from the central line of the back, and gracefully curls round both sides. The simile may be a fanciful one, but I thought the body of a man thus ornamented was like the trunk of a noble tree embraced by a delicate creeper.

Many of the elder people had their feet covered with small figures, so placed as to resemble a sock. This fashion, however, is partly gone by, and has been succeeded by others. Here, although fashion is far from immutable, everyone must abide by that prevailing in his youth. An old man has thus his age forever stamped on his body, and he cannot assume the airs of a young dandy. The women are tattooed in the same manner as the men, and very commonly on their fingers. One unbecoming fashion is now almost universal: namely, shaving the hair from the upper part of the head, in a circular form, so as to leave only an outer ring. The missionaries have tried to persuade the people to change this habit but it is the fashion, and that is a sufficient answer at

Tahiti, as well as at Paris. I was much disappointed in the personal appearance of the women: they are far inferior in every respect to the men. The custom of wearing a white or scarlet flower in the back of the head, or through a small hole in each ear, is pretty. A crown of woven coconut leaves is also worn as a shade for the eyes. The women appear to be in greater want of some becoming costume even than the men.

Nearly all the natives understand a little English— that is, they know the names of common things; and by the aid of this, together with signs, a lame sort of conversation could be carried on. In returning in the evening to the boat, we stopped to witness a very pretty scene. Numbers of children were playing on the beach and had lighted bonfires which illumined the placid sea and surrounding trees; others, in circles, were singing Tahitian verses. We seated ourselves on the sand and joined their party. The songs were impromptu, and I believe related to our arrival: one little girl sang a line, which the rest took up in parts, forming a very pretty chorus. The whole scene made us unequivocally aware that we were seated on the shores of an island in the far-famed South Sea.

17th. This day is reckoned in the logbook as Tuesday the 17th, instead of Monday the 16th, owing to our, so far, successful chase of the sun. Before breakfast the ship was hemmed in by a flotilla of canoes; and when the natives were allowed to come on board, I suppose there could not have been less than two hundred. It was the opinion of everyone that it would have been difficult to have picked out an equal number from any other nation who would have given so little trouble. Everybody brought something for sale: shells were the main article of trade. The Tahitians now fully understand the value of money and prefer it to old clothes or other articles. The various coins, however, of English and Spanish denomination puzzle them, and they never seem to think the small silver quite secure until changed into dollars. Some of the chiefs have accumulated considerable sums of money. One chief, not long since, offered $800 (about 160*l*. sterling) for a small vessel; and frequently they purchase whaleboats and horses at the rate of from $50 to $100.

After breakfast I went on shore and ascended the nearest slope to a height of between two and three thousand feet. The outer mountains are smooth and conical, but steep; and the old volcanic rocks of which they are formed have been cut through by many profound ravines, diverging from the central broken parts of the island to the coast. Having crossed the narrow low girt of inhabited and fertile land, I followed a smooth steep ridge between two of the deep ravines. The vegetation was singular, consisting almost exclusively of small dwarf ferns mingled, higher up, with coarse grass; it was not very dissimilar from that on some of the Welsh hills, and this so close above the orchard of tropical plants on the coast was very surprising. At the highest point, which I reached, trees again appeared. Of the three zones of comparative luxuriance, the lower one owes its moisture, and therefore fertility, to its flatness; for, being scarcely raised above the level of the sea, the water from the higher land drains away slowly. The intermediate zone does not, like the upper one, reach into a damp and cloudy atmosphere, and therefore remains sterile. The woods in the upper zone are very pretty, tree ferns replacing the coconuts on the coast. It must not, however, be supposed that these woods at all equal in splendor the forests of Brazil. The vast number of productions which characterize a continent cannot be expected to occur in an island.

From the highest point which I attained there was a good view of the distant island of Eimeo, dependent on the same sovereign with Tahiti. On the lofty and broken pinnacles, white massive clouds were piled up which

formed an island in the blue sky, as Eimeo itself did in
the blue ocean. The island, with the exception of one
small gateway, is completely encircled by a reef. At this
distance, a narrow but well-defined brilliantly white line
was alone visible, where the waves first encountered the
wall of coral. The mountains rose abruptly out of the
glassy expanse of the lagoon included within this narrow
white line, outside which the heaving waters of the
ocean were dark-colored. The view was striking: it may
aptly be compared to a framed engraving, where the
frame represents the breakers, the marginal paper the
smooth lagoon, and the drawing the island itself. When
in the evening I descended from the mountain a man
whom I had pleased with a trifling gift met me, bringing
with him hot roasted bananas, a pineapple, and coconuts.
After walking under a burning sun, I do not know anything more delicious than the milk of a young coconut.
Pineapples are here so abundant that the people eat them
in the same wasteful manner as we might turnips. They
are of an excellent flavor—perhaps even better than
those cultivated in England; and this I believe is the highest compliment which can be paid to any fruit. Before
going on board, Mr. Wilson interpreted for me to the
Tahitian who had paid me so adroit an attention that I
wanted him and another man to accompany me on a
short excursion into the mountains.

   18th. In the morning I came on shore early, bringing
with me some provisions in a bag and two blankets for
myself and servant. These were lashed to each end of a
long pole which was alternately carried by my Tahitian
companions on their shoulders. These men are accustomed thus to carry, for a whole day, as much as fifty
pounds at each end of their poles. I told my guides to provide themselves with food and clothing; but they said
that there was plenty of food in the mountains, and for
clothing that their skins were sufficient. Our line of
march was the valley of Tia-auru, down which a river

flows into the sea by Point Venus. This is one of the principal streams in the island, and its source lies at the base of the loftiest central pinnacles, which rise to a height of about 7,000 feet. The whole island is so mountainous that the only way to penetrate into the interior is to follow up the valleys. Our road, at first, lay through woods which bordered each side of the river; and the glimpses of the lofty central peaks, seen as through an avenue, with here and there a waving coconut tree on one side, were extremely picturesque. The valley soon began to narrow, and the sides to grow lofty and more precipitous. After having walked between three and four hours, we found the width of the ravine scarcely exceeded that of the bed of the stream. On each hand the walls were nearly vertical; yet, from the soft nature of the volcanic strata, trees and a rank vegetation sprang from every projecting ledge. These precipices must have been some thousand feet high; and the whole formed a mountain gorge far more magnificent than anything which I had ever before beheld. Until the midday sun stood vertically over the ravine, the air felt cool and damp, but now it became very sultry. Shaded by a ledge of rock, beneath a facade of columnar lava, we ate our dinner. My guides had already procured a dish of small fish and fresh-water prawns. They carried with them a small net stretched on a hoop; and where the water was deep and in eddies, they dived and like otters, with their eyes open followed the fish into holes and corners, and thus caught them.

The Tahitians have the dexterity of amphibious animals in the water. An anecdote mentioned by Ellis shows how much they feel at home in this element. When a horse was landing for Pomare in 1817 the slings broke and it fell into the water: immediately the natives jumped overboard, and by their cries and vain efforts at assistance almost drowned it. As soon, however, as it reached the shore, the whole population took to flight and tried to hide themselves from the man-carrying pig, as they christened the horse.

A little higher up, the river divided itself into three little streams. The two northern ones were impracticable, owing to a succession of waterfalls which descended from the jagged summit of the highest mountain; the other to all appearance was equally inaccessible, but we managed to ascend it by a most extraordinary road. The sides of the valley were here nearly precipitous; but, as frequently happens with stratified rocks, small ledges projected, which were thickly covered by wild bananas, liliaceous plants, and other luxuriant productions of the tropics. The Tahitians, by climbing amongst these ledges searching for fruit, had discovered a track by which the whole precipice could be scaled. The first ascent from the valley was very dangerous; for it was necessary to pass a steeply-inclined face of naked rock by the aid of ropes which we brought with us. How any person discovered that this formidable spot was the only point where the side of the mountain was practicable, I cannot imagine. We then cautiously walked along one of the ledges until we came to one of the three streams. This ledge formed a flat spot, above which a beautiful cascade, some hundred feet in height, poured down its waters, and beneath, another high cascade fell into the main stream in the valley below. From this cool and shady recess we made a circuit to avoid the overhanging waterfall. As before, we followed little projecting ledges, the danger being partly concealed by the thickness of the vegetation. In passing from one of the ledges to another, there was a vertical wall of rock. One of the Tahitians, a fine active man, placed the trunk of a tree against this, climbed up it, and then by the aid of crevices reached the summit. He fixed the ropes to a projecting point and lowered them for our dog and luggage, and then we clambered up ourselves. Beneath the ledge on which the dead tree was placed, the precipice must have been five or six hundred feet deep; and if the abyss had not been partly concealed by the overhanging ferns and lilies, my head would have turned giddy, and nothing should have induced me to have attempted it. We continued to ascend, sometimes along ledges, and sometimes along knife-edged ridges, having on each hand profound ravines. In the Cordillera I have seen mountains on a far grander scale, but for abruptness, nothing at all comparable with this. In the evening we reached a flat little spot on the banks of the same stream, which we had continued to follow, and which descends in a chain of waterfalls: here we bivouacked for the night. On each side of the ravine there were great beds of the mountain banana, covered with ripe fruit. Many of these plants were from twenty to twenty-five feet high, and from three to four in circumference. By the aid of strips of bark for rope, the stems of bamboos for rafters, and the large leaf of the banana for a thatch, the Tahitians in a few minutes built us an excellent house; and with withered leaves made a soft bed.

They then proceeded to make a fire, and cook our evening meal. A light was procured by rubbing a blunt-pointed stick in a groove made in another, as if with intention of deepening it, until by the friction the dust became ignited. A peculiarly white and very light wood (the Hibiscus tiliaceus) is alone used for this purpose: it is the same which serves for poles to carry any burden and for the floating outriggers to their canoes. The fire was produced in a few seconds: but to a person who does not understand the art it requires, as I found, the greatest exertion; but at last, to my great pride, I succeeded in igniting the dust. The Gaucho in the Pampas uses a different method: taking an elastic stick about eighteen inches long, he presses one end on his breast, and the other pointed end into a hole in a piece of wood and then rapidly turns the curved part, like a carpenter's center bit. The Tahitians, having made a small fire of sticks, placed a score of stones, of about the size of cricket balls, on the burning wood. In about ten minutes the sticks were consumed, and the stones hot. They had previously folded up, in small parcels of leaves, pieces of beef, fish, ripe and unripe bananas, and the tops of the wild arum. These green parcels were laid in a layer between two layers of the hot stones and the whole then covered up with earth, so that no smoke or steam could escape. In about a quarter of an hour, the whole was most deliciously cooked. The choice green parcels were now laid on a cloth of banana leaves and with a coconut shell we drank the cool water of the running stream; and thus we enjoyed our rustic meal.

I could not look on the surrounding plants without admiration. On every side were forests of banana, the fruit of which, though serving for food in various ways, lay in heaps decaying on the ground. In front of us there was an extensive brake of wild sugar cane; and the stream was shaded by the dark-green, knotted stem of the *ava*, so famous in former days for its powerful intoxicating effects. I chewed a piece and found that it had an acrid and unpleasant taste which would have induced anyone at once to have pronounced it poisonous. Thanks to the missionaries, this plant now thrives only in these deep ravines, innocuous to every one. Close by I saw the wild arum, the roots of which, when well baked, are good to eat, and the young leaves better than spinach. There was the wild yam, and a liliaceous plant called *ti*, which grows in abundance and has a soft brown root, in shape and size like a huge log of wood: this served us for dessert, for it is as sweet as treacle, and with a pleasant taste. There were, moreover, several other wild fruits and useful vegetables. The little stream, besides its cool water, produced eels and crayfish. I did indeed admire this scene when I compared it with an uncultivated one in the temperate zones. I felt the force of the remark that man, at least savage man, with his reasoning powers only partly developed, is the child of the tropics.

As the evening drew to a close, I strolled beneath the gloomy shade of the bananas up the course of the stream.

My walk was soon brought to a close by coming to a waterfall between two and three hundred feet high; and again above this there was another. I mention all these waterfalls in this one brook to give a general idea of the inclination of the land. In the little recess where the water fell, it did not appear that a breath of wind had ever blown. The thin edges of the great leaves of the banana, damp with spray, were unbroken instead of being, as is so generally the case, split into a thousand shreds. From our position, almost suspended on the mountainside, there were glimpses into the depths of the neighboring valleys; and the lofty points of the central mountains, towering up within sixty degrees of the zenith, hid half the evening sky. Thus seated, it was a sublime spectacle to watch the shades of night gradually obscuring the last and highest pinnacles.

Before we laid ourselves down to sleep, the elder Tahitian fell on his knees and with closed eyes repeated a long prayer in his native tongue. He prayed as a Christian should do, with fitting reverence, and without the fear of ridicule or any ostentation of piety. At our meals neither of the men would taste food without saying beforehand a short grace. Those travelers who think that a Tahitian prays only when the eyes of the missionary are fixed on him should have slept with us that night on the mountainside. Before morning it rained very heavily; but the good thatch of banana leaves kept us dry.

November 19th. At daylight my friends, after their morning prayer, prepared an excellent breakfast in the same manner as in the evening. They themselves certainly partook of it largely; indeed I never saw any men eat near so much. I suppose such enormously capacious stomachs must be the effect of a large part of their diet consisting of fruit and vegetables, which contain, in a given bulk, a comparatively small portion of nutriment. Unwittingly, I was the means of my companions breaking, as I afterwards learned, one of their own laws and resolutions. I took with me a flask of spirits, which they could not refuse to partake of; but as often as they drank a little, they put their fingers before their mouths and uttered the word "Missionary." About two years ago, although the use of the *ava* was prevented, drunkenness from the introduction of spirits became very prevalent. The missionaries prevailed on a few good men, who saw that their country was rapidly going to ruin, to join with them in a temperance society. From good sense or shame, all chiefs and the queen were at last persuaded to join. Immediately a law was passed that no spirits should be allowed to be introduced into the island, and that he who sold and he who bought the forbidden article should be punished by a fine. With remarkable justice, a certain period was allowed for stock in hand to be sold before the law came into effect. But when it did, a general search was made in which even the houses of the missionaries were not exempted, and all the *ava* (as the natives call all ardent spirits) was poured on the ground. When one reflects on the effect of intemperance on the aborigines of the two Americas, I think it will be acknowledged that every well-wisher of Tahiti owes no common debt of gratitude to the missionaries. As long as the little island of St. Helena remained under the government of the East India Company, spirits, owing to the great injury they had produced, were not allowed to be imported; but wine was supplied from the Cape of Good Hope. It is rather a striking, and not very gratifying fact, that in the same year that spirits were allowed to be sold in St. Helena their use was banished from Tahiti by the free will of the people.

After breakfast we proceeded on our journey. As my object was merely to see a little of the interior scenery, we returned by another track, which descended into the main valley lower down. For some distance we wound, by a most intricate path, along the side of the mountain which formed the valley. In the less precipitous parts we passed through extensive groves of the wild banana. The Tahitians, with their naked, tattooed bodies, their heads ornamented with flowers, and seen in the dark shade of these groves, would have formed a fine picture of man inhabiting some primeval land. In our descent we followed the line of ridges; these were exceedingly narrow, and for considerable lengths steep as a ladder; but all clothed with vegetation. The extreme care necessary in poising each step rendered the walk fatiguing. I did not cease to wonder at these ravines and precipices: when viewing the country from one of the knife-edged ridges, the point of support was so small that the effect was nearly the same as it must be from a balloon. In this descent we had occasion to use the ropes only once, at the point where we entered the main valley. We slept under the same ledge of rock where we had dined the day before: the night was fine but, from the depth and narrowness of the gorge, profoundly dark.

Before actually seeing this country, I found it difficult to understand two facts mentioned by Ellis; namely, that after the murderous battles of former times, the survivors on the conquered side retired into the mountains, where a handful of men could resist a multitude. Certainly half-a-dozen men, at the spot where the Tahitian reared the old tree, could easily have repulsed thousands. Secondly, that after the introduction of Christianity, there were wild men who lived in the mountains, and whose retreats were unknown to the more civilized inhabitants.

November 20th. In the morning we started early, and reached Matavai at noon. On the road we met a large party of noble athletic men, going for wild bananas. I found that the ship, on account of the difficulty in watering, had moved to the harbor of Papawa, to which place I immediately walked. This is a very pretty spot. The cove is surrounded by reefs, and the water as smooth as in a lake. The cultivated ground, with its beautiful productions, interspersed with cottages, comes close down to the water's edge.

From the varying accounts which I had read before reaching these islands, I was very anxious to form, from my own observation, a judgment of their moral state — although such judgment would necessarily be very imperfect. First impressions at all times very much depend on one's previously acquired ideas. My notions were drawn from Ellis's *Polynesian Researches*, an admirable and most interesting work, but naturally looking at everything under a favorable point of view; from Beechey's *Voyage;* and from that of Kotzebue, which is strongly adverse to the whole missionary system. He who compares these three accounts will, I think, form a tolerably accurate conception of the present state of Tahiti. One of my impressions, which I took from the two last authorities, was decidedly incorrect; viz., that the Tahitians had become a gloomy race, and lived in fear of the missionaries. Of the latter feeling I saw no trace, unless, indeed, fear and respect be confounded under one name. Instead of discontent being a common feeling, it would be difficult in Europe to pick out of a crowd half so many merry and happy faces. The prohibition of the flute and dancing is inveighed against as wrong and foolish; the more than presbyterian manner of keeping the sabbath is looked at in a similar light. On these points I will not pretend to offer any opinion, in opposition to men who have resided as many years as I was days on the island.

On the whole, it appears to me that the morality and religion of the inhabitants are highly creditable. There are many who attack, even more acrimoniously than Kotzebue, both the missionaries, their system, and the effects produced by it. Such reasoners never compare the present state with that of the island only twenty years ago; nor even with that of Europe at this day; but they compare it with the high standard of Gospel perfection. They expect the missionaries to effect that which the Apostles themselves failed to do. In as much as the condition of the people falls short of this high standard, blame is attached to the missionary, instead of credit for that which he has effected. They forget, or will not remember, that human sacrifices, and the power of an idolatrous priesthood—a system of profligacy unparalleled in any other part of the world—infanticide a consequence of that system—bloody wars, where the conquerors spared neither women nor children—that all these have been abolished; and that dishonesty, intemperance, and licentiousness have been greatly reduced by the introduction of Christianity. In a voyager to forget these things is base ingratitude; for should he chance to be at the point of shipwreck on some unknown coast, he will most devoutly pray that the lesson of the missionary may have extended thus far.

In point of morality, the virtue of the women, it has been often said, is most open to exception. But before they are blamed too severely, it will be well distinctly to call to mind the scenes described by Captain Cook and Mr. Banks, in which the grandmothers and mothers of the present race played a part. Those who are most severe should consider how much of the morality of the women in Europe is owing to the system early impressed by mothers on their daughters, and how much in each individual case to the precepts of religion. But it is useless to argue against such reasoners; I believe that, disappointed in not finding the field of licentiousness quite so open as formerly, they will not give credit to a morality which they do not wish to practice or to a religion which they undervalue, if not despise.

Sunday, 22nd. The harbour of Papeete, where the queen resides, may be considered as the capital of the island: it is also the seat of government and the chief resort of shipping. Captain Fitz Roy took a party there this day to hear divine service, first in the Tahitian language and afterwards in our own. Mr. Pritchard, the leading missionary in the island, performed the service. The chapel consisted of a large airy framework of wood; and it was filled to excess by tidy, clean people of all ages and both sexes. I was rather disappointed in the apparent degree of attention; but I believe my expectations were raised too high. At all events the appearance was quite equal to that in a country church in England. The singing of the hymns was decidedly very pleasing; but the language from the pulpit, although fluently delivered, did not sound well: a constant repetition of words, like *"tata ta, mata mai,"* rendered it monotonous. After English service, a party returned on foot to Matavai. It was a pleasant walk, sometimes along the sea beach and sometimes under the shade of the many beautiful trees.

About two years ago, a small vessel under English colors was plundered by some of the inhabitants of the Low Islands, which were then under the dominion of the Queen of Tahiti. It was believed that the perpetrators were instigated to this act by some indiscreet laws issued by her majesty. The British government demanded compensation; which was acceded to, and a sum of nearly three thousand dollars was agreed to be paid on the first of last September. The Commodore at Lima ordered Captain Fitz Roy to inquire concerning this debt, and to demand satisfaction if it were not paid. Captain Fitz Roy accordingly requested an interview with the Queen Pomare, since famous from the ill treatment she has received from the French; and a parliament was held to consider the question, at which all the principal chiefs attempt to describe what took place, after the interesting account given by Captain Fitz Roy. The money, it appeared, had not been paid; perhaps the alleged reasons were rather equivocal; but otherwise I cannot sufficiently express our general surprise at the extreme good sense, the reasoning powers, moderation, candor, and prompt resolution which were displayed on all sides. I believe we all left the meeting with a different opinion of the Tahitians, from what we entertained when we entered. The chiefs and people resolved to subscribe and complete the sum which was wanting; Captain Fitz Roy urged that it was hard that their private property should be sacrificed for the crimes of distant islanders. They replied that they were grateful for his consideration but that Pomare was their queen and that they were determined to help her in this her difficulty. This resolution and its prompt execution, for a book was opened early the next morning, made a perfect conclusion to this very remarkable scene of loyalty and good feeling.

After the main discussion was ended, several of the chiefs took the opportunity of asking Captain Fitz Roy many intelligent questions on international customs and laws relating to the treatment of ships and foreigners. On some points, as soon as the decision was made, the law was issued verbally on the spot. This Tahitian parliament lasted for several hours, and when it was over Captain Fitz Roy invited Queen Pomare to pay the *Beagle* a visit.

November 25th. In the evening four boats were sent for her majesty; the ship was dressed with flags, and the yards manned on her coming on board. She was accompanied by most of the chiefs. The behavior of all was very proper: they begged for nothing, and seemed much pleased with Captain Fitz Roy's presents. The Queen is a large awkward woman, without any beauty, grace, or dignity. She has only one royal attribute: a perfect immoveability of expression under all circumstances, and that rather a sullen one. The rockets were most admired; and a deep "Oh!" could be heard from the shore, all round the dark bay, after each explosion. The sailors' songs were also much admired; and the queen said she thought that one of the most boisterous ones certainly could not be a hymn! The royal party did not return on shore till past midnight.

26th. In the evening, with a gentle land-breeze, a

course was steered for New Zealand; and as the sun set we had a farewell view of the mountains of Tahiti— the island to which every voyager has offered up his tribute of admiration.

III. The Missionaries

Richard E. Lingenfelter

The First Printing Press in the Pacific

Christian missionary efforts in the nineteenth century frequently involved the translation and publication of the Bible and educational materials in the native languages. This was true when the London Missionary Society set up a station on Tahiti in 1797. The first publications, however, were printed in London and in Sydney, Australia, and it was not until 1817 that the first press was set up in the islands. The printing office was erected at Afareaitu on the island of Moorea, just across the channel from Papeete. Amid a horde of his excited subjects, King Pomare II, on the morning of June 30, pulled the first impression of a page of printing ever struck off in the islands of the Pacific Ocean.

Thereafter, through the years, presses were set up on more than a score of islands by missionary artisans who, aided by willing native workers, issued millions of hand-set pages of text and pictures, which were eagerly seized by avid converts. The story is well told by Richard E. Lingenfelter. The selection that follows forms the first chapter of his book, *Presses of the Pacific Islands: 1817-1867* (Los Angeles: Plantin Press, 1967).

PRINTING has flourished in China and Japan on the west shore of the Pacific since well before the seventh century and in Mexico and Peru on the east since its introduction by the Spanish in the sixteenth century. Before the end of the sixteenth century, the Manila galleons carried the press across the Pacific to the Philippines and two centuries later, in 1795, the British brought the press to Australia. But the first printing for any of the islands of the Pacific was not done until the early nineteenth century. Ironically, it was done on the opposite side of the globe. This was a Tahitian spelling book, *Te Aebi No Taheiti*, printed in London in 1810 for the London Missionary Society.

The first mission in the Pacific islands was established in Tahiti in 1797 by the London Missionary Society, two years after its founding. There the missionaries undertook to put the Tahitian language in written form, to make up a grammar, and to translate hymns, catechisms, and portions of the Gospel into Tahitian. By 1808 John Davies had completed the manuscript of a spelling book and it was sent to England for printing. The completed edition of 700 copies did not reach Tahiti until 1811, more than three years after it was ready for the press. Furthermore, since the proofs could not be corrected by the author or anyone familiar with the language, many errors were made, which the Tahitians themselves could soon "detect and censure with good-humored familiarity."

To remedy these problems the missionaries decided to have their next books printed in Australia. In the latter part of 1813 the second book of the islands, *Parau No Tahiti*, a collection of scriptures and hymns, was printed by George Howe at Sydney. This greatly reduced the delay, and also the typographical errors, so long as one of the missionaries went to Sydney to check the proofs. But this was still far from satisfactory, particularly since the number of manuscripts they wished to have printed was growing rapidly.

They soon decided that they must do their own printing, and Davies and others began to appeal to the directors of the society to send them out a press and type. At the same time one of the missionaries, William Pascoe Crook, who was then at Sydney, began to learn printing from George Howe, so that when a press was sent from England someone at Tahiti would be able to work it. Howe also drew up a list of materials for a small printing plant and Crook forwarded this to London but it was not known whether these recommendations were followed in preparing the plant which was finally sent.

In any event the directors decided in 1815 to send a press to Tahiti and they appointed a recent volunteer, William Ellis, to accompany it as a printer. Ellis, a former London gardener, was only twenty-one years old and had never before been outside of London. He had no experience in printing, but in the few months before his departure he tried hard to learn. Also, shortly before he intended to leave, Ellis was married.

Early in December he and his bride arrived with the press at Portsmouth to board the *Atlas*, a prison ship bound for New South Wales. Strong gales delayed their departure for nearly two months, however, and it was not until January 23, 1816, that they finally set sail for the Pacific. Six months later they reached Sydney, where they were delayed another five months, during which time Mrs. Ellis gave birth to a daughter. At last in December of 1816 Ellis, his family and the press, sailed on the brig, *Queen Charlotte*, for Tahiti.

On February 10, 1817, the *Queen Charlotte* drew in sight of the high peaks of Tahiti and three days later dropped anchor in the bay at Papetoai on the neighboring island of Moorea, then known as Eimeo. Ellis, his wife and child went ashore, where they were greeted by Davies, Crook, and the other missionaries. Following an uprising in 1808, Moorea was the only island on which there was a missionary station, but King Pomare II of Tahiti had requested the missionaries to reoccupy their former station at Tahiti and they were anxious to do so. However, the missionaries also felt that a station should be set up in the Leeward islands of the group, but as all wanted to go to Tahiti and none to the Leewards, a disagreement had arisen over the division of the mission, resulting in a stalemate.

When Ellis arrived with the press, a meeting of the missionaries was called and a majority at last agreed that the press with Ellis, Davies, and Crook should go to Tahiti, particularly since King Pomare had specifically requested the press. But after the missionaries had finally agreed among themselves, the captain of the *Queen Charlotte* refused to take them and the press was unloaded at Moorea. The quibbling then commenced anew and a week later, over the protests of Ellis, Davies, and Crook, the majority decision was set aside and the missionaries drew lots to determine the disposition of the press. By this lottery it was decided that the press, Ellis, and Davies should go to the Leewards. This decision was immediately opposed by Pomare and many of his following, who were already unhappy that the press had been unloaded at Moorea and not Tahiti and were even more disturbed at the prospect of its being moved a hundred miles farther away. Pomare wrote several strong letters expressing his disapproval of the plan but all to little avail. After a month of bickering, the missionaries finally agreed to try to partially appease the King by temporarily setting up the press on Moorea to print three books — an edition of the spelling book, a catechism, and the gospel of Luke — before it was taken to the Leewards. This they hoped would satisfy the curiosity of the King and his people. During its stay on Moorea the press was to be run by Ellis, Davies, and Crook at the village of Afareaitu on the southeast side of the island, facing Tahiti.

On March 18th the press and printing equipment, accompanied by Davies, were loaded into nine canoes and taken around the island to Afareaitu, where they arrived the following day. Crook and Ellis went overland and selected an attractive site for the printing office near the head of the bay beside a clear, rushing stream and only a few yards from the beach. The office was begun a few days later by the villagers, but heavy rains, delays in getting materials, and lack of cooperation from the others at Papetoai caused its construction to drag on for more than two months. Nevertheless it was to become the finest building on the island, boasting the island's first glass window and a floor paved with blocks of basalt from a nearby temple ruin. During this time the rift between the two missionary groups grew even wider as rumors were spread of Ellis' misappropriating £500 of the society's funds for such luxuries as two hogsheads of wine.

By the end of May the printing office was at last completed and Ellis and Crook set up the press, type cases, and other equipment. Davies wrote King Pomare inviting him to Afareaitu, since he had expressed his desire "to see the whole procedure of printing." Pomare arrived on the evening of June 9th and the following morning he and a large entourage packed into the printing office to watch the type set for the first page of the spelling book.

"I took the composing stick in my hand," Ellis recalled, "and observing Pomare looking with curious delight at the new and shining types, I asked him if he would like to put together the first A B or alphabet. His countenance was lighted up with evidence satisfaction as he answered in the affirmative. I then placed the composing stick in his hand; he took the capital letters, one by one, out of their respective compartments and, fixing them, concluded the alphabet. He put together the small letters in the same manner, and the few monosyllables composing the first page of the spelling book were afterwards added. He was delighted when he saw the first page complete, and appeared desirous to have it struck off at once; but when informed that it would not be printed till as many were composed as would fill a sheet, he requested that he might be sent for whenever it was ready." For the next two weeks Ellis and Crook were busy setting and correcting the other fifteen pages of the first sheet. Finally everything was in readiness for the first printing.

Early on the morning of June 30th, 1817, King Pomare, two of his favorite chiefs, and a long train of attendants arrived at the printing office. "Crowds of the natives were already collected around the door," Ellis wrote, "but they made way for him and, after he and his two companions had been admitted, the door was closed, and the small window next the sea darkened, as he did not wish to be overlooked by the people on the outside. The king examined, with great minuteness and pleasure, the form as it lay on the press, and prepared to try to take off the first sheet ever printed in his dominions. Having been told how it was to be done, he jocosely charged his companions not to look very particularly at him, and not to laugh if he should not do it right. I put the printer's ink ball into his hand and directed him to strike it two or three times upon the face of the letters; this he did, and then placing a sheet of clean paper upon the parchment, I covered it down and, turning it under the press, directed the king to pull the handle. He did so, and when the paper was removed from beneath the press, and the covering lifted up, the chiefs and attendants rushed towards it, to see what effect the king's pressure had produced. When they beheld the letters black, and large, and well defined, there was one simultaneous expression of wonder and delight.

"The king took up the sheet and having looked first at the paper and then at the types with attentive admiration handed it to one of his chiefs, and expressed a wish to take another. He printed two more; and while he was so engaged, the first sheet was shewn to the crowd without, who, when they saw it, raised one general shout of astonishment and joy." The first printing had been done in the Pacific, and Ellis concluded, "We cannot but view the introduction of printing as an auspicious event. The 30th of June, 1817, was, on this account, an important day in the annals of Tahiti; and there is no act of Pomare's life . . . that will be remembered with more grateful feeling than the circumstances of his printing the first page of the first book published in the South Sea Islands."

The crowd disbanded and Ellis and Crook set to work

intending to print 400 impressions before the end of the day. But very shortly they discovered that the leather from which the ink balls were made had rotted so on the long voyage out from England that the balls soon fell apart. A few days later, when they started printing again, the cast-iron chase broke after they had printed only 150 sheets and they were again delayed. But finally on the 17th of July they finished the first printing of 2592 copies of the spelling book. The exact number printed is not known, however, for three weeks later Crook wrote, "Bro. Ellis and I printed a few more spelling books."

The demand for the spelling books was immediate and exhausting. The two previous editions—one of 700 printed in London in 1810 and another of 2500 printed in Sydney in 1815—had long before been exhausted. By late August all of the new edition had also been distributed and Ellis lamented, "there is a call for double the number did our paper allow it. People are now daily coming from Tahiti for books but we are obliged to deny them. Some hundreds have thus been disappointed."

In view of the demand and the hard use to which they were doubtless put, it is not surprising that no copies of this edition seem to have survived and thus no accurate description of this first Pacific imprint can be given. However, from the meager description given in the journals and letters of the missionaries it is known that the book consisted of thirty-two pages, which contained in addition to the spelling lessons "several scripture lessons &c," and that it was printed on India paper purchased by Ellis in Sydney. Unlike the two previous editions, it also does not appear to have had a title page or cover.

In their letter to the directors in July Ellis requested a long list of items for the press, including some composition ink balls, a large stock of paper, sheepskin, calfskin, and millboards for binding, two new chases, parchment for tympans, and "a few Italic types . . . to print the supplementary words in the Scripture &c." As the standard English font contained many letters infrequently or never used in printing Tahitian, Ellis drew up a font more suitable to the needs of the language, requesting that the type be sent as follows:

a	800	A	50	á	20
b	100	B	30	é	20
d	150	D	20	î	40
e	700E	E	50	ó	20
f	150	F	50	ú	20
h	150	H	50	â	20
i	700	I	50	ê	20
m	150	M	50	î	20
n	150	N	30	ô	20
o	700	O	30	û	20
p	150	P	50	ä	20
r	150	R	30	ë	20
t	700	T	60	ï	50
u	700	U	40	ö	20
v	100	V	30	ü	20
	5500		620		350

To this he added a request for 50 each of C, s, and w for biblical names that they had introduced into the language.

In August Ellis began setting up the catecisms and scripture lessons that were to be their second book. By this time he was assisted both by Crook and by two young Tahitians who had begun "to be very handy at the printing office." The catechisms and scripture lessons each consisted of 16 pages, set in separate forms. On the 24th of September they finished printing about 2300 of the combined work and an additional 1100 of the scripture lessons for those who already had copies of the first edition of the catechism printed in Sydney in 1815. This nearly exhausted the supply of India paper brought from Australia. The paper brought from England was reserved for the printing of the gospel of Luke.

For some time Ellis had been waiting for Henry Nott at Papetoai to send the final draft of the gospel of Luke which he and King Pomare had prepared. When it finally arrived about the first of October, Ellis quickly composed the first page and sent a proof to Nott for comment on the orthography. There was some dispute among the missionaries over the inclusion of *b* and *d* in the Tahitian alphabet — Nott having made his translation without these letters and Ellis having set the first page with them wherever Davies thought it proper. This only added to the ill-feeling between the two factions and it was a full month before Nott finally agreed to their inclusion. Ellis, however, had already gone ahead setting the first sheet with them and by November 8th he had printed 1500 copies — all that their supply of paper would allow. But, ten days later, before he had distributed the type, the brig *Active* arrived at Papetoai with additional paper from England, and Ellis immediately decided to double the size of the edition.

Also aboard the *Active* were six new missionary reinforcements, which included Charles Barff, Robert Bourne, David Darling, and John Williams. Bourne was a printer, who had been sent out to assist Ellis, and in addition to the paper he brought considerable new type and other materials to supplement the printing office. But since the press was soon to be moved to the Leeward islands, Bourne decided to remain at Papetoai until the move rather than going to the "expense and ilconvenience" of joining the press at Afareaitu. Within a short time, however, he indicated that he would probably never join them, declaring "that he will not join any that may insist upon regulating missionary affairs by the voice of a majority, he will follow his own views, and will not be controlled by anyone."

A more compelling motive for Bourne's refusal became apparent in early February, when he and Darling announced that they would keep the type and other equipment that Bourne had brought and set it up at Tahiti with a new press they proposed to make. The great popularity of the press among the islanders was evident almost from its arrival and the station at Afareaitu became the immediate favorite of the King and most of his people—much to the consternation of those at Papetoai. Thus when Bourne arrived the missionaries at Papetoai persuaded him to join them and set up a press at Tahiti, as Bourne put it "to make the station respectable," for he felt certain that without a press "the Tahitian station will not be thought anything of."

Ellis and Davies objected that the material Bourne had brought out rightfully should go to their press, but they found little support for their claims, as most of those who were either remaining at Moorea or going to Tahiti were convinced that a press was needed to improve their status. Darling planned to make the wood frame for the press and Williams, though he said he didn't approve of the business, promised to cast an iron screw. In mid-February, Bourne and Williams visited Afareaitu to make careful drawings and measurements of the press that they might copy it. On this visit Bourne apparently made an agreement with Crook to join him on the new press at Tahiti—for after this Crook no longer worked with Ellis at the press and a month later he and his family left for Tahiti.

The need for a second press may have been problematical, but the popularity of the first was undeniable, as Ellis testified: "The curiosity awakened in the inhabitants of Afareaitu by the establishment of the press was not soon satisfied: day after day Pomare visited the printing office; the chiefs applied to be admitted inside, while the people thronged the windows, doors, and every crevice through which they could peep, often involuntarily exclaiming, *Beri-ta-nie! fenua paari:* Oh Britain! land of skill or knowledge. The press soon became a matter of universal conversation; and the facility with which books could be multiplied filled the minds of the people in general with wonderful delight.

"Multitudes arrived from every district of Eimeo, and even from other islands, to procure books, and to see this astonishing machine . . . . So great was the influx of strangers that for several weeks before the first portion of the Scriptures was finished the district of Afareaitu resembled a public fair. The beach was lined with canoes from distant parts of Eimeo and other islands; the houses of the inhabitants were thronged, and small parties had erected their temporary encampments in every direction . . . The printing office was daily crowded by the strangers, who thronged the door, &c. in such numbers as to climb upon each others backs, or on the sides of the windows, so as frequently to darken the place. The house had been enclosed with a fence five or six feet high; but this instead of presenting an obstacle to the gratification of their curiosity was converted into a means of facilitating it: numbers were constantly seen sitting on the top of the railing, whereby they were able to look over the heads of their companions who were round the windows."

Ellis in the meantime had been completing the printing of Luke, assisted now by six or seven Tahitians—two men working the press, two women folding and sewing, and the remaining women beating up tapa cloth to make boards for binding. The most welcome assistance was of course with the press, as Ellis wrote, "two natives were instructed to perform the most laborious parts; and, before the book was finished, they were able, under proper superintendence, to relieve us from the mechanical labor of press work—a department in which they with others have been ever since employed; receiving regular payment for the same." But even then the work was long and tiring. "We labored eight, and sometimes ten, hours daily," Ellis lamented, "yet found that the work advanced but slowly. Notwithstanding all the care that had been exercised in selecting the printing materials and accompanying apparatus, many things were either deficient or spoiled."

However, on March 5th, 1818, the printing of the gospel of Luke, *Te Evanelia na Luka,* was at last finished—with the exception of a title page. That afternoon Ellis left for Papetoai to see if Bourne would let him have enough display type for a title, but Bourne refused. Later Ellis set up a title page with the body type but only five hundred of these were printed. The following week Mrs. Ellis gave birth to a son and Ellis halted further work on the book for a month while he cared for his family.

Te Evanelia na Luka was by far the largest work to be published on the press for some time, both in length, 120 pages, and in size of the edition, totaling 3000 copies. The previous books at best had had only paper covers, but Ellis hoped to make *Luke* more durable by binding it in boards. He bound the first dozen or so in leather and gave them to the King, the Queen, the chiefs, and the other missionaries. But for most of the books he had to make do with native materials, although the result sounds rather attractive as he described it, "a large quantity of native cloth, made with the bark of a tree, was purchased, and females employed to beat a number of layers or folds together, usually, from seven to ten. These were afterwards submitted to the action of a powerful upright screw-press, and when gradually dried formed a good stiff paste board. For their covers, the few sheepskins brought from England were cut into slips for the backs and corners, and a large bundle of old newspapers dyed, for covers to the sides. In staining these papers, they were covered over with the juice of the stem of the mountain plantain, or *fei* . . . imparting to the sheet, when dried in the sun, a rich glossy purple color, which remained as long as the paper lasted. If lime juice was sprinkled upon it, a beautiful and delicate pink was produced."

Still the process was quite time consuming and it is doubtful that more than a few hundred books were ever bound. Fifteen hundred copies, nearly all as loose sheets, were divided among the missionaries at Papetoai and Tahiti, and the remaining copies were taken to the Leewards. Both the division of the books and the fact that they were not bound angered the other missionaries — particularly since they claimed there were more than three thousand people on Moorea and Tahiti who could read while there were yet but few in the Leewards. However, they appear to have vented their anger more on the Tahitians than on Ellis and Davies, for they distributed the sheets to the people before they were even sewed together and with little regard to insuring that each received the full five sheets that made up the complete text.

Previously all books had been given freely to the people, but for *Te Evanelia na Luka* the missionaries decided to demand a payment of three gallons of coconut oil for each copy — whether bound or not. In this way they hoped to defray the cost of the paper, and thereafter all of their books were sold either for coconut oil or arrow-root.

With the three books thus printed, as had been decided the previous year, Ellis and Davies now prepared to move the press to the Leeward islands. But before the press was taken down, one final imprint was made at Afareaitu. On May 18, 1818, the Tahitian Auxiliary Missionary Society was organized at Papetoai and ten days later Ellis printed an edition of the *Rules for the Tahitian Society*. No further information has been found regarding this pamphlet, although it probably ran to a couple dozen pages, as did a similar one later published for the Huahine Society.

The following week they commenced packing up the type and dismantling the press. On June 17th the brig *Hawies* anchored in the harbor of Haumi, a short distance away, and within a few days the printing equipment and all of their personal belongings were loaded aboard. Ellis, Davies and their families went overland to Papetoai, where they joined John Williams, who was to go with them to the Leewards. On July 1, 1818, they sailed aboard the *Hawies* for the island of Huahine.

The press was never again established on Moorea. But despite the squabbling that had attended it, the first press in the Pacific had been exceptionally productive. In the scant eleven months of its active existence it had produced over 9000 books, totaling over half a million pages, and this success was to spur the introduction of the press to other islands of the Pacific.

IV. The Explorers

George Robertson

The "Old Trade" at Matavai

Captain Samuel Wallis of H.M.S. *Dolphin* on June 19, 1767, discovered the Polynesian paradise of Tahiti. In his specially built, copper-bottomed vessel, then on its second voyage of discovery around the globe, Wallis spent four months battling storms in the Strait of Magellan. Then he cruised westward through the reef-studded Tuamotu Archipelago. A few days later the crew sighted the high peak of Tahiti. Following an initial brush with Polynesian warriors in their canoes at Matavai Bay, Wallis and his officers were greeted by "Queen Oberea" and for a month refreshed themselves on the island. At the end of that time, the queen wept when Wallis decided the time had come to set sail for further adventures.

George Roberton, master of the *Dolphin* for the two-year voyage, began service at about the age of thirty as master's mate in the Royal Navy in 1761 and, after successive promotions, was in command of several British vessels during the American Revolution. On the *Dolphin* voyage, both Wallis and First Lieutenant William Clarke were ill much of the time, and the success of the expedition can be credited mainly to Second Lieutenant Tobias Furneaux and to Robertson, the master. The latter's engaging personal journal of the voyage, written in direct and unadorned English, is one of the classics of South Sea discovery.

Particularly diverting is his straight-faced account of the "old trade" that went on between Wallis' lusty seamen and the complacent Tahitian women. At first the ladies were satisfied with a tenpenny nail for their favors, but soon inflation set in to a point where sailors were trading their hammock spikes and tearing cleats from the *Dolphin*'s deck, so that, when Captain Wallis found out about the commerce, he "no longer wondered that the ship was in danger of being pulled to pieces for the nails and iron that held her together."

JULY 6, 1767. At noon we returned on board and found our traders had but very indifferent success. They only brought off four pigs, a few fowls, and some fruit. I was told by one of the young gentlemen [midshipmen] that a new sort of trade took up the most of their attention this day, but it might be more properly called the old trade. He says a dear Irish boy, one of our marines, was the first that began the trade, for which he got a very severe cobbing [thrashing] from the liberty men for not beginning in a more decent manner, in some house or at the back of some bush or tree. Paddy's excuse was the fear of losing the honor of having the first . . . .

July 9. I this day went ashore for the first time and walked about a mile up the river, with two of the young gentlemen along with me . . . In returning back to the boats, three very fine young girls accosted us, and one of them made a signal and smiled in my face. This made me stop to inquire what the young lady wanted, and supposing the young gentlemen better acquainted than I, who had never seen any of the young ladies before but at a great distance, I desired one of them to explain the meaning of the signal. They both put on a very grave look and told me they did not understand her signs. I then supposed she had something to sell and made signs for her to show her goods, but this seemed to displease her and another repeated the same signal, which was this: She held up her right hand and first finger of the right hand straight, then laid hold of her right wrist with the left hand, and held the right hand and first finger up straight and smiled, then crooked all her fingers and kept playing with them and laughed very hearty, which set my young friends laughing as hearty as the young girl. This made me insist upon their explaining the sign, and they told me the young girls only wanted a long nail each, but they never before saw them make a sign for one longer than their fingers, but they supposed the young girls thought I carried longer nails than the rest because I was dressed in a different manner. I wanted them to explain the other part of the signal, that I might understand the whole, but the young men begged to be excused. I therefore gave the young girls a nail each, and parted good friends, then walked down to see how the traders went on. I told the gunner what had happened betwixt us and the young girls, and he explained the whole matter in few words, and told me my young friends were not so very ignorant as they pretended to be. He likewise told me that the price of the old trade is now fixed at a thirty-penny nail each time, and he told me that the liberty men dealt so largely in that way that he was much afraid of losing his trade of hogs, pigs, fowls, and fruit . . . .

July 16. By this time the natives and all our people were turned very sociable, and the instant our boats landed, numbers of them came flocking round, especially the young girls, who very seldom failed to carry off a nail from every man of the party.

I was told by a gentleman of the party that he had seen a very handsome little woman, who lived near to this long house, and he says he made her several little presents at differnt times that he saw her ashore, but could never find her so kind as the other young girls. This day he gave her some considerable presents—at least they appeared so to her—and she gave him the usual sign, which he readily obeyed, and walked after her into the woods. When she got clear out of sight of the rest she pointed to a little house, and made him understand that he should be happily rewarded for all his presents there. But just as my friend was going in, he observed a strong, well-made man coming toward the house. This made him stop, and the woman observed him waiting at the door. She ran out and saw it was her husband. She immediately looked frightened and called out *"Takena, takena,"* which made my friend suppose it was her husband.

She soon returned to the door with a very fine fowl and some fruit, and when the husband came she was selling the fowl, and my friend was offering double the price that any other fowl cost, but she could not agree until her husband came. Then she talked to him and he began to smell, and offered the fowl and fruit for what was offered to his wife, and my friend gladly accepted and, seeing the husband was a carpenter, he gave him several nails which gained the poor man's heart so much that he would have given him all that he had except his handsome wife.

My friend returned to his party very unhappy at so great a disappointment, but I told him I thought he had double reason to be happy, that the strong fellow did not catch him and give him a good drubbing. He allows he was well able if he had got hold of him without his sword. He told me the guard relieve one another regularly and got value for their nail, and returned back to their duty. Some of the fellows were so extravagant that while he was ashore, they spent two nails. He says this was owing to the great variety of goods which came to market . . .

July 17. A little after 9 a.m. the handsome little woman came off in a canoe with her husband, father and mother, and a young girl which we supposed to be her sister. We showed them all the different parts of the ship, and the husband took very great notice of everything he saw, especially the chairs, chests, and tables, and measured the length and breadth of every joint of our chairs and the gun-room table and marked his measures on a piece of line which he brought with him. I observed him make different knots for the length and breadth. He appears to be a very sensible fellow, and I dare say will be able to make a chair or table when he has a mind.

While the honest carpenter and I were taking the dimensions of the chairs and tables, my friend and the wife were endeavoring to get clear of the old man and his wife, and another hand took care of the sister and showed her some curious things which pleased the young lass. But the instant the carpenter saw his wife and my friend go into his cabin, he immediately went after them to see what curiosities they had there. This disappointment cost my friend a suit of old clothes to the honest carpenter, and a shirt to the wife, besides the trouble of showing the curious man everything in his cabin.

At this time the woman slipped out of the cabin and cast loose the canoe which she came off in, and let her run a good way from the ship. She then looked round and saw her father and mother were out of the gun room and one of the young gentlemen entertaining her sister. She then called out loudly to her husband and told him the canoe was gone adrift. This made the poor man throw off his clothes, to jump into the water to save his canoe. This alarmed my friend, who desired me to be so good as to order a boat to go after the canoe. Meantime he laid hold of the carpenter to prevent him from jumping overboard, but the little artful creature immediately put herself in such a passion that her husband twisted himself out of my friend's hands and jumped out at the gun-room port and swam after his canoe.

The instant that he was in the water, she immediately stepped into my friend's cabin and laid hold of his coat and pulled him in. While she was enjoying the reward of her art and cunning, the poor man's life was running the greatest risk imaginable, not knowing but he might be devoured every minute by some large shark such as we caught about a fortnight before. But the honest carpenter had better luck. In about ten minutes' time he brought his canoe back and made her fast to the gun-room port, where his wife cast her loose from, and jumped into the gun room, where his wife received him and gave him a few large nails which she gained in his absence, to make up for the loss he sustained. This greatly pleased the good man, as he knew nothing of the way and manner the nails were procured. They then all got a few presents and were sent ashore in one of our boats, which towed their canoe . . . .

July 20. The gunner told me this day that the old trade

has risen about 100 per cent. This made me inquire how the people came by the nails. I therefore sent for the carpenter and desired him to examine his stock of nails. He told me he had and took care to keep the people from thieving them . . . .

July 21. When I was ordering the liberty men into the boat, the carpenter came and told me every cleat in the ship was drawn, and all the nails carried off. At the same time the boatswain informed me that most of the hammock nails were drawn and two thirds of the men obliged to lie on the deck for want of nails to hang their hammocks. I immediately stopped the liberty men and called all hands and let them know that no man in the ship would have liberty to go ashore until they informed me who had drawn the nails and cleats and let me know what use they made of them. But not one would acknowledge that they knew anything about drawing the nails and cleats, but all said they knew what use they went to.

I told them it was very surprising that they knew the use they were put to, but knew none of the men.

Then some of the young gentlemen told me that all the liberty men carried on a trade with the young girls, who had now risen their price for some days past, from a twenty- or thirty-penny nail to a forty-penny, and some were so extravagant as to demand a seven- or nine-inch spike. This was a plain proof of the way the large nails went . . . .

This evening I observed a great murmuring among the people. I therefore stepped forward to see if I could find out who had drawn the nails and cleats. At this time the galley was full, dressing their suppers, and some blamed one, some another. It being dark, none of them observed me and therefore told their minds plain. At last I found out that most of them were concerned, and several said they had rather receive a dozen lashes than have their liberty stopped. At last there was a trial among them, and six were condemned for spoiling the old trade by giving large spike nails when others had only a hammock nail, which three declared were refused, they being much smaller than the spikes, but two cleared themselves by proving that they got double value for the spikes. After that a battle ensued, about the one interfering with the other in the way of trade, that obliged me to call out what was the matter, and all was quiet immediately.

At sunrise I sent all the boats ashore, but sent no liberty men.

At noon the boats returned and brought off ten hogs, six fowls, and plenty of fruit. I told the traders they were to go ashore after dinner, but none should go on liberty unless some of them who drew the nails were found out.

At last three concurring witnesses proved that a poor fellow, who was flogged some time before for thieving, had drawn one of the cleats. This unhappy fellow was a proper object to make an example of. I therefore acquainted the captain, who ordered me to cause him to run the gantlet three times round the ship. I then called all hands and placed the men in proper order with a nettle in each of their hands. I several times asked him if there was any of the rest concerned with him, but he still said no. This made the men very merciful the first round, but when I ordered him the second round he began to impeach some of the rest, and hoped to be excused himself. I told him it was then too late, and sent him the second round, but the poor fellow got a hard drubbing that time, which made me excuse him from going the third time. At the same time I acquainted the whole that if any such complaint came again they might rely on a much severer punishment and none of them would be ever allowed to go on liberty any more. Then they all declared to a man that they should take great care that no such thing should ever be done again.

Louis Antoine de Bougainville

The French Find the New Cytherea

Born in Paris, De Bougainville (1729-1811) became the first of the great French navigators to explore the Pacific. He entered the army and served in Canada during the Seven Years' War, winning before its end the rank of colonel. Thereafter he was an officer in the navy. In 1766, in command of the ships *Boudeuse* and *Etoile*, he was commissioned to sail around the world on a voyage of discovery.

Entering the Pacific through the Strait of Magellan, he visited the Tuamotus, Tahiti (where Captain Samuel Wallis had preceded him by eight months), Samoa, the New Hebrides, and the Solomon Islands. Returning to France in 1769, with many important geographical discoveries to his credit, he wrote his famous *Voyage autour du Monde* (1771-1772), which was translated into English by John Reinhold Foster and printed in 1772 as *A Voyage Round the World.*

In France and England at this time there was a widespread interest in Rousseau's doctrine of primitivism, which held that civilization corrupted human nature and that mankind could be noble and happy only in a primitive society. Since De Bougainville gave a detailed and colorful picture of a newly discovered primitive people, the Tahitians, living happily in the "state of nature," his narrative was eagerly read for its illustration of Rousseau's theories operating in practice. This and the fact that De Bougainville wrote with raciness and humor made the book one of the most popular of all Pacific voyages.

THE second of April [1768], at ten in the morning, we perceived to the NNE a high and very steep mountain, seemingly surrounded by the sea. I called it the Boudoir, or the Peak of the Boudeuse. We stood to the northward, in order to make it plain, when we saw another land bearing W by N, the coast of which was not so high but afforded an indeterminate extent to our eyes. We had a very urgent necessity for touching at some place where we might get refreshments and wood, and we flattered ourselves to find them on this land. It was a calm almost the whole day. In the evening a breeze sprung up, and we stood toward the land till two in the morning, when we stood off shore again, for three hours together. The sun rose obscured by clouds and haze; and it was nine o'clock in the morning before we could see the land again, its southernmost point then bearing W by N. We could no longer see the Peak of Boudeuse, but from the masthead. The wind blew N and NNE and we stood as close upon it as we could, in order to fall in to the windward of the island. As we came nearer we saw, beyond its northernmost point, a distant land, still further to the northward, without being able at that time to distinguish whether it joined to the first isle, or whether it formed a second.

During the night, between the third and fourth, we turned to windward, in order to get more to the northward. With joy we saw fires burning on every part of the coast, and from thence concluded that it was inhabited.

The 4th, at daybreak, we discovered that the two islands, which before appeared separate, were united together by a low land, which was bent like a bow, and formed a bay open to the NE. We run with all sails set towards the land, standing to the windward of this bay, when we perceived a piragua coming from the offing, and standing for the land, and making use of her sail and paddles. She passed athwart us, and joined a number of others, which sailed ahead of us, from all parts of the island. One of them went before all the rest; it was manned by twelve naked men, who presented us with branches of bananas; and their demonstrations signified that this was their olive branch. We answered them with all the signs of friendship we could imagine; they then came alongside of our ship; and one of them, remarkable for his prodigious growth of hair, which stood like bristles divergent upon his head, offered us, together with his branch of peace, a little pig and a cluster of bananas. We accepted his present, which was fastened to a rope which was thrown over to him; we gave him caps and handkerchiefs; and these first presents were the pledges of our alliance with these people.

The two ships were soon surrounded with more than a hundred piraguas of different sizes, all of which had outriggers. They were laden with coconuts, bananas, and other fruits of the country. The exchange of these fruits, which were delicious to us, was made very honestly for all sorts of trifles; but without any of the islanders venturing to come aboard. We were obliged either to come into their piraguas, or show them at a distance what we offered in exchange; when both parties were agreed, a basket or a net was let down by a rope; they put their goods in it, and so we did ours, giving before they had received, or receiving before they gave indifferently, with a kind of confidence, which made us conceive a good opinion of their character. We further saw no kind of arms in their piraguas, in which there were no women at this first interview. The piraguas kept alongside of the ships, till the approach of night obliged us to stand off shore, when they all retired.

We endeavored, during night, to go to the northward, never standing further than three leagues from the land. All the shore was, till near midnight, covered as the night before, with little fires at a short distance from each other: it seemed as if it was an illumination made on purpose, and we accompanied it with several skyrockets from both our ships.

The 5th we spent in plying, in order to work to the windward of the island, and letting the boats sound for an anchoring place. The aspect of this coast, elevated like an amphitheater, offered us the most enchanting prospect. Notwithstanding the great height of the mountains, none of the rocks has the appearance of barrenness; every part is covered with woods. We hardly believed our eyes when we saw a peak covered with trees up to its solitary summit, which rises above the level of the mountains, in the interior parts of the southernmost quarter of the island. Its apparent size seemed to be more than of thirty toises in diameter, and grew less in breadth as it rose higher. At a distance it might have been taken for a pyramid of immense height, which the hand of an able sculptor had adorned with garlands and foliage. The less elevated lands are interspersed with meadows and little woods; and all along the coast there runs a piece of low and level land, covered with plantations, touching on one side the sea, and on the other bordering the mountainous parts of the country. Here we saw the houses of the islanders amidst bananas, coconuts, and other trees loaded with fruit.

As we ran along the coast, our eyes were struck with the sight of a beautiful cascade, which came from the tops of the mountains and poured its foaming waters into the sea. A village was situated at the foot of this cascade, and there appeared to be no breakers in this part of the coast. We all wished to be able to anchor within reach of this beautiful spot; we were constantly sounding aboard the ships, and our boats took sounding close under the shore; but we found a bottom of nothing but rocks in this port, and were forced to go in search of another anchorage.

The piraguas returned to the ship at sun rising, and continued to make exchanges all the day. We likewise opened new branches of commerce; for, besides the fruit, which they brought the day before, and other refreshments such as fowls and pigeons, the islanders brought with them several instruments for fishing;

stone chisels, strange kinds of cloth, shells, etc. They wanted iron and earrings in exchange. This bartering trade was carried on very honestly, as the day before: this time some pretty and almost naked women came in the piraguas. One of the islanders went aboard the *Etoile* and stayed there all night, without being in the least uneasy.

This night was likewise spent in plying; and on the 6th in the morning we were got to the most northerly extremity of the island. Another isle came within sight; but seeing several breakers that seemed to obstruct the passage between the two isles, I determined to return in search of anchorage in the first bay, which we saw on the day of our landfall. Our boats which sounded ahead of us toward shore found the north side of the bay everywhere surrounded at a quarter of a league's distance, by a reef which appears at low water. However, about a league from the north point, they discovered a gap in the reef, of the width of twice a cable's length at most, where there was thirty and thirty-five fathoms of water, and within it a pretty extensive road, where the bottom varied from nine to thirty fathoms. This road was bounded to the south by a reef, which, proceeding from the land, joined that which surrounded the shore. Our boats had constantly found a sandy bottom, and discovered several rivers fit for watering at. Upon the reef, on the north side, there are three little islands.

This account determined me to come to an anchor in the road, and we immediately made sail to enter into it. We ranged the point of the starboard reef in entering; and as soon as we were got within it, we let go our best bower at thirty-four fathoms, bottom of gray sand, shells, and gravel; and we immediately carried out the stream-anchor to the northwest, in order to let go our small bower there. The *Etoile* went to windward, and came to an anchor a cable's length to the northward of us. As soon as we were moored, we struck yards and topmasts.

As we came nearer the shore, the number of islands surrounding our ships increased. The piraguas were so numerous all about the ships that we had much to do to warp in amidst the crowd of boats and noise. All these people came out crying *tayo*, which means friend, and gave a thousand signs of friendship; they all asked nails and earrings of us. The piraguas were full of females; who, for agreeable features, are not inferior to most European women; and who on the point of beauty of the body might, with much reason, vie with them all. Most of these fair females were naked; for the men and old women that accompanied them had stripped them of the garments which they generally dress themselves in. The glances which they gave us from the piraguas seemed to discover some degree of uneasiness, notwithstanding the innocent manner in which they were given; perhaps because nature everywhere embellished their sex with a natural timidity; or because even in those countries where the ease of the golden age is still in use, women seem to least desire what they most wish for. The men, who were more plain, or rather more free, soon explained their meaning more clearly. They pressed us to choose a woman and to come on shore with her; and their gestures, which were nothing less than equivocal, denoted in what manner we should form an acquaintance with her. It was very difficult, amidst such a sight, to keep at their work four hundred young French sailors, who had seen no women for six months. In spite of all our precautions, a young girl came on deck and placed herself upon the quarterdeck, near one of the hatchways, which was open in order to give air to those who were heaving at the capstan below it. The girl carelessly dropped a cloth, which covered her, and appeared to the eyes of all beholders, such as Venus showed herself to the Phyrgian shepherd, having, indeed, the celestial form of that goddess. Both sailors and soldiers endeavored to come to the hatchway; and the capstan was never hove with more alacrity than on this occasion.

At last our cares succeeded in keeping these bewitched fellows in order, though it was no less difficult to keep the command of ourselves. One single Frenchman, who was my cook, having found means to escape against my orders, soon returned more dead than alive. He had hardly set his feet on shore, with the fair whom he had chosen, when he was immediately surrounded by a crowd of Indians, who undressed him from head to feet. He thought he was utterly lost, not knowing where the exclamation of these people would end, who were tumultuously examining every part of his body. After having considered him well, they returned him his clothes, put into his pockets whatever they had taken out of them, and brought the girl to him, desiring him to content those desires which had brought him on shore with her. All their persuasive arguments had no effect; they were obliged to bring the poor cook on board, who told me that I might reprimand him as much as I pleased, but that I could never frighten him so much as he had just been frightened on shore . . . .

I have pointed out the obstacles with which we met in coming to an anchor. When we were moored, I went on shore with several officers to survey the watering place. An immense crowd of men and women received us there, and could not be tired with looking at us; the boldest of them came to touch us; they even pushed aside our clothes with their hands, in order to see whether we were made exactly like them; none of them wore any arms, not so much as a stick. They sufficiently expressed their joy at our arrival. The chief of this district conducted and introduced us into his house, in which we found five or six women and a venerable old man. The women saluted us by laying their hands on their breasts and saying several times *tayo*. The old man was the father of our host. He had no other character of old age than that respectable one which is imprinted on a fine figure. His head adorned with white hair, and a long beard; all his body, nervous and fleshy, had neither wrinkles, nor showed any marks of decrepitude. This venerable man seemed to be rather displeased with our arrival; he even retired without answering our civilities, without giving any signs of fear, astonishment, or curiosity; very far from taking part in the raptures all this people was in at our sight, his thoughtful and suspicious air seemed to show that he feared the arrival of a new race of men would trouble those happy days which he had spent in peace.

We were at liberty to examine the interior parts of the house. It had no furniture, no ornament to distinguish it from the common huts, except its extent. It was eighty feet long and twenty feet wide. In it we observed a cylinder of osier, three or four feet long, set with black feathers, which was suspended from the thatch; and besides it, there were two wooden figures which we took for idols. One, which was their god, stood upright against one of the pillars; the goddess was opposite, leaned against the wall, which she surpassed in height, and was fastened to the reeds, of which their walls are made. These figures, which were ill made and without any proportion, were about three feet high, but stood on a cylindrical pedestal, hollow within and carved right through. This pedestal was made in the shape of a tower, was six or seven feet high, and about a foot in diameter. The whole was made of a black and very hard wood.

The chief then proposed that we should sit down upon the grass in front of his house, where he ordered some fruit, broiled fish, and water to be set in front of us: during the meal he sent for several pieces of cloth, and for two great collars of gorgets of osiers, covered with black feathers and shark's teeth. They are pretty like in form to the immense ruffs worn in the time of Francis the First. One of these he put on the neck of Chevalier D'Oraison, another upon mine, and distributed the cloths. We were just going to return on board when the

Chevalier de Suzannet missed a pistol, which had been very dexterously stolen out of his pocket. We informed the chief of it, who was immediately for searching all the people who surrounded us, and even treated some of them very harshly. We stopped his researches, endeavoring only to make him understand that the thief wold fall a victim of his own crime and that what he had stolen could kill him.

The chief and all his people accompanied us to our boats. We were almost come to them when we were stopped by an islander of a fine figure who, lying under a tree, invited us to sit down by him on the grass. We accepted his offer: he learned toward us, and with a tender air he slowly sung a song, without doubt of the Anacreontic kind, to the tune of a flute, which another Indian blew with his nose: this was a charming scene, and worthy the pencil of a Boucher. Four islanders came with great confidence to sup and lie on board. We let them hear the music of our flutes, bass viols, and violins, and we entertained them with a firework of skyrockets and fire-snakes. This sight caused a mixture of surprise and horror in them.

On the 7th in the morning, the chief, whose name was Ereti, came on board. He brought us a hog, some fowls, and the pistol which had been stolen at his house the day before. This act of justice gave us a good opinion of him. However, we made everything ready in the morning for landing our sick people and our water casks, and leaving a guard for their defense. In the afternoon I went on shore with arms and implements, and we began to make a camp on the banks of a little brook, where we were to fill our water. Ereti saw the men under arms and the preparations for the encampment, without appearing at first surprised or discontented. However, some hours after he came to me, accompanied by his father and the principal people of the district, who had made remonstrances to him on this occasion, and gave me to understand that our stay on shore displeased them, that we might stay there during daytime as long as we pleased, but that we should lie on board our ships at night. I insisted upon establishing the camp, making him comprehend that it was necessary to us in order to get wood and water and to facilitate the exchange between both nations. They then held a second council, the result of which was that Ereti came to ask me whether we intended to stay here forever, or whether we intended to go away again, and how soon that would be. I told him that we should set sail in eighteen days, in sign of which I gave him eighteen little stones. Upon this they held a new conference, at which they desired that I would be present. A grave man, who seemed to have much weight with the members of the council, wanted to reduce the number of days of our encamping to nine; but as I insisted on the number that I had at first required, they at last gave their consent.

From that moment their joy returned; Ereti himself offered us an extensive building like a shed, close to the river, under which there were some piraguas, which he immediately got taken away. Under this shed we raised the tent for those who were ill of the scurvy, being thirty-four in number, twelve from the *Boudeuse* and twenty-two from the *Etoile,* and for some necessary hands. The guard consisted of thirty soldiers, and I likewise landed muskets enough to arm the workmen and the sick. I stayed on shore the first night, which Ereti likewise chose to pass under our tents. He ordered his supper to be brought, and joined it to ours, driving away the crowd that surrounded the camp, and retaining only five or six of his friends. After supper he desired to see some sky-rockets played off, and they frightened him at least as much as they gave him pleasure. Towards the end of the night he sent for one of his wives, whom he sent to sleep in Prince Naffau's tent. She was old and ugly.

The next day was spent in completing our camp. The

shed was well made and entirely covered over by a kind of mats. We left only one entrance to it, which we provided with a barrier, and placed a guard there. Ereti, his wives, and his friends alone were allowed to come in; the crowd kept on the outside of the shed, and only a single man of our people with a switch in his hand was sufficient to clear the way. Hither the natives from all sides brought fruits, fowls, hogs, fish, and pieces of cloth, which were exchanged for nails, tools, beads, buttons, and numberless other trifles, which were treasures to them. They were, upon the whole, very attentive to learn what would give us pleasure; they saw us gathering antiscorbutic plants and searching for shells: their women and children soon vied with each other in bring-us bundles of the same plants, which they had seen us collecting, and baskets full of shells of all sorts. Their trouble was paid at a small expense.

This same day I desired the chief to show me where I might cut wood. The low country where we were was covered only with fruit trees, and a kind of wood full of gum and of little consistence; the hardwood grows upon the mountains. Ereti pointed out to me the trees which I might cut down, and even showed towards which side I should fell them. The natives assisted us greatly in our works; our workmen cut down the trees and made them into faggots, which the islanders brought to the boats; they likewise gave us their assistance in making our provision of water, filling the caulks and bringing them to the boats. Their labor was paid in nails, of which the number was proportionate to the work they had done. The only constraint which their preference put upon us was that they obliged us to have our eyes upon everything that was brought on shore, and even to look to our pockets; for even in Europe itself one cannot see more expert filchers than the people of this country.

However, it does not appear that stealing is usual among themselves. Nothing is shut up in their houses;

every piece of furniture lies on the ground or is hung up, without being under locks or under any person's care. Doubtless their curiosity for new objects excited violent desires in them; and besides that, there are always base-minded people everywhere. During the first two nights we had some things stolen from us, notwithstanding our guards and patrols, at whom the thieves had even thrown stones. These thieves hid themselves in a marsh full of grass and reeds extending behind our camp. This marsh was partly cleared by my orders, and I commanded the officer upon duty to fire upon any thieves who should come in the future. Ereti himself told me to do it, but took great care to show me several times the spot where his house was situated, earnestly recommending it to me to fire toward the opposite quarter. I likewise sent every evening three of our boats, armed with pedereroes and swivel guns, to lie at anchor before the camp.

All our transactions were carried on in as friendly a manner as possible, if we except thieving. Our people were daily walking on the isle without arms, either quite alone, or in little companies. There were invited to enter the houses, where the people gave them to eat. Nor did the civility of their landlords stop at a slight collation; they offered them young girls. The hut was immediately filled with a curious crowd of men and women, who made a circle around the guest and the young victim of hospitality. The ground was spread with leaves and flowers, and their musicians sung an hymeneal song to the tune of their flutes. Here Venus is the goddess of hospitality, her worship does not permit of any mysteries, and every tribute paid to her is a feast for the whole nation. They wre surprised at the confusion which our people appeared to be in, as our customs do not permit of these public proceedings. However, I would not answer for it that every one of our men had found it very hard to conquer their repugnance and conform to the custom of the country.

I have often, in the company of one or two of our people, been out walking in the interior part of the isles. I thought I was transported into the garden of Eden. We crossed a turf covered with fine fruit trees and intersected with little rivulets, which kept up a pleasant coolness in the air, without any of those inconveniences which humidity occasions. A numerous people there enjoy the blessings which nature flowers liberally down upon them. We found companies of men and women sitting under the shade of their fruit trees: they all greeted us with signs of friendship: those who met us upon the road stood aside to let us pass by; everywhere we found hospitality, ease, innocent joy, and every appearance of happiness amongst them.

James Cook

Captain Cook at Point Venus

When the *Dolphin* returned to England, Captain Wallis learned that the bark *Endeavour* was fitting out for a scientific voyage to the Pacific. Her crew, under the command of Lieutenant James Cook, was supplemented by a group of scientists led by young Joseph Banks, later to be president of the Royal Society for more than thirty years. Part of the ship's mission was to study, from a distant position, the "transit" of the planet Venus across the face of the sun, and Wallis suggested to Cook that the best viewing spot would be on King George III Island, as he had christened Tahiti.

Cook (1728-1789), called "the greatest explorer-seaman the world has known," was born of Scottish parentage in a humble Yorkshire cottage, and at an early age followed the call of the sea. Learning the skills of the navigator during service in the merchant marine, he rose to the rank of master's mate in the Royal Navy, and served off American shores during the Seven Years' War. For four years he mapped the coasts of Newfoundland, and early in 1769 put to sea in the *Endeavour* on one of the great voyages of maritime history. After rounding Cape Horn, the bark anchored on April 13 at Matavai Bay to begin a three-month visit. Cook's daily journal is one of the best sources of ethnographic lore concerning the natives of the group he named the Society Islands. He was to use Tahiti as his base in two later explorations of the Pacific during the following decade.

During his stay he was unaware that a French expedition under Bougainville had stopped on the southern shore of the island eight months after Wallis had anchored at Matavai Bay. Like Wallis and other early visitors, Cook's command suffered from the Polynesian propensity that Westerners harshly termed "stealing." His reception was both aided and hindered by acquaintance with chiefs who had been friendly with Wallis — especially the lady known as "Queen Oberea." Cook's remedy for insuring the return of stolen goods was to hold hostage a high chief or chiefess — a remedy that was to have fatal results for him when he tried to employ it in 1779 on a beach at the island of Hawaii.

THURSDAY, April 13, 1769. As soon as the ship was properly secured, I went on shore accompanied by Mr. Banks and the other gentlemen, with a party of men under arms. We took along with us Owhaa, who conducted us to the place where the *Dolphin* watered and made signs, as well as we could undertand, that we might occupy that ground, but it happened not to be fit for our purpose. No one of the natives made the least opposition at our landing, but came to us with all imaginable marks of friendship and submission. We afterwards made a circuit thorough the woods and then came on board.

We did not find the inhabitants to be numerous and therefore at first imagined that several of them had fled from their habitations upon our arrival in the bay [Matavai]. But Mr. Gore and some others who had been here before observed that a very great revolution must have happened — not near the number of inhabitants, and a great number of houses razed, hardly a vestige of some to be seen, particularly what was called the queen's — and not so much as a hog or fowl was to be seen; no very agreeable discovery to us whose ideas of plenty on our arrival at this island (from the report of the *Dolphin*) were carried to the very highest pitch.

Friday, 14th. This morning we had a great many canoes about the ship. The most of them came from the westward but brought nothing with them but a few coconuts, etc. Two that appeared to be chiefs we had on board, together with several others, for it was a hard matter to keep them out of the ship, as they climb like monkeys. But it was still harder to keep them from stealing everything that came within their reach. In this they are progidies expert. I made each of the two chiefs a present of a hatchet, things that they seemed mostly to value.

As soon as we had partly got clear of these people, I took two boats and went to the westward, all the gentlemen being along with me. My design was to see if there was not a more commodious harbor and to try the disposition of the natives, having along with us the two chiefs abovementioned. The first place we landed at was in the Great Canoe Harbor (so called by Captain Wallis). Here the natives flocked about us in great numbers and in as friendly a manner as we could wish, only that they showed a great inclination to pick out pockets.

We were conducted to a chief who for distinction's sake we called Hercules. After staying a short time with him and distributing a few presents about us, we proceeded further and came to a chief whom I shall call Lycurgus. This man entertained us with broiled fish, breadfruit, coconuts, etc., with great hospitality, and all the time took great care to tell us to take care of our pockets, as a great number of people had crowded about us. Notwithstanding the care we took, Dr. Solander and Dr. Monkhouse had each of them their pockets picked, the one of his spyglass and the other his snuffbox. As soon as Lycurgus was made acquainted with the theft, he dispersed the people in a moment; and the method he made use of was to lay hold of the first thing that came in his way and throw it at them, and happy was he or she that could get first out of his way. He seemed very much concerned for what had happened, and by way of recompense offered us but everything that was in his house; but we refused to accept of anything and made signs to him that we only wanted the things again. He had already sent people out after them, and it was not long before they were returned. We found the natives very numerous wherever we came, and from what we could judge seemed very peaceably inclined. About six o'clock in the evening we returned on board, very well satisfied with our little excursion.

Saturday, 15th. . . . This morning several of the chiefs we had seen yesterday came on board and brought with them hogs, breadfruit, etc. For these we gave them hatchets, linen, and such things as they valued. Having not met with yesterday a more convenient situation for every purpose we wanted than the place where we are now, I therefore without delay resolved to pitch upon some spot upon the northeast point of the bay properly situated for observing the transit of Venus and at the same time under the command of the ship's guns, and there to throw up a small fort for our defense.

Accordingly I went ashore with a party of men accompanied by Mr. Banks, Dr. Solander, and Mr. Green [astronomer]. We took along with us one of Mr. Banks' tents, and after we had fixed upon a place fit for our purpose we set up the tent and marked out the ground we intended to occupy.

By this time a great number of the natives had got collected together about us, seemingly only to look on, as not one of them had any weapon either offensive or defensive. I would suffer none to come within the lines I had marked out excepting one who appeared to be a chief and old Owhaa. To these two men we endeavored to explain as well as we could that we wanted that ground to sleep upon such a number of nights, and then we should go away. Whether they understood us or no is uncertain, but no one appeared the least displeased at what we were about. Indeed, the ground we had fixed upon was of no use to them, being part of the sandy beach upon the shore of the bay and not near to any of their habitations. It being too late in the day to do anything more, a party with a petty officer was left to guard the tent while we, with another party, took a walk into the woods and with us most of the natives.

We had just crossed the river when Mr. Banks shot

three ducks at one shot, which surprised them so much that the most of them fell down as though they had been shot likewise. I was in hopes this would have had some good effect, but the event did not prove it, for we had not been gone long from the tent before the natives again began to gather about it and one of them, more daring than the rest, pushed one of the sentinels down, snatched the musket out of his hand, and made a push at him and then made off, and with him all the rest. Immediately upon this the officer ordered the party to fire, and the man who took the musket was shot dead before he had got far from the tent. But the musket was carried quite off.

When this happened I and Mr. Banks with the other party were about half a mile off, returning out of the woods. Upon hearing the firing of muskets and the natives leaving us at the same time, we suspected that something was the matter and hastened our march; but before we arrived the whole was over and every one of the natives fled except old Owhaa, who stuck by us the whole time. I believe from the first he either knew or had some suspicion that the people would attempt something at the tent, as he was very much against our going into the woods out of sight of this tent. However, he might have other reasons, for Mr. Hicks being ashore the day before the natives would not permit him to go into the woods. This made me resolve to go to see whether they meant to prescribe bounds to us or no. Old Owhaa as I have said before was the only one of the natives that stayed by us and by his means we prevailed on about twenty of them to come to the tent and there sit down with us, and we endeavored by every means in our power to convince them that the man was killed for taking away the musket, and that we still would be friends with them. At sunset they left us, seemingly satisfied, and we struck our tent and went on board.

Sunday, 16th. This day warped the ship nearer the shore

and moored her in such a manner as to command all the shore of the northeast part of the bay, but more particularly the place where we intended to erect a fort. Punished Richard Hutchins, seaman, with twelve lashes for disobeying command.

Several of the natives came down to the shore of the bay but not one of them came off to the ship during the whole day. In the evening I went ashore with only a boat's crew and some of the gentlemen. The natives gathered about us to the number of about thirty or forty and brought us coconuts, etc., and seemed as friendly as ever . . . .

Monday, 17th. . . . This morning several chiefs from the westward made us a visit. They brought with them emblems of peace, which are young plantain trees. These they put on board the ship before they would venture themselves. They brought us a present of two hogs (an article we find here very scarce) and some breadfruit; for these they had hatchets and other things. In the afternoon we set up one of the ship's tents ashore, and Mr. Green and myself stayed ashore the night to observe an eclipse of Jupiter's first satellite, which we were hindered from seeing by clouds.

Tuesday, 18th. Cloudy weather with some showers of rain. This morning took as many people out of the ship as could possibly be spared and set about erecting a fort. Some were employed in throwing up entrenchments, while others were cutting fascines, pickets, etc. The natives were so far from hindering us that several of them assisted in bringing the pickets and fascines out of the woods and seemed quite unconcerned at what we were about. The wood we made use of for this occasion we purchased of them, and we cut no tree down before we had first obtained their consent. By this time all the ship's sails were unbent and the armorers' forge set up to repair the ironwork, etc. Served fresh pork to the ship's company today for the first time. This is like to be a very scarce article with us, but as to breadfruit, coconuts, and plantains the natives supply us with as much as we can destroy.

Wednesday, 19th. This morning Lycurgus, whose real name is Toobouratomita, came with his family from the westward in order, from what we could understand, to live near us. He brought with him the covering of a house with several other materials for building one. We intend to requite the confidence this man seems to put in us by treating him with all imaginable kindness. Got on shore some empty casks, which we placed in a double row along the bank of the river by way of a breastwork on that side.

Thursday, 20th. Wind at southeast and squally with rain. All hands employed ashore, and nothing remarkable excepting that a hog weighing about ninety pounds was brought alongside the ship for sale. But those who brought it would not part with it for anything we could offer them but a carpenter's broadax, and as this was what we could not part with, they carried it away. Thus we see those very people who but two years ago preferred a spike nail to an ax of any sort have now so far learned the use of them that they will not part with a pig of ten or twelve pounds' weight for anything under a hatchet, and even those of an inferior or small sort are in no great esteem with them. Small nails such as tenpenny, twenty-penny, or any under forty-penny are of no value at all; but beads, particularly white cut glass beads, are much valued by them.

Mr. Banks and Dr. Solander lay ashore tonight for the first time, their marquee being set up within the walls of the fort and fit for their reception.

Friday, 21st. Got the copper oven ashore and fixed it in the bank of the breastworks . . . .

Saturday, 22nd to *Thursday, 27th.* Nothing worthy of note happened. The people [crew] were continually at work upon the fort, and the natives were so far reconciled to us that they rather assisted us than not . . . .

Friday, 28th. This morning a great number of the natives came to us in their canoes from different parts of the island, several of whom we had not seen before. One of these was the woman called by the *Dolphin* the queen of the island. She first went to Mr. Banks' tent at the fort, where she was not known till the master happening to go ashore, who knew her, brought her on board with two men and several women who seemed to be all of her family. I made them all some presents or other, but to Oberea — for such is this woman's name — I gave several things, in return for which, as soon as I went ashore with her, she gave me a hog and several bunches of plantains. These she caused to be carried from her canoes up to the fort in a kind of procession, she and I bringing up the rear. This woman is about forty years of age and like most of the other women very masculine. She is head or chief of her own family or tribe, but to all appearance has no authority over the rest of the inhabitants, whatever she might have had when the *Dolphin* was here.

Hercules, whose real name is Tootaha, is to all appearances the chief man of the island and has generally visited us twice a week since we have been here, and came always attended by a number of canoes and people. At those times we were sure to have a supply, more or less, of everything the island afforded, both from himself and from those that came with him, and it is a chance thing that we got a hog at any other time. He was with us at this time and did not appear very well pleased at the notice we took of Oberea, but I soon put him into a good humor by taking him on board and making him some presents.

Saturday, 29th. This day got the four guns out of the hold and mounted two of them on the quarterdeck, and the other two in the fort on the bank of the river. For this day or two past, about thirty double canoes, in which might be between two and three hundred people, had come into our neighborhood. This made us keep a very good lookout and a strict eye over all their motions.

Sunday, 30th. This being the day that Owhaa told us that we should fire our guns, no one of us went from the fort except such as were sent out to watch the motions of the natives. However, the day passed over without any visible alteration in the behavior of any of them.

Queen Oberea visited this morning pretty early and made me sensible that I must give her a hatchet and then she would give me a pig. I agreed to her plan and the pig was produced.

Monday, May 1st. This morning Tootaha came on board the ship and was very desirous of seeing into every chest and drawer in the cabin. I satisfied his curiosity so far as to open most of those that belong to me. He saw several things that he took a fancy to and collected them together. But at last he cast his eye upon the adze I had from Mr. Stephens [in London] that was made in imitation of one of their stone adzes or axes. The moment he laid his hands upon it he of his own accord put away everything he had got before and asked me if I would give him that, which I very readily did; and he went away without asking for any one thing more, which I by experience knew was a sure sign that he was well pleased with what he had got . . . .

This afternoon we set up the observatory and took the astronomical quadrant ashore for the first time, together with some other instruments. The fort being now finished and made as tenable as the time, nature, and situation of the ground, and materials we had to work upon, would admit of. The north and south parts consisted of a bank of earth 4½ feet high on the inside, and a ditch without ten feet broad and six feet deep; on the west side facing the bay a bank of earth four feet high and palisades upon that, but no ditch, the works being at high-water mark. On the east side upon the bank of the river was placed a double row of casks; and as this was the weakest side, the two four-pounders were planted there, and the whole was defended, besides these two guns, with six swivels, and generally about forty-five men with small arms, including the officers and gentlemen who resided ashore. I now thought myself perfectly secure from anything these people could attempt.

Tuesday, 2nd. This morning about nine o'clock, when Mr. Green and I went to set up the quadrant, it was not to be found. It had never been taken out of the packing case (which was about eighteen inches square) since it came from Mr. Bird the maker, and the whole was pretty heavy, so that it was a matter of astonishment to us all how it could be taken away, as a sentinel stood the whole night within five yards of the door of the tent where it was put, together with several other instruments, but none of them was missing but this. However, it was not long before we got information that one of the natives had taken it away and carried it to the eastward.

Immediately a resolution was taken to detain all the large canoes that were in the bay, and to seize upon Tootaha and some others of the principal people and keep them in custody until the quadrant was produced. But this last we did not think proper immediately to put in execution, as we had only Oberea in our power and the detaining of her by force would have alarmed all the rest.

In the mean time Mr. Banks (who is always very alert upon all occasions wherein the natives are concerned) and Mr. Green went into the woods to inquire of Toobouratomita which way and where the quadrant had gone. I very soon was informed that these three were gone to the eastward in quest of it and some time after I followed myself with a small party of men, but before I went away I gave orders that if Tootaha came either to the ship or to the fort, he was not to be detained, for I found that he had no hand in taking away the quadrant, and that there was almost a certainty of getting it again.

I met Mr. Banks and Mr. Green about four miles from

310

the fort, returning with the quadrant. This was about sunset, and we all got back to the fort about eight o'clock, where I found Tootaha in custody and a number of the natives crowding about the gate of the fort. My going into the woods with a party of armed men so alarmed the natives that in the evening they began to move off with their effects, and a double canoe putting off from the bottom of the bay was observed by the ship and a boat sent after her. In this canoe happened to be Tootaha, and as soon as our boat came up with her he and all the people that were in the canoe jumped overboard. He only was taken up and brought on board the ship, together with the canoe; the rest were permitted to swim ashore. From the ship, Tootaha was sent to the fort, where Mr. Hicks thought proper to detain him until I returned.

The scene between Toobouratomita and Tootaha when the former came into the fort and found the latter in custody was really moving. They wept over each other for some time. As For Tootaha, he was so far prepossed with the thought that he was to be killed that he could not be made sensible to the contrary till he was carried out of the fort to the people, many of whom expressed their joy by embracing him. And after all he would not go away until he had give us two hogs, notwithstanding we did all in our power to hinder him, for it is very certain that the treatment he had met with from us did not merit such a reward. However, we had it in our power to make him a present of equal value whenever we pleased.

We had now time to consider how the quadrant was stolen. It is very probable that the man who took it had seen the box brought into the tent, or else had been well informed by others and had from that moment resolved to steal it. About sunset last night a man was seen crawling along the bank of the river behind the fort, but on being spoken to he went away. However, it was very clear that he was watching for an opportunity to get into the fort in the dusk of the evening before the sentinels were called in and while the most of our people, after leaving off work, were diverting themselves with the natives. However, myself and some others were never out of the fort, and I did not stir out of the tent where the quadrant was till sunset, then walked several times round the inside of the fort, after which I went into Mr. Banks' marquee and ordered the drummer to beat the tattoo. In the doing of which he went three times round the works, yet in one of these short intervals when either mine or the drummer's back was turned the man found the means to carry off the box, for immediately upon beating the tattoo everybody came into the fort and the sentinels were called and placed inside, when it would have been impossible for him to have done it. Indeed, we found it difficult to believe that a naked Indian, frightened of firearms as they are, would have made such an attempt at the certain risk of his life . . . .

Thursday, 4th. Some people came to the fort today from York Island [Moorea]. One of them gave us an account of twenty-two islands lying in the neighborhood of this . . . .

Tuesday, 9th, Wednesday, 10th, and Thursday, 11th. Nothing remarkable happened for the three days. Oberea, the *Dolphin*'s queen, made us a visit for the first time since the quadrant was stolen. She introduced herself with a small pig, for which she had a hatchet, and as soon as she got it she lugged out a broken ax and several pieces of old iron. These I believe she must have had from the *Dolphin*. The ax she wanted to be mended and axes made of old iron. I obliged her in the first but excused myself from the latter. Since the natives have seen the forge at work they have frequently brought pieces of iron to be made into one sort of tool or other, which has generally been done whenever it did not hinder our own work, being willing to oblige them in everything in our power. These pieces of old iron the natives must have got from the *Dolphin*, as we know of no other ship being here and very prob-

312

ably some from us; for there is no species of theft they will not commit to get this article, and I may say the same of the common seamen when in these parts.

Friday, 12th. Cloudy weather with showers of rain. This morning a man and two young women with some others came to the fort whom we had not seen before, and as their manner of introducing themselves was a little uncommon I shall insert it.

Mr. Banks was as usual at the gate of the fort trading with the people when he was told that some strangers were coming, and therefore stood to receive them. The company had with them about a dozen young plantain trees and some other small plants. These they laid down about twenty feet from Mr. Banks. The people then made a lane between him and them. When this was done the man (who appeared to be only a servant of the women) brought the young plantains singly, together with some of the other plants, and gave them to Mr. Banks, and at the delivery of each pronounced a short sentence, which we understood not. After he had thus disposed of all his plantain trees he took several pieces of cloth and spread them on the ground. One of the young women then stepped upon the cloth and with as much innocence as one could possibly conceive exposed herself entirely naked from the waist downwards. In this manner she turned herself once or twice around, I am not certain which, then stepped off the cloth and dropped down her clothes. More cloth was then spread upon the former, and she again performed the same ceremony. The cloth was the rolled up and given to Mr. Banks, and the two young women went and embraced him, which ended the ceremony.

Saturday, 13th. Nothing worthy of note happened during the day. In the night one of the natives attempted to get into the fort by climbing over the walls, but being discovered by the sentinels he made off. The iron and iron tools daily in use at the armorer's forge are temptations that these people cannot possibly withstand.

Sunday, 14th. This day we performed divine service in one of the tents in the fort, where several of the natives attended and behaved with great decency the whole time. This day closed with an odd scene at the gate of the fort, where a young fellow above six feet high lay with a little girl about ten or twelve years of age, publicly before several of our people and a number of natives. What makes me mention this is because it appeared to be done more from custom than lewdness; for there were several women present — particularly Oberea and several others of the better sort — and these were so far from showing the least disapprobation that they instructed the girl how she should act her part, which young as she was did not seem to want it . . . .

Thursday, 1st June. This day I sent Lieutenant Gore in the longboat to York Island with Dr. Monkhouse and Mr. Sporing (a gentleman belonging to Mr. Banks) to observe the Transit of Venus, Mr. Green having furnished them with instruments for that purpose. Mr. Banks and some of the natives of this island went along with them.

Friday, 2nd. Very early this morning Lieutenant Hicks, Mr. Clerk, Mr. Petersgill, and Mr. Saunders went away in the pinnace to the eastward, with orders to fix upon some convenient situation on this island and there to observe the Transit of Venus — they being likewise provided with instruments for that purpose.

Saturday, 3rd. This day proved as favorable to our purpose as we could wish. Not a cloud was to be seen the whole day and the air was perfectly clear, so that we had every advantage we could desire in observing the whole of the passage of the planet Venus over the sun's disk. We very distinctly saw an atmosphere or dusky shade round the body of the planet, which very much disturbed the times of the contacts, particularly the two internal ones. Dr. Solander observed, as well as Mr. Green and myself, and we differed from one another in observing the times of the contact much more than could be expected. Mr. Green's telescope and mine were of the same magnifying power but that of the doctor was greater than ours. It was nearly calm the whole day and the thermometer exposed to the sun about the middle of the day rose to a degree of heat we have not before met with.

Sunday, 4th. Punished Archibald Wolf with two dozen lashes for theft, having broken into one of the storerooms and stolen from thence a large quantity of spike nails; some few of them were found upon him. This evening the gentlemen that were sent to observe the Transit of Venus returned with success. Those that were sent to York Island were well received by the natives; that island appeared to them not to be very fruitful ....

Wednesday, 14th. Between two and four o'clock this morning one of the natives stole out of the fort an iron rake made use of for the oven. It happened to be set up against the wall, and by that means was visible from the outside and had been seen by them in the evening, as a man had been seen lurking about the fort some hours before the thing was missed. I was informed by some others of the natives that he watched an opportunity when the sentinel's back was turned and hooked it with a long, crooked stick and haled it over the wall.

When I came to be informed of this theft in the morning, I resolved to recover it by some means or other, and accordingly went and took possession of all the canoes of any value I could meet with and brought them into the river behind the fort, to the number of twenty-two, and told the natives then present (most of them being the owners of the canoes) that unless the principal things they had stolen from us were restored, I would burn them every one. Not that I ever intend to put this into execution, and yet I was very much displeased with them, as they were daily either committing or attempting to commit one theft or another, when at the same time (contrary to the opinion of everybody) I would not suffer them to be fired upon. This would have been putting it in the power of the sentinels to have fired upon them upon the most slight occasions, as I had before experienced, and I have a great objection to firing with powder only amongst people who know not the difference. By this they would learn to despise firearms and think their own arms superior, and if ever such an opinion prevailed they would certainly attack you, the event of which might prove as unfavorable to you as them.

About noon the rake was restored us, when they wanted to have their canoes again. But now as I had them in my possession I was resolved to try if they would not redeem them by restoring what they had stolen from us before. The principal things which we had lost were the marine musket, a pair of pistols belonging to Mr. Banks, a sword belonging to one of the petty officers, and a water cask with some articles not worth mentioning. Some said that these things were not in the island, others that Tootaha had them, and those of Tootaha's friends laid the whole to Oberea, and I believe the whole was between these two persons . . . .

Monday, 19th. Punished James Tunley with twelve lashes for taking rum out of the cask on the quarterdeck . . . .

Tuesday, 20th. . . . Last night Oberea made us a visit, whom we have not seen for some time. We were told of her coming and that she would bring with her some of the stolen things—which we gave credit to because we knew several of them were in her possession, but we were surprised to find this woman put herself wholly in our power and not bring with her one article of what we had lost. The excuse she made was that her gallant, a man that used to be along with her, did steal them, and she had beat him and turned him away. She was so sensible of her own guilt that she was ready to drop down through fear—and yet she had resolution enough to insist upon sleeping in Mr. Banks' tent all night, and was with difficulty prevailed upon to go to her canoe, although no one took the least notice of her.

In the morning she brought her canoe with everything she had to the gate of the fort, after which we could not help admiring her for her courage and the confidence she seemed to place in us, and thought that we could do no less than to receive her into favor and accept the presents she had brought us, which consisted of a hog, a dog, some breadfruit, and plantains. We refused to accept of the dog as being an animal we had no use for, at which she seemed a little surprised, and told us that it was very good eating. We very soon had an opportunity to find that it was so, for Mr. Banks having bought a basket of fruit in which happened to be the thigh of a dog ready dressed, of this several of us tasted and found that it was meat not to be despised . . . .

I now gave over all thought of recovering any of the things the natives had stolen from us and therefore intend to give them up their canoes whenever they apply for them . . . .

Thursday, July 13th. Winds easterly, a light breeze. This morning we were visited by Oberea and several others of our acquaintances, a thing we did not expect after what had happened but two days ago. This was in some measure owing to Mr. Banks, Dr. Solander, and myself going to Apparra last night, where we so far convinced them of our friendly disposition that several of them were in tears at our coming away.

Between eleven and twelve o'clock we got under sail and took our final leave of this people after a stay of just three months, the most part of which time we have been upon good terms with them. Some few differences have now and then happened, owing partly to the want of rightly understanding one another and partly to their natural thievish disposition, which we could not at all times neither bear with or guard against. But these have been attended with no ill consequences to either side except the first, in which one of them was killed. This I was very sorry for, because from what happened to them by the *Dolphin* I thought it would have been no hard matter to have got and kept a footing with them without bloodshed.

William Bligh

Captain Bligh and the Breadfruit

William Bligh (1754-1817), who first visited Tahiti as the sailing master of the *Resolution* on Captain Cook's third Pacific voyage, was appointed in 1787 to command the armed transport *Bounty*. This vessel set sail from England with orders to go to Tahiti and load a cargo of young breadfruit trees, to be transplanted to the West Indies to supply a possible food for slaves.

For almost a month, the *Bounty* fought furious weather off Cape Horn, and on April 22 the captain ordered that the ship should sail clear around the world and enter the Pacific by way of the Cape of Good Hope. He arrived at Tahiti at a time when it was impossible to collect proper breadfruit seedlings, and the delay of almost six months caused the crew to make a number of amorous connections among the complaisant Tahitian women. The reluctance of such an officer as master's mate Fletcher Christian to return to England was a main cause of what was to follow. On the morning of April 28, 1789, off the Tongan island of Tofua, Christian led the most notorious sea mutiny in maritime history. Eighteen other officers and men not involved in the rebellion joined Bligh in the ship's launch, only twenty-three feet long. After forty-one days of danger and privation, sailing 3,600 miles westward, all but one man reached the Dutch outpost at Timor, on one of the most amazing open-boat voyages on record.

A hero in the eyes of the British public, Bligh made a second —and successful—breadfruit voyage in command of H.M.S. *Providence* in 1791, but as it turned out, the people of the Caribbean declined to modify their diet to include this Polynesian staple, and stuck to their daily ration of bananas. Later, Bligh rose in the ranks of the Royal Navy, serving under Lord Nelson in the battle of Copenhagen. In 1805 he was appointed governor of the colony of New South Wales, where he faced another mutiny against his rule. The best account of his first breadfruit

319

voyage is to be found in his volume *A Voyage to the South Sea* ... (1792), which was a best-seller in its day and is still highly readable. Its author was termed by Dr. Bengt Danielsson "a first-rate anthropologist."

Sunday, October 26, 1788. The ship being anchored, our number of visitors continued to increase; but as yet we saw no person that we could recollect to have been of much consequence. Some inferior chiefs made me presents of a few hogs, and I made them presents in return. We were supplied with coconuts in great abundance, but breadfruit was scarce.

Many inquiries were made after Captain Cook, Sir Joseph Banks, and many of their former friends. They said a ship had been here, from which they had learned that Captain Cook was dead. But the circumstances of his death they did not appear to be acquainted with; and I had given particular directions to my officers and ship's company that they should not be mentioned. The ship spoken of, they [the natives] informed me, stayed at Tahiti one month and had been gone four months, by some of their accounts; according to others, only three months. The captain they called Tonah. I understood likewise from them that Lieutenant Watts was in the ship, who, having been here in the *Resolution* with Captain Cook, was well known to them . . . . Otoo, who was the chief of Matavai when Captain Cook was here the last time, was absent at another part of the island. They told me messengers were sent to inform him of our arrival, and that he was expected to return soon. There appeared among the natives in general great good will toward us, and they seemed to be much rejoiced at our arrival.

This whole day we experienced no instance of dishonesty. We were so much crowded that I could not undertake to remove to a more proper station without danger of disobliging our visitors by desiring them to leave the ship. This business was, therefore, deferred till the next morning.

Tuesday, 28th. . . . I had sent Nelson [the gardener] and his assistant to look for plants, and it was no small pleasure to me to find, by their report, that according to appearances the object of my mission would probably be accomplished with ease. I had given directions to everyone on board not to make known to the islanders the purpose of our coming, lest it might enhance the value of the breadfruit plants or occasion other difficulties. Perhaps so much caution was not necessary, but at all events I wished to reserve to myself the time and manner of communication.

Thursday, 30th. . . . Tinah, understanding from my conversation that I intended visiting some of the other islands in the neighborhood, very earnestly desired I would not think of leaving Matavai. "Here," said he, "you shall be supplied plentifully with everything you want. All here are your friends and friends of King George. If you go to the other islands, you will have everything stolen from you."

I replied that, on account of their good will, and from a desire to serve him and his country, King George had sent out those valuable presents to him; "And will not you, Tinah, send something to King George in return?"

"Yes," he said, "I will send him anything I have," and then began to enumerate the different articles in his power, among which he mentioned the breadfruit. This was the exact point to which I wished to bring the conversation and, seizing an opportunity which had every appearance of being undesigned and accidental, I told him the breadfruit trees were what King George would like. Upon which he promised me a great many should be put on board, and seemed much delighted to find it so easily in his power to send anything that would be well received by King George . . . .

Nelson, who accompanied me in this expedition, had but little opportunity to search after plants, the natives having crowded so much about him. He saw enough, however, to assure him that they were to be procured here [Oparre, called One-tree Hill by visitors] as plentifully as at Matavai.

Sunday, November 2nd. . . . The principal use of the tents on shore was for a lodgment for the plants; and I had now, instead of appearing to receive a favor, brought the chiefs to believe that I was doing them a kindness in carrying the plants as a present from them to the *Earee Rabie no Britanee.* The party at the tent consisted of nine persons, including Nelson and his assistant . . .

Monday, 3rd. . . . I showed Tinah the preparations I was making to take on board the breadfruit plants, which pleased him exceedingly. But he did not forget to remind me when the next ship came out he hoped King George would send him large axes, files, saws, cloths of all kinds, hats, chairs, and bedsteads, with arms, ammunition, and in short everything he could think of mentioning . . . .

Wednesday, 5th. . . . This was the first day of our beginning to take up plants. We had much pleasure in collecting them, for the natives offered their assistance and perfectly understood the method of taking them up and pruning them . . . .

Thursday 6th. . . . We got on successfully with our plants, having a hundred potted at the tent and in a fair way of doing well. The cabin also was completed, and ready to receive them on board . . . .

Saturday, 8th. Our plants had now increased to 252. As they were all kept on shore at the tent, I augmented the guard there; though, from the general conduct of the natives, there did not appear the least occasion for so much caution . . . .

Monday, 17th. Our collection of breadfruit plants at the tents continued increasing. This morning I sent twelve on board in pots, to discover where they would thrive the best, the air being more temperate on board the ship than on shore . . . .

Tuesday, 25th. [A visit from "Queen Oberea"] This morning I sent a boat to Oparre, which returned in the afternoon with Oberea and two women, her servants. As she was old and corpulent, it was with difficulty that we helped her up the ship's side. As soon as she was in the ship, she sat down on the gangway and, clasping my knees in her arms, expressed her pleasure at seeing me by a flood of tears. Her servants then produced three pieces of cloth which, with a large hog, some breadfruit, plantains, and coconuts, she had brought as a present. As she was fatigued by her journey, she wished to remain on board all night. I directed accommodations to be prepared, which was done with little trouble, as nothing was more necessary than a mat and some cloth spread on deck. She had with her a favorite cat, bred from one that had been given her by Captain Cook. She told me all the misfortunes that had befallen her son and friends since Captain Cook left Tahiti . . . .

Monday, December 8. . . . The plants received no injury from the bad weather, having been carefully covered from the spray of the sea. Some were in a dormant state and others were striking out young shoots. Nelson thought that it was better to refrain a few days from taking them on board; I therefore consented to defer it. He was of opinion that the plants could be propagated from the roots only, and I directed some boxes to be filled, as we could stow them where no others could be placed . . . .

Wednesday, 24th. This day we took the plants on board, being 774 pots, all in a healthy state; for whenever any plant had an unfavorable appearance it was replaced by another. The number of those rejected was 302, of which not one in ten but was found to be growing at the root.

Friday, 26th. [At a more interesting harbor at Oparre]

. . . . I gave directions for the plants to be landed, and the same party to be with them as at Matavai . . . . Breadfruit began to be scarce, though we purchased without difficulty a sufficient quantity for our consumption; there was, however, another harvest approaching, which they expected would be fit for use in five or six weeks . . . .

Monday, January 5, 1789. [Three crewmen deserted in the small cutter; they were brought back by the Tahitians on the 22nd.]

Tuesday, March 31st. Today all the plants were on board, being in 774 pots, 39 tubs, and 24 boxes. The number of breadfruit plants were 1,015; besides which we had collected a number of other plants . . . .

Saturday, April 4th. . . . At sunset the boat returned and we made sail, bidding farewell to Tahiti, where for twenty-three weeks we had been treated with the utmost affection and regard, and which seemed to increase in proportion to our stay. That we were not insensible to their kindness the events which followed more than sufficiently proves; for to the friendly and endearing behavior of these people may be ascribed the motives for that event which effected the ruin of an expedition that, there was every reason to hope, would have been completed in the most fortunate manner . . . .

[When Bligh and eighteen loyal crewmen were put into the launch, the mutineers tossed overboard all the breadfruit and other plants, shouted "Huzzah for Tahiti!," and began the return to that island that led finally to the settlement of lonely Pitcairn Island by a refugee band of English seamen and men and women of the island of Tahiti.]

TALES OF THE PACIFIC

Stories of Hawaii by Jack London
Thirteen yarns drawn from the famous author's love affair with Hawaii Nei.
$3.95   ISBN 0-935180-08-7

A Hawaiian Reader
Thirty-seven selections from the literature of the past hundred years including such writers as Mark Twain, Robert Louis Stevenson and James Jones.
$3.95   ISBN 0-935180-07-9

Best South Seas Stories
Fifteen writers capture all the romance and exotic adventure of the legendary South Pacific including James A. Michener, James Norman Hall, W. Somerset Maugham, and Herman Melville.
$3.95   ISBN 0-935180-12-5

The Spell of Hawaii
A companion volume to *A Hawaiian Reader*. Twenty-four selections from the exotic literary heritage of the islands.
$3.95   ISBN 0-935180-13-3

South Sea Tales by Jack London
Fiction from the violent days of the early century, set among the atolls of French Oceania and the high islands of Samoa, Fiji, Pitcairn, and "the terrible Solomons."
$3.95   ISBN 0-935180-14-1

The Trembling of a Leaf by W. Somerset Maugham
Stories of Hawaii and the South Seas, including "Red," the author's most successful short story, and "Rain," his most notorious one.
$3.95   ISBN 0-935180-21-4

Kona by Marjorie Sinclair
The best woman novelist of post-war Hawaii dramatizes the conflict between a daughter of Old Hawaii and her straitlaced Yankee husband. Nor is the drama resolved in their children.
$3.95   ISBN 0-935180-20-6

Love in the South Seas by Bengt Danielsson
The noted Swedish anthropologist who served as a member of the famed **Kon-Tiki** expedition here reveals the sex and family life of the Polynesians, based on early accounts as well as his own observations during many years in the South Seas.
$3.95   ISBN 0-935180-25-7

The Lure of Tahiti selected and edited by A. Grove Day
Fifteen stories and other choice extracts from the rich
literature of "the most romantic island in the world."
Authors include Jack London, James A. Michener, James
Norman Hall, W. Somerset Maugham, Paul Gauguin,
Pierre Loti, Herman Melville, William Bligh, and James
Cook.
$3.95   0-935180-31-1

The Wild Wind a novel by Marjorie Sinclair
On the Hana Coast of Maui, Lucia Gray, great-grand-
daughter of a New England missionary, seeks solitude but
embarks on an interracial marriage with a Hawaiian cowboy. Then she faces some of the mysteries of the Polynesia
of old.
$3.95   0-935180-30-3

Captain David Grief by Jack London
Captain David Grief, South Sea tycoon, came to the
Pacific at the age of twenty, and two decades later he protected a vast trading empire. Eight long tales of daring and
adventure by the famous American storyteller who did
some of his best writing in that region.
$3.95   0-935180-34-6

Teller of Tales by Eric Knudsen
Son of a pioneer family of Kauai, the author spent most of
his life on the Garden Island as rancher, hunter of wild
cattle, lawyer, and legislator. Here are sixty campfire yarns
of gods and goddesses, ghosts and heroes, cowboy adventures, and legendary feats among the valleys and peaks of
the island.
$3.95   0-935180-33-8

**Coronado's Quest: The Discovery of the American
Southwest** by A. Grove Day
The story of the expedition that first entered the American
Southwest in 1540. A pageant of exploration with a cast
of dashing men and women—not only Hispanic adven-
turers and valiant Indians of a dozen tribes, but gray-robed
friars like Marcos de Niza—as well as Esteban, the black
Moorish slave who was slain among the Zuni pueblos he
had discovered.
$3.95   0-935180-370

How to Order

Send check or money order with an additional 20 percent
to cover mailing and handling to:

Mutual Publishing
2055 North King Street, Suite 202, Honolulu, Hawaii 96819

For airmail delivery add an additional 30 percent
For further information and trade inquiries telephone (808) 924-7732